WORKERS' COMPENSATION LAWS OF CALIFORNIA

February 2020 Supplement

THIS SUPPLEMENT IS TO BE USED IN CONJUNCTION
WITH THE 2020 EDITION.

An update to the California Code of Regulations:
- *WCAB Rule Changes*
- *Additional Rule Changes*

The California Code of Regulations is updated through
Register 2020, No. 1 [January 3, 2020].

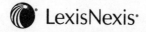

QUESTIONS ABOUT THIS PUBLICATION?

For questions about the **Editorial Content** appearing in these volumes or reprint permission, please call:

Robin Kobayashi, J.D. at .... 1-800-424-0651 EXT. 3352
or
Katie Komer at .... (925) 284-0168
or
E-mail .... CalCodes@lexisnexis.com

For assistance with replacement pages, shipments, billing or other customer service matters, please call:

Customer Service Department at .... (800) 833-9844

Outside the United States and Canada, please call .... (518) 487-3000

Fax number .... (518) 487-3584

Customer Service Website .... http://www.lexisnexis.com/custserv/

For information on other Matthew Bender publications, please call:

Your account manager .... (800) 223-1940

Outside the United States and Canada, please call .... (518) 487-3000

TABLE OF AMENDMENTS
2019–2020 State Regulatory Action

Effective on dates shown below.

California Code of Regulations

TITLE 8

Regulation	Effect	Effective Date
9789.25	Amended	11-1-19
9792.23.10	Amended	10-7-19
Subch. 1.7 (comm. w/§10175)	Repealed	11-6-19
10175–10181	Repealed	11-6-19
10300	Repealed / Added	1-1-20
10301	Renumbered to 10305	1-1-20
10302	Repealed / Added	1-1-20
10304	Repealed	1-1-20
10305	Amended & Renumbered from 10301	1-1-20
Art. 2 (comm. w/§10320)	Added	1-1-20
10320	Amended & Renumbered from 10340	1-1-20
10322	Repealed	1-1-20
10324	Renumbered to 10410	1-1-20
10325	Amended & Renumbered from 10341	1-1-20
10330	Amended & Renumbered from 10348	1-1-20
10338	Amended & Renumbered from 10342	1-1-20
Art. 2 (comm. w/§10340)	Repealed	1-1-20
10340	Renumbered to 10320	1-1-20
10341	Renumbered to 10325	1-1-20
10342	Renumbered to 10338	1-1-20
10344	Amended	1-1-20
10346	Amended	1-1-20
10348	Renumbered to 10330	1-1-20
10349	Repealed	1-1-20
10350	Repealed	1-1-20
10351	Repealed	1-1-20
10352	Repealed	1-1-20
10353	Repealed	1-1-20
10355	Added	1-1-20
Art. 3 (comm. w/§10360)	Repealed	1-1-20
10360	Renumbered to 10380 / Amended & Renumbered from 10593	1-1-20
10364	Repealed	1-1-20
10370	Added	1-1-20
Art. 3 (comm. w/§10380)	Added	1-1-20
10380	Repealed / Amended &	

Regulation	Effect	Effective Date
	Renumbered from 10360	1-1-20
10382	Added	1-1-20
Art. 4 (comm. w/§10390)	Repealed	1-1-20
10390	Repealed / Amended &	
	Renumbered from 10550	1-1-20
10391	Repealed	1-1-20
10392	Repealed	1-1-20
10393	Repealed	1-1-20
10396	Amended & Renumbered	
	from 10589	1-1-20
10397	Renumbered to 10617	1-1-20
10398	Amended & Renumbered	
	from 10592	1-1-20
Art. 4 (comm. w/§10400)	Added	1-1-20
Art. 5 (comm. w/§10400)	Repealed	1-1-20
10400	Repealed & Added	1-1-20
10401	Repealed & Added	1-1-20
10402	Repealed / Amended &	
	Renumbered from 10774	1-1-20
10403	Repealed / Added	1-1-20
10404	Renumbered to 10470 / Added	1-1-20
10405	Renumbered to 10460	1-1-20
10408	Renumbered to 10500	1-1-20
10409	Renumbered to 10480	1-1-20
10410	Renumbered to 10488 /	
	Amended & Renumbered	
	from 10324	1-1-20
10411	Renumbered to 10490	1-1-20
10412	Repealed	1-1-20
10414	Renumbered to 10742	1-1-20
10416	Renumbered to 10744	1-1-20
10417	Renumbered to 10789	1-1-20
10420	Renumbered to 10745	1-1-20
10421	Amended & Renumbered	
	from 10561	1-1-20
10430	Repealed / Amended &	
	Renumbered from 10782	1-1-20
10440	Repealed & Added	1-1-20
10445	Repealed / Amended &	
	Renumbered from 10779	1-1-20
10447	Renumbered to 10528	1-1-20
Art. 5 (comm. w/§10450)	Added	1-1-20
10450	Renumbered to 10510 / Added	1-1-20
10451.1	Repealed	1-1-20
10451.2	Repealed	1-1-20
10451.3	Renumbered to 10545	1-1-20
10451.4	Renumbered to 10570	1-1-20
10452	Renumbered to 10960	1-1-20
10453	Renumbered to 10788	1-1-20

California Code of Regulations

TITLE 8

Regulation	Effect	Effective Date
10454	Repealed	1-1-20
10455	Renumbered to 10534 / Added	1-1-20
10458	Renumbered to 10534	1-1-20
10460	Amended & Renumbered from 10405	1-1-20
10462	Repealed / Added	1-1-20
10464	Repealed	1-1-20
10465	Added	1-1-20
10466	Repealed	1-1-20
10470	Renumbered to 10530 / Amended & Renumbered from 10404	1-1-20
Art. 6 (comm. w/§10480)	Added	1-1-20
10480	Repealed / Amended & Renumbered from 10409	1-1-20
10482	Added	1-1-20
10484	Repealed	1-1-20
10488	Amended & Renumbered from 10410	1-1-20
10490	Renumbered to 10515 / Amended & Renumbered from 10411	1-1-20
10492	Renumbered to 10517	1-1-20
10496	Repealed	1-1-20
10497	Repealed	1-1-20
10498	Renumbered to 10520	1-1-20
Art. 6 (comm. w/§10500)	Repealed	1-1-20
Art. 7 (comm. w/§10500)	Added	1-1-20
10500	Repealed / Amended & Renumbered from 10408	1-1-20
10501	Repealed	1-1-20
10505	Repealed	1-1-20
10506	Repealed	1-1-20
10507	Renumbered to 10605	1-1-20
10508	Renumbered to 10600	1-1-20
10510	Repealed / Amended & Renumbered from 10450	1-1-20
10515	Amended & Renumbered from 10490	1-1-20
10517	Amended & Renumbered from 10492	1-1-20
10520	Amended & Renumbered from 10498	1-1-20
10525	Added	1-1-20
10528	Amended & Renumbered from 10447	1-1-20
Art. 7 (comm. w/§10530)	Repealed	1-1-20
10530	Renumbered to 10640 / Amended & Renumbered	

Regulation	Effect	Effective Date
	from 10470	1-1-20
10532	Renumbered to 10642	1-1-20
10534	Renumbered to 10644 /	
	Renumbered from 10455	1-1-20
10536	Renumbered to 10647 /	
	Amended & Renumbered	
	from 10458	1-1-20
10537	Renumbered to 10650	1-1-20
10538	Renumbered to 10655	1-1-20
10540	Added	1-1-20
Art. 8 (comm. w/§10541)	Repealed	1-1-20
10541	Renumbered to 10761	1-1-20
10544	Renumbered to 10750	1-1-20
10545	Amended & Renumbered	
	from 10451.3	1-1-20
10547	Added	1-1-20
10548	Renumbered to 10748	1-1-20
10549	Renumbered to 10757	1-1-20
10550	Renumbered to 10390 /	
	Amended & Renumbered	
	from 10582	1-1-20
10552	Renumbered to 10782	1-1-20
10555	Renumbered to 10785 / Added	1-1-20
Art. 8 (comm. w/§10560)	Added	1-1-20
10560	Repealed / Added	1-1-20
10561	Renumbered to 10421	1-1-20
10562	Repealed	1-1-20
10563	Repealed	1-1-20
10563.1	Repealed	1-1-20
10564	Renumbered to 10790	1-1-20
10565	Added	1-1-20
10566	Repealed	1-1-20
10567	Amended & Renumbered	
	from 10957	1-1-20
10570	Renumbered to 10833 /	
	Amended & Renumbered	
	from 10451.4	1-1-20
10575	Amended & Renumbered	
	from 10957.1	1-1-20
10578	Repealed	1-1-20
10580	Renumbered to 10672 /	
	Amended & Renumbered	
	from 10959	1-1-20
10582	Renumbered to 10550	1-1-20
10582.5	Repealed	1-1-20
10583	Repealed	1-1-20
10589	Renumbered to 10396	1-1-20
10590	Amended & Renumbered	
	from 10953	1-1-20

California Code of Regulations
TITLE 8

Regulation	Effect	Effective Date
10592	Renumbered to 10398	1-1-20
10593	Renumbered to 10360	1-1-20
Art. 9 (comm. w/§10600)	Amended	1-1-20
10600	Repealed / Amended & Renumbered from 10508	1-1-20
10601	Repealed	1-1-20
10602	Renumbered to 10675	1-1-20
10603	Renumbered to 10677	1-1-20
10604	Repealed	1-1-20
10605	Renumbered to 10680 / Amended & Renumbered from 10507	1-1-20
10606	Renumbered to 10682	1-1-20
10606.5	Renumbered to 10685	1-1-20
10607	Repealed	1-1-20
10608	Repealed	1-1-20
10608.5	Repealed	1-1-20
10610	Added	1-1-20
10615	Repealed / Added	1-1-20
10616	Repealed	1-1-20
10617	Amended & Renumbered from 10397	1-1-20
10618	Renumbered to 10660	1-1-20
10620	Added	1-1-20
10622	Repealed	1-1-20
10625	Added	1-1-20
10626	Repealed	1-1-20
10628	Added	1-1-20
10629	Repealed / Added	1-1-20
10631	Renumbered to 10683	1-1-20
10632	Repealed / Added	1-1-20
10633	Repealed	1-1-20
10634	Repealed	1-1-20
10635	Added	1-1-20
10637	Added	1-1-20
Art. 10 (comm. w/§10640)	Added	1-1-20
10640	Amended & Renumbered from 10953	1-1-20
10642	Renumbered from 10532 & Note Amended	1-1-20
10644	Amended & Renumbered from 10534	1-1-20
10647	Renumbered from 10536 & Note Amended	1-1-20
10650	Amended & Renumbered from 10537	1-1-20
10655	Amended & Renumbered from 10538	1-1-20
10660	Amended & Renumbered	

Regulation	Effect	Effective Date
	from 10618	1-1-20
Art. 11 (comm. w/§10670)	Added	1-1-20
10670	Added	1-1-20
10672	Renumbered from 10580	1-1-20
10675	Amended & Renumbered from 10602	1-1-20
10677	Amended & Renumbered from 10603	1-1-20
10680	Amended & Renumbered from 10605	1-1-20
10682	Amended & Renumbered from 10606	1-1-20
10683	Amended & Renumbered from 10631	1-1-20
10685	Amended & Renumbered from 10606.5	1-1-20
Art. 10 (comm. w/§10700)	Repealed	1-1-20
Art. 12 (comm. w/§10700)	Added	1-1-20
10700	Added	1-1-20
10702	Amended & Renumbered from 10886	1-1-20
10705	Amended & Renumbered from 10875	1-1-20
Art. 11 (comm. w/§10740)	Repealed	1-1-20
10740	Renumbered to 10800	1-1-20
Art. 13 (comm. w/§10742)	Added	1-1-20
10742	Amended & Renumbered from 10414	1-1-20
10744	Amended & Renumbered from 10416	1-1-20
10745	Amended & Renumbered from 10420	1-1-20
10748	Amended & Renumbered from 10548	1-1-20
Art. 12 (comm. w/§10750)	Repealed	1-1-20
10750	Repealed / Amended & Renumbered from 10544	1-1-20
10751	Repealed / Added	1-1-20
10752	Added	1-1-20
10753	Repealed	1-1-20
10754	Renumbered to 10813	1-1-20
10755	Renumbered to 10811 / Added	1-1-20
10756	Added	1-1-20
10757	Amended & Renumbered from 10549	1-1-20
10758	Added	1-1-20
10759	Added	1-1-20
10760	Renumbered to 10818	1-1-20
10761	Amended & Renumbered	

California Code of Regulations

TITLE 8

Regulation	Effect	Effective Date
	from 10541	1-1-20
Art. 13 (comm. w/§10770)	Repealed	1-1-20
10770	Repealed	1-1-20
10770.1	Repealed	1-1-20
10770.5	Renumbered to 10863	1-1-20
10770.6	Renumbered to 10874	1-1-20
10770.7	Repealed	1-1-20
10772	Repealed	1-1-20
10773	Repealed	1-1-20
Art. 14 (comm. w/§10774)	Repealed	1-1-20
10774	Renumbered to 10402	1-1-20
10774.5	Repealed	1-1-20
10775	Renumbered to 10844	1-1-20
10776	Renumbered to 10840	1-1-20
10778	Renumbered to 10842	1-1-20
10779	Renumbered to 10445	1-1-20
Art. 15 (comm. w/§10780)	Repealed	1-1-20
10780	Renumbered to 10850	1-1-20
10782	Renumbered to 10430 / Amended & Renumbered from 10552	1-1-20
10785	Repealed / Amended & Renumbered from 10555	1-1-20
10786	Added	1-1-20
10787	Added	1-1-20
10788	Amended & Renumbered from 10453	1-1-20
10789	Amended & Renumbered from 10417	1-1-20
10790	Amended & Renumbered from 10564	1-1-20
Art. 14 (comm. w/§10800)	Added	1-1-20
10800	Amended & Renumbered from 10740	1-1-20
10803	Added	1-1-20
10807	Added	1-1-20
10811	Amended & Renumbered from 10755	1-1-20
10813	Amended & Renumbered from 10754	1-1-20
10818	Amended & Renumbered from 10760	1-1-20
Art. 16 (comm. w/§10820)	Repealed	1-1-20
10820	Amended	1-1-20
10825	Amended	1-1-20
10828	Repealed	1-1-20
Art. 15 (comm. w/§10832)	Added	1-1-20
10832	Added	1-1-20
10833	Amended & Renumbered	

Regulation	Effect	Effective Date
	from 10570	1-1-20
10835	Added	1-1-20
Art. 17 (comm. w/§10840)	Repealed	1-1-20
10840	Repealed / Amended & Renumbered from 10776	1-1-20
10842	Renumbered to 10945 / Amended & Renumbered from 10778	1-1-20
10843	Renumbered to 10955	1-1-20
10844	Repealed / Amended & Renumbered from 10775	1-1-20
10845	Repealed	1-1-20
10846	Renumbered to 10972	1-1-20
10848	Renumbered to 10964	1-1-20
10850	Repealed / Amended & Renumbered from 10780	1-1-20
10852	Repealed	1-1-20
10856	Renumbered to 10974	1-1-20
10858	Renumbered to 10966	1-1-20
10859	Renumbered to 10961	1-1-20
10860	Renumbered to 10962	1-1-20
Art. 16 (comm. w/§10862)	Added	1-1-20
10862	Renumbered to 10984 / Added	1-1-20
10863	Amended & Renumbered from 10770.5	1-1-20
10864	Renumbered to 10986	1-1-20
10865	Renumbered to 10990	1-1-20
10866	Renumbered to 10995	1-1-20
10868	Added	1-1-20
Art. 18 (comm. w/§10870)	Repealed	1-1-20
10870	Repealed	1-1-20
10872	Added	1-1-20
10873	Added	1-1-20
10874	Repealed / Amended & Renumbered from 10770.6	1-1-20
10875	Renumbered to 10705 / Added	1-1-20
10876	Added	1-1-20
10878	Repealed / Added	1-1-20
10880	Added	1-1-20
10882	Repealed	1-1-20
10886	Renumbered to 10702	1-1-20
10888	Repealed / Added	1-1-20
10899	Amended & Renumbered from 10772	1-1-20
Art. 17 (comm. w/§10900)	Added	1-1-20
10900	Added	1-1-20
10905	Added	1-1-20
10910	Added	1-1-20
10912	Amended & Renumbered	

California Code of Regulations

TITLE 8

Regulation	Effect	Effective Date
	from 10998	1-1-20
10914	Added	1-1-20
10920	Amended & Renumbered	
	from 10999	1-1-20
Art. 18 (comm. w/§10940)	Added	1-1-20
Art. 19 (comm. w/§10940)	Repealed	1-1-20
10940	Repealed / Added	1-1-20
10942	Repealed	1-1-20
10945	Amended & Renumbered	
	from 10842	1-1-20
10946	Repealed	1-1-20
Art. 20 (comm. w/§10950)	Repealed	1-1-20
10950	Repealed	1-1-20
10953	Renumbered to 10590	1-1-20
10955	Amended & Renumbered	
	from 10843	1-1-20
10957	Renumbered to 10567	1-1-20
10957.1	Renumbered to 10575	1-1-20
10959	Renumbered to 10580	1-1-20
Art. 21 (comm. w/§10960)	Repealed	1-1-20
10960	Amended & Renumbered	
	from 10452	1-1-20
10961	Amended & Renumbered	
	from 10859	1-1-20
10962	Amended & Renumbered	
	from 10860	1-1-20
10964	Amended & Renumbered	
	from 10848	1-1-20
10966	Renumbered from 10858 &	
	Note Amended	1-1-20
10972	Renumbered from 10846 &	
	Note Amended	1-1-20
10974	Amended & Renumbered	
	from 10856	1-1-20
10984	Amended & Renumbered	
	from 10862	1-1-20
10986	Amended & Renumbered	
	from 10864	1-1-20
10990	Amended & Renumbered	
	from 10865	1-1-20
Art. 22 (comm. w/§10995)	Repealed	1-1-20
10995	Repealed / Amended &	
	Renumbered from 10866	1-1-20
10996	Repealed	1-1-20
10997	Repealed	1-1-20
10998	Renumbered to 10912	1-1-20
10999	Renumbered to 10920	1-1-20
14300.35	Certificate of Compliance &	
	Note Amended	12-11-19

California Code of Regulations

TITLE 8

WCAB RULES CONCORDANCE
Reprinted with permission

Number	Old Title	New Title/Repeal	New Number
10300	Adoption, Amendment or Rescission of Rules.	Construction of Rules.	10300
		Rulemaking Notices.	10302
10301	Definitions.	Definitions.	10305
10302	Working Titles of Workers' Compensation Judges.	Definitions.	10305
10304	Article and Section Headings.	Construction of Rules.	10300
10322	Workers' Compensation Appeals Board Records Not Subject to Subpoena.	Inspection of Workers' Compensation Appeals Board Records.	10807
10324	Ex Parte Communications.	Ex Parte Communications.	10410
10340	Appeals Board Decisions and Orders.	Appeals Board Decisions and Orders.	10320
10341	En Banc Decisions.	En Banc and Significant Panel Decisions.	10325
10342	Appeals Board Member Orders.	Authority of Commissioners of the Appeals Board.	10338
10344	Appeals Board, Commissioner, Deputy Commissioner and Presiding Workers' Compensation Judges Orders.	Authority of Commissioners, Deputy Commissioners and Presiding Workers' Compensation Judges.	10344
10346	Assignment or Transfer of Cases.	Authority of Presiding Workers' Compensation Judge to Assign or Transfer Cases.	10346

10393	Filing of Medical Reports, Medical Legal Reports, and Various Records.	Filing Proposed Exhibits.	10620
		Documentary Evidence.	10670
		Approval of Settlements	10700
		Mandatory Settlement Conferences	10759
10397	Restrictions on the Rejection for Filing of Documents Subject to a Statute of Limitations or a Jurisdictional Time Limitation.	Restrictions on the Rejection for Filing of Documents Subject to a Statute of Limitations or a Jurisdictional Time Limitation.	10617
10400	Filing and Service of Applications.	Invoking the Jurisdiction of the Workers' Compensation Appeals Board.	10450
		Applications.	10455
10401	Separate Application for Each Injury.	Applications.	10455
10402	Minors and Incompetents as Applicants.	Applications.	10455
10403	Application Required Before Jurisdiction Invoked and Before Compelled Discovery May Be Commenced.	Invoking the Jurisdiction of the Workers' Compensation Appeals Board.	10450
10404	Labor Code Section 4906(g) Statement.	Labor Code Section 4906(h) Statement.	10470
10405	Request for Findings of Fact.	Request for Findings of Fact.	10460

10408	Application for Adjudication of Claim Form and Other Forms.	Form Pleadings.	10500
10409	Venue.	Venue.	10480 10482
10410	Objection to Venue Under Labor Code Section 5501.5(c).	Objection to Venue Based on an Attorney's Principal Place of Business.	10488
10411	Petition for Change of Venue Under Labor Code Section 5501.6.	Petition for Change of Venue for Good Cause.	10490
10412	Proceedings and Decision After Venue Change.	**Repeal.**	**Repeal.**
10414	Declaration of Readiness to Proceed.	Declaration of Readiness to Proceed.	10742
10416	Objection to Declaration of Readiness to Proceed.	Objection to Declaration of Readiness to Proceed.	10744
10417	Walk-Through Documents.	Walk-Through Documents.	10789
10420	Setting the Case.	Setting the Case.	10745.
10430	Letters of Appointment for Medical Examiners.	**Repeal.**	**Repeal.**
10440	Pleadings—Serious and Willful Misconduct.	Petition for Increased or Decreased Compensation – Serious and Willful Misconduct.	10525
10445	Allegations.	Petition for Increased or Decreased Compensation – Serious and Willful Misconduct.	10525

10447	Pleadings –Discrimination.	Petition for Increased Compensation– Discrimination under Labor Code section 132a.	10528
10450	Petitions and Answers.	Petitions and Answers to Petitions.	10510
10451.1	Determination of Medical-Legal Expense Disputes.	Determination of Medical-Legal Expense Dispute.	10786
10451.2	Determination of Medical Treatment Disputes.	**Repeal.**	**Repeal.**
10451.3	Petition for Costs.	Petition for Costs.	10545
New Rule		Petition for Labor Code Section 5710 Attorney's Fees.	10547
10451.4	Petition to Enforce Independent Bill Review Determination.	Petition to Enforce an Administrative Director Determination.	10570
10452	Petition for Disqualification of Judge.	Petition for Disqualification of Judge.	10960.
10453	Petition for Automatic Reassignment of Trial or Expedited Hearing to Another Workers' Compensation Judge.	Petition for Automatic Reassignment of Trial or Expedited Hearing to Another Workers' Compensation Judge.	10788
10454	Automatic Reassignment After Reversal.	**Repeal.**	**Repeal.**
10455	Petition to Reopen.	Petition to Reopen.	10534

10498	Special Requirements for Pleadings Filed or Served by Attorneys or by Non-Attorney Employees of an Attorney or Law Firm.	Special Requirements for Pleadings Filed or Served by Representatives.	10520
10500	Service by the Workers' Compensation Appeals Board.	Service by the Workers' Compensation Appeals Board.	10628
New Rule		Designated Service	10629
10501	Service in Death Cases.	Service on the Division of Workers' Compensation and the Director of Industrial Relations.	10632
10505	Service by Parties or Lien Claimants.	Service.	10625
10506	Service: Mail Box.	Service by the Workers' Compensation Appeals Board.	10628
10507	Time Within Which to Act When a Document is Served by Mail, Fax, or E-Mail.	Time Within Which to Act When a Document is Served by Mail, Fax or E-Mail.	10605
10508	Extension of Time for Weekends and Holidays.	Time for Actions.	10600
10510	Service on Represented Employees or Dependents and on Attorneys or Agents.	Service.	10625
New Rule		**Filing and Service of Documents.**	10610
10530	Subpoenas.	Subpoenas.	10640

10532	Notice to Appear or Produce.	Notice to Appear or Produce.	10642
10534	Microfilm.	Subpoenas of Electronic Records.	10644
10536	Witness Fees and Subpoenas.	Witness Fees and Subpoenas.	10647
10537	Subpoena for Med Witness.	Subpoena for Medical Witness.	10650
10538	Subpoenas for Medical Information by Non-Physician Lien Claimants.	Subpoenas for Medical Information by Non-Physician Lien Claimants.	10655
10541	Submission at Conference.	Submission at Conference.	10761
10544	Notice of Hearing.	Notice of Hearing.	10750
10548	Continuances.	Continuances.	10748
10549	Appearances in Settled Cases.	Appearances in Settled Cases.	10757
10550	Proper Identification of the Parties and Lien Claimants.	Proper Identification of Parties.	10390
10552	Expedited Hearing Calendar.	Expedited Hearing.	10782
10555	Priority Conference Calendar.	Priority Conference.	10785
10560	Submission at Single Trial.	Trials.	10787
10561	Sanctions.	Sanctions.	10421
10562	Failure to Appear.	Failure to Appear at Mandatory Settlement Conference or Trial.	10755
		Dismissal of Lien Claims.	10888

New Rule		Appearances by Representatives Not Identified on Notice of Representation	10751
10563	Appearances Required of Parties to Case-in-Chief.	Appearances Required.	10752
10563.1	Other Appearances Required.	Appearances Required.	10752
New Rule		Status Conferences.	10758
10564	Interpreters.	Interpreters.	10790
10566	Minutes of Hearing and Summary of Evidence.	Trials.	10787
10570	Minute Orders.	Minute Orders.	10833
10578	Waiver of Summary of Evidence.	Trials.	10787
10580	Evidence Taken Without Notice.	Evidence Taken Without Notice.	10672
10582	Inactive Cases.	Petition to Dismiss Inactive Case.	10550
10582.5	Dismissal of Inactive Lien Claimants for Lack of Prosecution.	Dismissal of Lien Claims.	10888
10583	Dismissal of Claim Form—Labor Code Section 5404.5.	**Repeal.**	**Repeal.**
10589	Consolidation of Cases.	Consolidation of Cases.	10396
10592	Assignment of Consolidated Cases.	Assignment of Consolidated Cases.	10398
10593	Testimony of Judicial or Quasi-Judicial Officers.	Testimony of Judicial or Quasi-Judicial Officers.	10360
10600	Evidence and Reports.	Documentary Evidence.	10670

10601	Copies of Reports and Records.	Duty to Serve Documents.	10635
10602	Formal Permanent Disability Rating Determinations.	Formal Permanent Disability Rating Determinations.	10675
10603	Oversized Exhibits, Diagnostic Imaging, Physical Exhibits, and Exhibits on Media.	Oversized Exhibits, Diagnostic Imaging, Physical Exhibits and Exhibits on Media.	10677
10604	Certified Copies.	Documentary Evidence.	10670
10605	Reproductions of Documents.	Reproductions of Documents.	10680
10606	Physicians' Reports as Evidence.	Physicians' Reports as Evidence.	10682
10606.5	Vocational Experts' Reports as Evidence.	Vocational Experts' Reports as Evidence.	10685
10607	Computer Printouts of Benefits Paid.	Duty to Serve Documents.	10635
10608	Service of Medical Reports, Medical-Legal Reports, and Other Medical Information.	Duty to Serve Documents.	10635
		Service of Medical Reports, Medical-Legal Reports, and Other Medical Information on a Non-Physician Lien Claimant.	10637
10608.5	Service by Parties and Lien Claimants of Reports and Records on Other Parties and Lien Claimants.	Service.	10625
10615	Continuing Duty to Serve.	Duty to Serve Documents.	10635

10616	Employer-Maintained Medical Records.	Duty to Serve Documents.	10635
10618	X-Rays.	X-Rays.	10660
10622	Failure to Comply.	Documentary Evidence.	10670
10626	Examining and Copying Hospital and Physicians' Records.	**Repeal.**	**Repeal.**
10629	Filing and Listing of Exhibits.	Mandatory Settlement Conferences.	10759
10631	Specific Finding of Fact—Labor Code section 139.2(d)(2).	Specific Finding of Fact—Labor Code section 139.2(d)(2).	10683
10632	Labor Code Section 4065–Evidence.	**Repeal.**	**Repeal.**
10633	Proposed Rating–Labor Code Section 4065.	**Repeal.**	**Repeal.**
10634	Labor Code Section 4628(k) Requests.	Documentary Evidence.	10670
10740	Transcripts.	Transcripts.	10800
10750	Record of Proceedings.	Record of Proceedings Maintained in Adjudication File.	10803
10751	Adjudication File.	Record of Proceedings Maintained in Adjudication File.	10803
10753	Inspection of Files.	Inspection of Workers' Compensation Appeals Board Records.	10807
10754	Sealing Documents.	Sealed Documents.	10813
10755	Destruction of Records.	Destruction of Records.	10811

10760	Recording of Trial Level Proceedings.	Recording of Proceedings.	10818
10770	Filing and Service of Lien Claims.	Filing and Service of Lien Claims and Supporting Documents.	10862
		Notification of Resolution or Withdrawal of Lien Claims.	10872
10770.1	Lien Conferences and Lien Trials.	Lien Conferences and Lien Trials.	10875
		Fees Required at Lien Conference.	10877
		Submission at Lien Conferences.	10880
		Dismissal of Lien Claims.	10888
10770.5	Verification to Filing of Lien Claim or Application by Lien Claimant.	Verification of Compliance with Labor Code section 4906.3 on Filing o Lien Claim or Application by Lien Claimant.	10890
10770.6	Verification to Filing Declaration of Readiness By or on Behalf of Lien Claimant.	Verification to Filing Declaration of Readiness to Proceed by or on Behalf of Lien Claimant.	10874
10770.7	Requirement for Liens Filed Before January 1, 2017.	Requirement for Liens Filed Before January 1, 2017.	10863

10772	Unemployment Compensation Disability Liens.	Unemployment Compensation Disability Liens.	10899
10773	Law Firm Employees.	Non-Attorney Representatives.	10400
10774	Substitution or Dismissal of Attorneys	Substitution or Dismissal of Attorneys and Non-Attorney Representatives.	10405
10774.5	Notices of Representation, Change of Representation, and Non-Representation for Lien Claimants.	Notices of Representation, Change of Representation and Non-Representation for Lien Claimants.	10868
10775	Reasonable Attorney's Fee.	Reasonable Attorney's Fee.	10844
10776	Approval of Attorney's Fee.	Approval of Attorney's Fee by Workers' Compensation Appeals Board Required.	10840
10778	Request for Increase of Attorney's Fee.	Request for increase of Attorney's Fee.	10842
10779	Disbarred and Suspended Attorneys.	Non-Attorney Representatives.	10440
		Disbarred and Suspended Attorneys.	10445
10780	Dismissal Orders.	Order Dismissing Application.	10850
10782	Vexatious Litigants.	Vexatious Litigants.	10430

New Rule		Contempt.	10440
10785	Electronically filed decisions	**Repeal**	**Repeal**
10820	When Certified Copies Will Issue.	When Certified Copies Will Issue.	10820
10825	Withholding Certified Copies.	Withholding Certified Copies.	10825
10828	Necessity for Bond.	**Repeal.**	**Repeal.**
10840	Filing Petitions for Reconsideration, Removal, and Disqualification and Answers.	Filing and Service of Petitions for Reconsideration, Removal, Disqualification and Answers.	10940
10842	Contents of Petitions for Reconsideration, Removal, and Disqualification and Answers.	Required Content of Petitions for Reconsideration, Removal, and Disqualification and Answers.	10945
10843	Petitions for Removal and Answers.	Petitions for Removal and Answers.	10955
10844	Petitions for Disqualification and Answers.	Filing and Service of Petitions for Reconsideration, Removal, Disqualification and Answers.	10940

10845	General Requirements for Petitions for Reconsideration, Removal, and Disqualification, and for Answers and Other Documents.	Filing and Service of Petitions for Reconsideration, Removal, Disqualification and Answers.	10940
10846	Skeletal Petitions.	Skeletal Petitions.	10972
10848	Supplemental Petitions.	Supplemental Petitions.	10964
10850	Proof of Service.	Filing and Service of Petitions for Reconsideration, Removal, Disqualification and Answers.	10940
10852	Insufficiency of Evidence.	**Repeal.**	**Repeal.**
10856	Allegations of Newly Discovered Evidence and Fraud.	Allegations of Newly Discovered Evidence and Fraud.	10974
10858	Correction of Errors.	Correction of Errors.	10966
10859	Orders After Filing of Petition for Reconsideration.	Actions by Workers' Compensation Judge After Petition for Reconsideration is Filed.	10961
10860	Report of Workers' Compensation Judge.	Report of Workers' Compensation Judge.	10962
10862	Hearing After Reconsideration is Granted.	Hearing After Reconsideration is Granted.	10984

10864	Authority of Workers' Compensation Judge After Decision After Reconsideration.	Authority of Workers' Compensation Judge After Decision After Reconsideration.	10986
10865	Reconsideration of Arbitration Decisions Made Pursuant To–Labor Code Sections 3201.5 and 3201.7.	Reconsideration of Arbitration Decisions Made Pursuant To–Labor Code Sections 3201.5 and 3201.7.	10990
10866	Reconsideration of Arbitrator's Decisions or Awards Made Pursuant to the Mandatory or Voluntary Arbitration Provisions of Labor Code Sections 5270 through 5275.	Reconsideration of Arbitrator's Decisions or Awards Made Pursuant to the Mandatory or Voluntary Arbitration Provisions of Labor Code Sections 5270 through 5275.	10995
10870	Approval of Compromise and Release.	Approval of Settlements.	10700
10874	Form.	**Repeal.**	**Repeal.**
10875	Procedures–Labor Code section 3761.	Procedures–Labor Code section 3761.	10705
10878	Settlement Document as an Application.	**Repeal.**	**Repeal.**
10882	Action on Settlement Agreement.	Approval of Settlements.	10700
10886	Service on Lien Claimants.	Service of Settlements on Lien Claimants.	10702
10888	Resolution of Liens.	**Repeal.**	**Repeal.**

10940	Application.	Subsequent Injuries Benefits Trust Fund Application.	10462
10942	Service.	Service on the Division of Workers' Compensation and the Director of Industrial Relations.	10632
10946	Medical Reports in Subsequent Injuries Benefits Trust Fund Cases.	Subsequent Injuries Benefits Trust Fund Application.	10462
10950	Petitions Appealing Orders Issued by the Administrative Directors.	Petitions Related to Orders Issued by the Division of Workers' Compensation Administrative Director or the Director of Industrial Relations.	10560
10953	Petition Appealing Audit Penalty Assessment– Labor Code Section 129.5(g).	Petition Appealing Audit Penalty Assessment– Labor Code Section 129.5(g).	10590
10957	Petition Appealing Independent Bill Review determination of the Administrative Director.	Petition Appealing Independent Bill Review Determination.	10567
10957.1	Petition Appealing Independent Medical Review Determination of the Administrative Director.	Petition Appealing Independent Medical Review Determination.	10575
New Rule		**Petition Appealing Denial of Return-to-Work Supplement.**	10565

10959	Petition Appealing Medical Provider Network Determination of the Administrative Director.	Petition Appealing Medical Provider Network Determination of the Administrative Director.	10580
10995	Mandatory Arbitration.	Mandatory Arbitration.	10900
		Selection of Arbitrator.	10910
10996	Voluntary Arbitration.	Voluntary Arbitration.	10905
		Selection of Arbitrator.	10910
10997	Request for Arbitration.	**Repeal.**	**Repeal.**
10998	Disqualification of Arbitrator.	Disqualification of Arbitrator.	10912
10999	Arbitrator Fee and Cost Disputes.	Arbitrator Fee and Cost Disputes.	10920
New Rule		Complaints Regarding Violations of Labor Code Section 4907	10401
New Rule		Complaints Regarding Violations of Labor Code Section 4907	10402

SELECTED PROVISIONS
Of The
CALIFORNIA CODE OF REGULATIONS

TITLE 8
INDUSTRIAL RELATIONS

DIVISION 1
Department of Industrial Relations

CHAPTER 4.5
DIVISION OF WORKERS'
COMPENSATION

SUBCHAPTER 1
ADMINISTRATIVE DIRECTOR—
ADMINISTRATIVE RULES

ARTICLE 5.3
Official Medical Fee Schedule

§9789.25. Federal Regulations, Federal Register Notices, and Payment Impact File by Date of Discharge.

(a) Federal Regulations by Date of Discharge

(1) The Federal Regulations can be accessed at: http://www.cms.gov/AcuteInpatientPPS/ and the referenced sections are incorporated by reference and will be made available upon request to the Administrative Director.

	Discharges Occurring On or After 1/1/2004	*Discharges Occurring On or After 11/29/2004*	*Discharges Occurring On or After 12/1/2005*	*Discharges Occurring On or After 12/1/2006*
Title 42, Code of Federal Regulations, §412.2	Effective October 1, 2003			
Title 42, Code of Federal Regulations, §412.23(e)	Effective date October 1, 2002 and revised as of October 1, 2003			

1

Title 42, Code of Federal Regulations, §412.23(f)	Effective October 1, 2002 and revised as of October 1, 2003			
Title 42, Code of Federal Regulations, Section 412.64	Effective October 1, 2004			
Title 42, Code of Federal Regulations, Section 412.87	Effective September 7, 2001 and revised as of October 1, 2003	Amended; effective October 1, 2004		
Title 42, Code of Federal Regulations, Section 412.88	Effective September 7, 2001 and amended August 1, 2002 and August 1, 2003 and revised as of October 1, 2003	Amended; effective October 1, 2004		
Title 42, Code of Federal Regulations, §412.92(a)	Effective October 1, 2002 and revised as of October 1, 2003		Amended; effective October 1, 2005	
Title 42, Code of Federal Regulations, §412.92(d)	Effective October 1, 2002 and revised as of October 1, 2003		Amended; effective October 1, 2005	
Title 42, Code of Federal Regulations, Section 412.316(b)	Effective November 11, 2003, large urban add-on is an additional 3%	Amended; effective October 1, 2004, large urban add-on is an additional 3%	Amended; effective October 1, 2004, large urban add-on is an additional 3%	Amended; effective October 1, 2006, large urban add-on is an additional 3%
		Discharges Occurring On or After 1/1/2008	*Discharges Occurring On or After 12/1/2008*	*Discharges Occurring On or After 12/1/2009*	*Discharges Occurring On or After 3/01/2011*
Title 42, Code of Federal Regulations, §412.2				Amended; effective October 1, 2010
Title 42, Code of Federal Regulations, §412.23(e)			Amended; effective October 1, 2009	Amended; effective October 1, 2010
Title 42, Code of Federal Regulations, §412.23(f)				
Title 42, Code of Federal Regulations, Section 412.64				
Title 42, Code of Federal Regulations, Section 412.87		Amended; effective October 1, 2008	Amended; effective October 1, 2009	
Title 42, Code of Federal Regulations, Section 412.88	Amended; effective October 1, 2007			
Title 42, Code of Federal Regulations, Section 412.92(a)				
Title 42, Code of Federal Regulations, Section 412.92(d)		Amended; effective October 1, 2008		

	Discharges Occurring On or After 12/01/2011	Discharges Occurring On or After 03/15/2013	Discharges Occurring On or After 03/05/2015	Discharges Occurring On or After 03/05/2015 (These 2015 factors are updated by AD Order dated 02/05/2015, and supersedes 2014 factors adopted under the OMFS rulemaking filed with the Secretary of State on 02/04/2015)
Title 42, Code of Federal Regulations, Section 412.316(b)	Amended; effective October 1, 2007, large urban add-on is eliminated			
Title 42, Code of Federal Regulations, §412.2				Amended; effective October 1, 2010
Title 42, Code of Federal Regulations, §412.23(e)	Amended; effective October 1, 2011			Amended; effective October 1, 2014
Title 42, Code of Federal Regulations, §412.23(f)				Effective October 1, 2002 and revised as of October 1, 2003
Title 42, Code of Federal Regulations, §412.64	Amended; effective October 1, 2011	Amended	Amended	Amended; effective October 1, 2014
Title 42, Code of Federal Regulations, Section 412.87				Amended; effective October 1, 2009
Title 42, Code of Federal Regulations, Section 412.88				Amended; effective October 1, 2007
Title 42, Code of Federal Regulations, Section 412.92(a)				Amended; effective October 1, 2005
Title 42, Code of Federal Regulations, Section 412.92(d)				Amended; effective October 1, 2008
Title 42, Code of Federal Regulations, Section 412.106			Amended; effective October 1, 2013	Amended; effective October 1, 2014
Title 42, Code of Federal Regulations, Section 412.316(b)				Amended; effective October 1, 2007

	Discharges Occurring On or After 3/01/2016	Discharges Occurring On or After 01/01/2017	Discharges Occurring On or After 12/01/2017	Discharges Occurring On or After 12/01/2018
Title 42, Code of Federal Regulations, §412.2	Amended; effective October 1, 2010	Amended; effective October 1, 2010	Amended; effective October 1, 2010	Amended; effective October 1, 2010

Title 42, Code of Federal Regulations, §412.23(e)	Amended; effective October 1, 2015	Amended; effective October 1, 2015	Amended; effective October 1, 2017	Amended; effective October 1, 2018
Title 42, Code of Federal Regulations, §412.23(f)	Effective October 1, 2002 and revised as of October 1, 2003	Effective October 1, 2002 and revised as of October 1, 2003	Effective October 1, 2002 and revised as of October 1, 2003	Effective October 1, 2002 and revised as of October 1, 2003
Title 42, Code of Federal Regulations, §412.64	Amended; effective October 1, 2015	Amended; effective October 1, 2016	Amended; effective October 1, 2017	Amended; effective October 1, 2018
Title 42, Code of Federal Regulations, Section 412.87	Amended; effective October 1, 2009	Amended; effective October 1, 2009	Amended; effective October 1, 2017	Amended; effective October 1, 2017
Title 42, Code of Federal Regulations, Section 412.88	Amended; effective October 1, 2007	Amended; effective October 1, 2007	Amended; effective October 1, 2007	Amended; effective October 1, 2007
Title 42, Code of Federal Regulations, Section 412.92(a)	Amended; effective October 1, 2005	Amended; effective October 1, 2005	Amended; effective October 1, 2005	Amended; effective October 1, 2018
Title 42, Code of Federal Regulations, Section 412.92(d)	Amended; effective October 1, 2008	Amended; effective October 1, 2008	Amended; effective October 1, 2008	Amended; effective October 1, 2018
Title 42, Code of Federal Regulations, Section 412.106	Amended; effective October 1, 2015	Amended; effective October 1, 2016	Amended; effective October 1, 2017	Amended; effective October 1, 2018
Title 42, Code of Federal Regulations, Section 412.316(b)	Amended; effective October 1, 2007	Amended; effective October 1, 2007	Amended; effective October 1, 2007	Amended; effective October 1, 2007

Discharges Occurring On or After 11/01/2019

Title 42, Code of Federal Regulations, § 412.2	Amended; effective October 1, 2010
Title 42, Code of Federal Regulations, § 412.23(e)	Amended; effective October 1, 2015
Title 42, Code of Federal Regulations, § 412.23(f)	Effective October 1, 2002 and revised as of October 1, 2003
Title 42, Code of Federal Regulations, Section 412.64	Amended effective Octobter 1, 2019
Title 42, Code of Federal Regulations, § 412.87	Amended effiective October 1, 2019
Title 42, Code of Federal Regulations, Section 412.88	Amended effective October 1, 2019
Title 42, Code of Federal Reguiations, Section 412.92(a)	Amended effective October 1, 2005

Title 42, Code of Amended effective
Federal Regulations, October 1, 2008
Section 412.92(d)

Title 42, Code of Amended effective
Federal Regulations, October 1, 2019
Section 412.106

Title 42, Code of Amended effective
Federal Regulations, October 1, 2007
Section 412.316(b)

(b) Federal Register Notices by Date of Discharge

(1) The Federal Register Notices can be accessed at: http://www.cms.gov/AcuteInpatientPPS/ and the referenced sections are incorporated by reference and will be made available upon request to the Administrative Director.

	Discharges Occurring On or After 1/1/2004	Discharges Occurring On or After 11/29/2004	Discharges Occurring On or After 7/1/2005	Discharges Occurring On or After 12/1/2005
Applicable FR Notices	(A) August 1, 2003 (CMS-1470-F; 68 FR 45346) final rule (B) October 6, 2003 (CMS-1470-CN; 68 FR 57732) correction notice	(A) August 11, 2004 (CMS-1428-F; 69 FR 48916) final rule (B) October 7, 2004 (CMS-1428-CN2; 69 FR 60242) correction notice (C) 69 FR 78526 (CMS-1428-F2) correction notice	(A) August 11, 2004 (CMS-1428-F; 69 FR 48916) final rule (B) October 7, 2004 (CMS-1428-CN2; 69 FR 60242) correction notice (C) 69 FR 78526 (CMS-1428-F2) correction notice	(A) August 12, 2005 (CMS-1500-F; 70 FR 47278) final rule (B) September 30, 2005 70 FR 57161 (CMS-1500-CN) correction notice
Capital wage index	Tables 4A–4C beginning on (A) page 57736	Tables $4A_1$–$4C_2$ beginning on (C) page 78619		Tables 4A–4C beginning on (A) page 47580 as corrected by Tables 4A–4C beginning on (B) page 57163
Capital market basket	Not applicable	0.7% ((A) page 49285)		0.8% ((A) page 47500)
Capital standard federal payment rate	$414.18 ((B) page 57735, Table 1D)	$416.73 ($413.83 × 1.007)		$420.06 ($416.73 × 1.008)
Complex Spinal Surgery DRGs	496, 497, 498, 519, 520, 531, 532			496, 497, 498, 519, 520, 531, 532, 546 (page 47308 of (A))
Fixed Loss Outlier Threshold	$31,000 ((A) page 45477)	$25,800 ((A) page 49278)		$23,600 ((A) page 47494)
National Standard Operating Rate	$3,136.39 ((B) page 57735, Table 1A)	$4,569.83 ($4,423.84 × 1.033)		$4,738.91 ($4,569.83 × 1.037)
Operating Wage Index	Tables 4A–4C beginning on (A) page 57736; PIF: Operating Wage Index location (WIGRN)	Tables $4A_1$–$4C_2$ beginning on (C) page 78619; PIF: Final Wage Index location (WIGRN)		Tables 4A–4C beginning on (A) page 47580 as corrected by Tables 4A–4C beginning on (B) page 57163; PIF: Post Reclass Wage Index location

		Discharges Occurring On or After 12/1/2006	*Discharges Occurring On or After 3/1/2007*	*Discharges Occurring On or After 1/1/2008*	*Discharges Occurring On or After 12/1/2008*
Labor-Related Portion	Table 1A beginning on B page 57735	For wage indexes greater than 1.0, the labor-related portion is 71.066% of the standard operating rate. For wage indexes less than or equal to 1.0, the labor-related portion is 62%. (A) page 49070			For wage indexes greater than 1.0, the labor-related portion is 69.731% of the standard operating rate. For wage indexes less than or equal to 1.0, the labor-related portion is 62%. (A) page 47393
Post-acute care transfer to a rehabilitation hospital or unit or long-term hospital qualifying DRGs	DRGs 12, 14, 24, 25, 89, 90, 113, 121, 122, 130, 131, 236, 239, 243, 263, 264, 277, 278, 296, 297, 320, 321, 429, 462, 483, or 468 (A) beginning at page 45413			DRGs 12, 14, 24, 25, 88, 89, 90, 113, 121, 122, 127, 130, 131, 236, 239, 277, 278, 294, 296, 297, 320, 321, 395, 429, 468, 541 or 542 (B) beginning at page 60246	DRGs designated with a "yes" in "FY06 Final Rule Post-acute Care DRG" column in Table 5 (A) beginning at page 47617 and (B) beginning at page 57163
Post-acute care transfer qualifying DRGs	DRGs 209, 210 or 211 (A) beginning at page 45413				DRGs 7, 8, 210, 211, 233, 234, 471, 497, 498, 544, 545, 549, or 550 (A) beginning at page 47617 and (B) beginning at page 57163
Applicable FR Notices	(A) August 18, 2006 (CMS-1488-F; 71 FR 47870) (B) October 11, 2006 (CMS-1488-N; 71 FR 59886) additional notice	(A) August 18, 2006 (CMS-1488-F; 71 FR 47870) (B) October 11, 2006 (CMS-1488-N; 71 FR 59886) additional notice (C) January 5, 2007 (CMS-1488-CN2; 72 fr 569) correction notice	(A) August 22, 2007 (CMS-1533-FC; 72 FR 47130) final rule (B) October 10, 2007 72 FR 57634 (CMS-1533-CN2) correction notice	(A) August 19, 2008 (CMS-1390-F; 73 FR 48434) final rule (B) October 3, 2008 73 FR 57888 (CMS-1390-N) correction notice
Capital wage index	Tables 4A-1–4C-1 (for discharges before 4/1/2007) and Tables 4A-2–4C-2 (for discharges occurring on or after 4/1/2007) beginning on (B) page 59975		Tables 4A–4C beginning on (B) page 57698	Tables 4A–4C beginning on (B) page 57956
Capital market basket	1.10% ((A) page 48163)		1.3% ((A) page 47426)	1.4% ((A) page 48776)
Capital standard federal payment rate	$424.68 ($420.06 × 1.0110)		$430.20 ($424.68 × 1.013)	$436.22 ($430.20 × 1.014)
Complex Spinal Surgery DRGs			028, 029, 030, 453, 454, 455, 456, 457, 458, 459, 460, 471, 472, 473	

Fixed Loss Outlier Threshold	$24,485 ((A) page 59890)		$22,185 ((A) Page 66887)	$20,045 ((A) page 57891)
National Standard Operating Rate	$4,900.03 ($4,738.91 × 1.034)		$5,061.73 ($4,900.03 × 1.033)	$5,243.95 ($5,061.73 × 1.036)
Operating Wage Index	Tables 4A-1–4C-1 (for discharges before 4/1/2007) and Tables 4A-2–4C-2 (for discharges occurring on or after 4/1/2007) beginning on (B) page 59975; PIF: Post Reclass Wage Index_a (for first half FY 2007) and Post Reclass Wage Index_b (for second half FY 2007)		Tables 4A–4C beginning on (B) page 57698; PIF: Post Reclass Wage Index location	Tables 4A–4C beginning on (B) page 57956; PIF: Post Reclass Wage Index location
Labor-Related Portion	For wage indexes greater than 1.0, the labor-related portion is 69.731% of the standard operating rate. For wage indexes less than or equal to 1.0, the labor-related portion is 62%. (A) page 48029		For wage indexes greater than 1.0, the labor-related portion is 69.731% of the standard operating rate. For wage indexes less than or equal to 1.0, the labor-related portion is 62%. (A) page 47344	For wage indexes greater than 1.0, the labor-related portion is 69.731% of the standard operating rate. For wage indexes less than or equal to 1.0, the labor-related portion is 62%. (A) page 48592
Post-acute care transfer to a rehabilitation hospital or unit or long-term hospital qualifying DRGs	DRGs designated with a "yes" in the "FY 07 Final Rule Post-acute Care DRG" column in Table 5 (B) beginning at page 60013	DRGs designated with a "yes" in the "FY 07 Final Rule Post-acute Care DRG" column in Table 5 (B) beginning at page 60013 and (C) beginning at page 573	Medicare Severity DRGs designated with a "yes" in the "FY08 Final Rule Post-Acute DRG" column in Table 5 (A) beginning at page 47539 and (B) at page 57727	Medicare Severity DRGs designated with a "yes" in the "FY09 Final Rule Post-Acute DRG" column in Table 5 (A) beginning at page 48899
Post-acute care transfer qualifying DRGs	DRGs 7, 8, 210, 211, 233, 234, 471, 497, 498, 545, 549, or 550 (B) beginning at page 60013	DRGs 7, 8, 210, 211, 233, 234, 471, 497, 498, 544, 545, 549, or 550 (B) beginning at page 60013 and (C) beginning at page 573	Medicare-Severity DRGs designated with a "yes" in the "FY08 Final Rule Special Pay DRG" column in Table 5 (A) beginning at page 47539 and (B) at page 57727	Medicare-Severity DRGs designated with a "yes" in the "FY09 Final Rule Special Pay DRG" column in Table 5 (A) beginning at page 48899
	Discharges Occurring On or After 12/1/2009	*Discharges Occurring On or After 3/01/2011*	*Discharges Occurring On or After 12/01/2011*	*Discharges Occurring On or After 1/1/2013 but Before 1/1/2014*
Applicable FR Notices	(A) August 27, 2009 (CMS-1406-F; FR 43754) final rule (B) October 7, 2009 (CMS-1406-CN; 74 FR 51496) correction notice	(A) August 16, 2010 (CMS-1498-F; FR 50042) final Rule (B) October 1, 2011 (CMS-1498-F; 75 FR 60640) correction	(A) August 18, 2011 (CMS-1518-F; FR 51476) final Rule (B) September 26, 2011 (CMS-1518-CN3; 76 FR 59263) correction	

Capital wage index	Tables 4A–4C beginning on page (A) 44085 as corrected by Tables 4A–4C beginning on (B) page 51505 for certain areas	Tables 4A–C Beginning on page (A) 50511	Tables 4A–C at https://www.cms.gov/AcuteInpatientPPS/01_overview.asp	
Capital market basket	1.2% ((B) page 51498)	1.2%, (A) page 50442	1.5%, (A) page 51806	
Capital standard federal payment rate	$441.46 ($436.22 × 1.012)	$446.75 ($441.46 × 1.012	$453.46 (446.75 × 1.015)	
Complex Spinal Surgery DRGs				028, 029, 030, 453, 454, 455, 456
Fixed Loss Outlier Threshold	$23,140 ((A) page 44011)	$23,075, (A) page 50441	$22,385, (A) page 51795	
National Standard Operating Rate	$5,354.08 ($5,243.95 × 1.021)	$5,493.28 ($5,354.08 × 1.026)	$5,658.08 ($5,493.28 × 1.03)	
Operating Wage Index	Tables 4A–4C beginning on page (A) 44085 as corrected by Tables 4A–4C beginning on (B) page 51505 for certain areas; PIF: Post Reclass Wage Index location	Tables 4A–C Beginning on page (A) 50511; PIF: FY 2011 Wage Index Location	Tables 4A–C at https://www.cms.gov/AcuteInpatientPPS/01_overview.asp; PIF: FY 2012 Wage Index Location	
Labor-Related Portion	For wage indexes greater than 1.0, the labor-related portion is 68.802% of the standard operating rate. For wage indexes less than or equal to 1.0, the labor-related portion is 62%. (A) page 43856	For wage indexes greater than 1.0, the labor-related portion is 68.8% of the standard operating rate. For wage indexes less than or equal to 1.0, the labor-related portion is 62% (A) page 50422	For wage indexes greater than 1.0, the labor-related portion is 68.8% of the standard operating rate. For wage indexes less than or equal to 1.0, the labor-related portion is 62% (A) page 51786	
Post-acute care transfer to a rehabilitation hospital or unit or long-term hospital qualifying DRGs	Medicare-Severity DRGs designated with a "yes" in the "FY 2010 Final Rule Post-Acute DRG" column in Table 5 (A) beginning at page 44126	Medicare-Severity DRGs designated with a "yes" in the "FY 2011 Final Rule Post-Acute DRG" Column in Table 5 (A) beginning at page 50547	Medicare-Severity DRGs designated with a "yes" in the "FY 2012 Final Rule Post-Acute DRG" Column in Table 5 https://www.cms.gov/AcuteInpatientPPS/	
Post-acute care transfer qualifying DRGs	Medicare-Severity DRGs designated with a "yes" in the "FY2010 Final Rule Special Pay DRG" column in Table 5 (A) beginning at page 44126	Medicare-Severity DRGs designated with a "yes" in the "FY 2011 Final Rule Special Pay DRG" column in Table 5 (A) Beginning at page 50547	Medicare-Severity DRGs designated with a "yes" in the "FY 2012 Final Rule Special Pay DRG" column in Table 5 https://www.cms.gov/AcuteInpatientPPS/	

	Discharges Occurring On or After 3/15/2013	*Discharges Occurring On or After 03/05/2015*	*Discharges Occurring On or After 03/05/2015 (These 2015 factors are updated by AD Order dated 02/05/ 2015, and supersedes 2014 factors adopted under the OMFS rulemaking filed with the Secretary of State on 02/04/2015)*	*Discharges Occurring On or After 03/01/2016*
Applicable FR Notices	(A) August 31, 2012 (CMS-1588-F; 77 FR 53258) final rule (B) October 3, 2012 (CMS-1588-CN2; 77 FR 60315; correction notice) (C) October 29, 2012 (CMS-1588-CN3; 77 FR 65495; correction notice)	(A) August 19, 2013 (CMS-1599-F; 78 FR 50496) Final Rule (B) October 3, 2013 (CMS-1599-CN2; 78 FR 61197; corrections) (C) October 3, 2013 (CMS-1599-IFC; 78 FR 61191; interim final rule) (D) January 2, 2014 (CMS-1599-CN3; 79 FR 61; corrections) (E) January 10, 2014 (CMS-1599-CN4; 79 FR 1741; corrections) (F) March 18, 2014 (CMS-1599-IFC2; 79 FR 15022; Interim final rule)	(A) August 22, 2014 (CMS-1607-F; 79 FR 49854) Final Rule (B) October 3, 2014 (CMS-1607-CN; 79 FR 59675; Corrections)	(A) August 17, 2015 (CMS-1632-F and IFC; 80 FR 49326; Final Rule) (B) October 5, 2015 (CMS-1632-CN; 80 FR 60055; Correction)
Capital wage index	Tables 4A–C at https://www.cms.gov/AcuteInpatientPPS/01_overview.asp	Tables 4A–4C-CN2 at https://www.cms.gov/AcuteInpatientPPS/01_overview.asp	Tables 4A-1 Through 4C-2CN at https://www.cms.gov/Medicare/Medicare-Fee-for-Service-Payment/AcuteInpatientPPS/index.html	Table 3 at https://www.cms.gov/Medicare/Medicare-Fee-for-Service-Payment/AcuteInpatientPPS/index.html Note: Table 3 contains information by CBSA and information from the following tables that have been provided in previous fiscal years: Tables 3A, 3B, 4A, 4B, 4C, 4D, and 4F.
Capital market basket	1.2% (A) page 53703	1.2% (A) page 50507	1.5% (A) page 50390	1.3% (A) page 49795
Capital standard federal payment rate	$458.90 ($453.46 × 1.012)	$464.41 ($458.90 × 1.012)	$471.37 ($464.41 × 1.015)	$477.50 ($471.37 x 1.013)

Complex Spinal Surgery DRGs			N/A	N/A
Fixed Loss Outlier Threshold	$21,821 ((A) page 53696)	$21,748 ((A) page 50983)	$24,626 (B) page 59680	$22,539 (B) page 60058
National Standard Operating Rate	$5,805.19 ($5,658.08 × 1.026)	$5,950.32 ($5,805.19 × 1.025)	$6,122.88 ($5,950.32 × 1.029)	$6,269.83 ($6,122.88 × 1.024)
Operating Wage Index	Tables 4A–C at https://www.cms.gov/AcuteInpatientPPS/01_overview.asp; PIF: FY 2013 Wage Index Location	Tables 4A–C at https://www.cms.gov/AcuteInpatientPPS/01_overview.asp; PIF: FY 2014 Wage Index Location	Tables 4A-1 Through 4C-2CN at https://www.cms.gov/Medicare/Medicare-Fee-for-Service-Payment/AcuteInpatientPPS/index.html	Table 3 at https://www.cms.gov/Medicare/Medicare-Fee-for-Service-Payment/AcuteInpatientPPS/index.html Note: Table 3 contains information by CBSA and information from the following tables that have been provided in previous fiscal years: Tables 3A, 3B, 4A, 4B, 4C, 4D, and 4F.
Labor-Related Portion	For wage indexes greater than 1.0, the labor-related portion is 68.8% of the standard operating rate. For wage indexes less than or equal to 1.0, the labor-related portion is 62% (A) page 53685	For wage indexes greater than 1.0, the labor-related portion is 69.6% of the standard operating rate. For wage indexes less than or equal to 1.0, the labor-related portion is 62% (A) page 50972	For wage indexes greater than 1.0, the labor-related portion is 69.6% of the standard operating rate. For wage indexes less than or equal to 1.0, the labor-related portion is 62% (A) page 49991	For wage indexes greater than 1.0, the labor-related portion is 69.6% of the standard operating rate. For wage indexes less than or equal to 1.0, the labor-related portion is 62% (A) page 49505
Post-acute care transfer to a rehabilitation hospital or unit or long-term hospital qualifying DRGs	Medicare-Severity DRGs designated with a "yes" in the "FY 2013 Final Rule Post-Acute DRG" Column in Table 5 https://www.cms.gov/AcuteInpatientPPS/	Medicare-Severity DRGs designated with a "yes" in the "FY 2014 FR Post-Acute DRG" Column in Table 5 https://www.cms.gov/AcuteInpatientPPS/	Medicare-Severity DRGs designated with a "yes" in the "FINAL Post-Acute DRG" Column in Table 5 https://www.cms.gov/Medicare/Medicare-Fee-for-Service-Payment/AcuteInpatientPPS/index.html?redirect=/AcuteInpatientPPS/01_overview.asp	Medicare-Severity DRGs designated with a "yes" in the "FY 2016 Final Post-Acute DRG" Column in Table 5 https://www.cms.gov/Medicare/Medicare-Fee-for-Service-Payment/AcuteInpatientPPS/index.html?redirect=/AcuteInpatientPPS/01_overview.asp

Post-acute care transfer qualifying DRGs	Medicare-Severity DRGs designated with a "yes" in the "FY 2013 Final Rule Special Pay DRG" column in Table 5 https://www.cms.gov/AcuteInpatientPPS/	Medicare-Severity DRGs designated with a "yes" in the "FY 2014 FR Special Pay DRG" column in Table 5 https://www.cms.gov/AcuteInpatientPPS/	Medicare-Severity DRGs designated with a "yes" in the "FY 2015 NPRM Special Pay DRG" column in Table 5 https://www.cms.gov/Medicare/Medicare-Fee-for-Service-Payment/Acute InpatientPPS/index.html?redirect=/AcuteInpatientPPS/01_overview.asp	Medicare-Severity DRGs designated with a "yes" in the "FY 2016 Final Special Pay DRG" column in Table 5 https://www.cms.gov/Medicare/Medicare-Fee-for-Service-Payment/Acute InpatientPPS/index.html?redirect=/AcuteInpatientPPS/01_overview.asp
Uncompensated Care Adjustment		0.943 (A) page 50634	0.7619 (A) page 50014	0.6369 (A) page 49522
	Discharges Occurring on or After 01/01/2017	*Discharges Occurring on or After 12/01/2017*	*Discharges Occurring on or After 12/01/2018*	*Discharges Occurring on or After 11/01/2019*
Applicable FR Notices	(A) August 22, 2016 (CMS-1655-F; 81 FR 56762) final rule (B) October 5, 2016 (CMS-1655-F; 81 FR 68947; final rule; correction)	(A) August 14, 2017 (CMS-1677-F; 82 FR 37990 (B) October 4, 2017 (CMS-1677-CN; 82 FR 46138; Final rule; correction)	(A) August 17, 2018 (CMS-1694-F; 83 FR 41144) (B) October 3, 2018 (CMS-1694-CN2; 83 FR 49836; Correction)	(A) August 16, 2019 (CMS-1716-F; 84 FR 42044 (B) October 8, 2019 (CMS-1716-CN2; 84 FR 53603; correction)
Capital wage index	Table 3 at https://www.cms.gov/Medicare/Medicare-Fee-for-Service-Payment/AcuteInpatientPPS/index.html	Table 3 at https://www.cms.gov/Medicare/Medicare-Fee-for-Service-Payment/AcuteInpatientPPS/index.html	Table 3 at https://www.cms.gov/Medicare/Medicare-Fee-for-Service-Payment/AcuteInpatientPPS/index.html	Table 3 (CN), at https://www.cms.gov/Medicare/Medicare-Fee-for-Service-Payment/AcuteInpatientPPS/index.html
Capital market basket	1.2% (A) page 57295	1.3% (A) page 38174	1.4% (A) page 41730	1.5% (A) page 42640
Capital standard federal payment rate	$483.23 ($477.50 × 1.012)	$489.51 ($483.23 × 1.013)	$496.36 ($489.51 × 1.014)	$503.81 ($496.36 × 1.015)
Complex Spinal Surgery DRGs	N/A	N/A	N/A	N/A
Fixed Loss Outlier Threshold	$23,573 ((B) page 68952)	$26,537 ((B) page 46143)	$25,743 ((B) page 49844)	$26.552 ((B) page 53609)
National Standard Operating Rate	$6,439.11 ($6,269.83 × 1.027)	$6,612.97 ($6,439.11 × 1.027)	$6,804.75 ($6,612.97 × 1.029)	$7,008.89 ($6,804.75 × 1.030)
Operating Wage Index	Table 3 at https://www.cms.gov/Medicare/Medicare-Fee-for-Service-Payment/AcuteInpatientPPS/index.html	Table 3 at https://www.cms.gov/Medicare/Medicare-Fee-for-Service-Payment/AcuteInpatientPPS/index.html	Table 3 at https://www.cms.gov/Medicare/Medicare-Fee-for-Service-Payment/AcuteInpatientPPS/index.html	Table 3 (CN) at https://www.cms.gov/Medicare/Medicare-Fee-for-Service-Payment/AcuteInpatientPPS/index.html

Labor-Related Portion	For wage indexes greater than 1.0, the labor-related portion is 69.6% of the standard operating rate. For wage indexes less than or equal to 1.0, the labor-related portion is 62% (A) page 57276	For wage indexes greater than 1.0, the labor-related portion is 68.3% of the standard operating rate. For wage indexes less than or equal to 1.0, the labor-related portion is 62% (A) page 38157	For wage indexes greater than 1.0, the labor-related portion is 68.3% of the standard operating rate. For wage indexes less than or equal to 1.0, the labor-related portion is 62% (A) page 41713	For wage indexes greater than 1.0, the labor-related portion is 68.3% of the standard operating rate. For wage indexes less than or equal to 1.0, the labor-related portion is 62% (A) page 42325
Post-acute care transfer to a rehabilitation hospital or unit or long-term hospital qualifying DRGs	Medicare-Severity DRGs designated with a "yes" in the "FY 2017 FINAL Post-Acute DRG" Column in Table 5 https://www.cms.gov/Medicare/Medicare-Fee-for-Service-Payment/AcuteInpatientPPS/index.html?redirect=/AcuteInpatientPPS/01_overview.asp	Medicare-Severity DRGs designated with a "yes" in the "FY 2018 Final Post-Acute DRG" Column in Table 5 https://www.cms.gov/Medicare/Medicare-Fee-for-Service-Payment/AcuteInpatientPPS/index.html?redirect=/AcuteInpatientPPS/01_overview.asp	Medicare-Severity DRGs designated with a "yes" in the "FY 2019 FINAL Post-Acute DRG" Column in Table 5 https://www.cms.gov/Medicare/Medicare-Fee-for-Service-Payment/AcuteInpatientPPS/index.html	Medicare-Severity DRGs designated with a "yes" in the "FY 2020 FINAL Post-Acute DRG" Column in Table 5, (Final Rule and Correction Notice) https://www.cms.gov/Medicare/Medicare-Fee-for-Service-Payment/AcuteInpatientPPS/index.html
Post-acute care transfer qualifying DRGs	Medicare-Severity DRGs designated with a "yes" in the "FY 2017 FINAL Special Pay DRG" column in Table 5 https://www.cms.gov/Medicare/Medicare-Fee-for-Service-Payment/AcuteInpatientPPS/index.html?redirect=/AcuteInpatientPPS/01_overview.asp	Medicare-Severity DRGs designated with a "yes" in the FY 2018 Final Special Pay DRG" column in Table 5 https://www.cms.gov/Medicare/Medicare-Fee-for-Service-Payment/AcuteInpatientPPS/index.html?redirect=/AcuteInpatientPPS/01_overview.asp	Medicare-Severity DRGs designated with a "yes" in the "FY 2019 FINAL Special Pay DRG" column in Table 5 https://www.cms.gov/Medicare/Medicare-Fee-for-Service-Payment/AcuteInpatientPPS/index.html	Medicare-Severity DRGs designated with a "yes" in the "FY 2020 FINAL Special Pay DRG" column in Table 5, (Final Rule and Correction Notice) https://www.cms.gov/Medicare/Medicare-Fee-for-Service-Payment/AcuteInpatientPPS/index.html
Uncompensated Care Adjustment	0.5536 (A) page 56950	0.5801 (A) page 38200	0.6751 (A) page 41409	0.6714 (A) page 42358

(c) Payment Impact File by Date of Discharge

(1) The Payment Impact File can be accessed at: http://www.cms.gov/AcuteInpatientPPS/ and the referenced sections are incorporated by reference and will be made available upon request to the Administrative Director.

	Discharges Occurring On or After 1/1/2004	*Discharges Occurring On or After 11/29/2004*	*Discharges Occurring On or After 12/1/2005*	*Discharges Occurring On or After 12/1/2006*
Applicable Payment Impact File (PIF)	FY2004 Final Rule Impact File	FY2005 Final Rule Impact File	FY2006 Final Rule Impact File	FY2007 Final Rule Impact File

Capital geographic adjustment factor	PIF: Capital Wage Index	PIF: POST RECLASS GAF	PIF: WICGRN	PIF: Post Reclass GAF_a (for first half FY 2007) and Post Reclass GAF_b (for capital second half FY 2007)
Large Urban Add-on	PIF: Post-Reclassification Urban/Rural location	PIF: Standardized payment location	PIF: URSPA	PIF: URSPA
Capital Disproportionate Share Adjustment Factor	PIF: Capital Disproportionate Share Adjustment location (DSHCPG)	PIF: Capital Disproportionate Share (DSH) Adjustment location (CAPITAL DSH ADJ.)	PIF: Capital Disproportionate Share (DSH) Adjustment location (DSHCPG)	PIF: Capital Disproportionate Share (DSH) Adjustment location (DSHCPG)
Capital Indirect Medical Education Adjustment Factor	PIF: Capital IME Adjustment location (TCHCP)	PIF: IME adjustment factor for capital PPS location (IME ADJUSTMENT-CAPITAL)	PIF: IME adjustment factor for capital PPS location (TCHCP)	PIF: IME adjustment factor for capital PPS location (TCHCP)
Operating Wage Index	Tables 4A–4C beginning on (A) page 57736; PIF: Operating Wage Index location (WIGRN)	Tables $4A_1$–$4C_2$ beginning on (C) page 78619; PIF: Final Wage Index location (WIGRN)	Tables 4A–4C beginning on (A) page 47580 as corrected by Tables 4A–4C beginning on (B) page 57163; PIF: Post Reclass Wage Index location	Tables 4A-1–4C-1 (for discharges before 4/1/2007) and Tables 4A-2–4C-2 (for discharges occurring on or after 4/1/2007) beginning on (B) page 59975; PIF: Post Reclass Wage Index_a (for first half FY 2007) and Post Reclass Wage Index_b (for second half FY 2007)
Operating Disproportionate Share Adjustment Factor	PIF: Operating DSH Adjustment Factor location (DSHOPG)	PIF: Operating Disproportionate Share (DSH) Adjustment Factor location (OPERATING DSH ADJ.)	PIF: Operating Disproportionate Share (DSH) Adjustment Factor location (DSHOPG)	PIF: Operating Disproportionate Share (DSH) Adjustment Factor location (DSHOPG)
Operating Indirect Medical Education Adjustment	PIF: Operating IME Adjustment location (TCHOP)	PIF: IME Adjustment Factor for Operating PPS location (IME ADJUSTMENT OPERATING)	PIF: IME Adjustment Factor for Operating PPS location (TCHOP)	PIF: IME Adjustment Factor for Operating PPS location (TCHOP)
Sole Community Hospital — Hospital Specific Rate	PIF: Hospital — Specific Rate location (HSPPUB)	PIF: Sole Community Hospital Cost/Case 1982/ 1987 and Sole Community Hospital Cost/Case 1996 locations	PIF: 82/87 Hospital Specific Rate Updated to FY 2006 (OLDHSPPS) and 1996 Hospital Specific Rate Updated to FY 2006 (HSP96) locations	PIF: 82/87/96 Hospital Specific Rate Updated to FY 2007 for SCH Providers location (HSP Rate)

Cost-to-Charge Ratio	PIF: Operating Cost-to-Charge Ratio location (OPCCR) and Capital Cost-to-Charge location (CPCCR)	PIF: Operating Cost-to-Charge Ratio location (OPCCR) and Capital Cost-to-Charge location (CPCCR)	PIF: Operating Cost-to-Charge Ratio location (OPCCR) and Capital Cost-to-Charge location (CPCCR)	PIF: Operating Cost-to-Charge Ratio location (OPCCR) and Capital Cost-to-Charge location (CPCCR)
	Discharges Occurring On or After 1/1/2008	*Discharges Occurring On or After 12/1/2008*	*Discharges Occurring On or After 12/1/2009*	*Discharges Occurring On or After 3/01/2011*
Applicable Payment Impact File (PIF)	FY2008 Final Rule	FY2009 Final Rule	FY2010 Correction Notice	FY 2011 Final Rule
Capital Geographic Adjustment Factor	Post Reclass GAF	Post Reclass GAF	Post Reclass GAF	FY 2011 GAF
Capital Disproportionate Share Adjustment Factor	PIF: Capital Disproportionate Share (DSH) Adjustment location (DSHCPG)	PIF: Capital Disproportionate Share (DSH) Adjustment location (DSHCPG)	PIF: Capital Disproportionate Share (DSH) Adjustment location (DSHCPG)	PIF: Capital Disproportionate Share (DSH) adjustment location (DSHCPG)
Capital Indirect Medical Education Adjustment Factor	PIF: IME adjustment factor for capital PPS location (TCHCP)	PIF: IME adjustment factor for capital PPS location (TCHCP)	PIF: IME adjustment factor for capital PPS location (TCHCP)	PIF: IME adjustment factor for capital PPS location (TCHCP)
Operating Wage Index	Tables 4A–4C beginning on (B) page 57698; PIF: Post Reclass Wage Index location	Tables 4A–4C beginning on (B) page 57956; PIF: Post Reclass Wage Index location	Tables 4A–4C beginning on page (A) 44085 as corrected by Tables 4A–4C beginning on (B) page 51505 for certain areas; PIF: Post Reclass Wage Index location	Tables 4A–C Beginning on page (A) 50511; PIF: FY 2011 Wage Index Location
Operating Disproportionate Share Adjustment Factor	PIF: Operating Disproportionate Share (DSH) Adjustment Factor location (DSHOPG)	PIF: Operating Disproportionate Share (DSH) Adjustment Factor location (DSHOPG)	PIF: Operating Disproportionate Share (DSH) Adjustment Factor location (DSHOPG)	PIF: Operating Disproportionate Share (DSH) Adjustment Factor location (DSHOPG)
Operating Indirect Medical Education Adjustment	PIF: IME Adjustment Factor for Operating PPS location (TCHOP)	PIF: IME Adjustment Factor for Operating PPS location (TCHOP)	PIF: IME Adjustment Factor for Operating PPS location (TCHOP)	PIF: IME Adjustment Factor for Operating PPS location (TCHOP)
Sole Community Hospital — Hospital Specific Rate	PIF: 82/87/96 Hospital Specific Rate Updated to FY 2008 for SCH Providers location (HSP Rate)	PIF: 82/87/96 Hospital Specific Payment (HSP) Rate Updated to FY 2009 for SCH Providers location (HSP Rate)	PIF: 82/87/96/06 Hospital Specific Payment (HSP) Rate Updated to FY 2010 for SCH Providers location (FY10 HSP Rate)	PIF: 82/87/96/06 Hospital Specific Payment (HSP) Rate Updated to FY2011 for SCH Providers location (FY11 HSP Rate)
Cost-to-Charge Ratio	PIF: Operating Cost-to-Charge Ratio location (OPCCR) and Capital Cost-to-Charge location (CPCCR)	PIF: Operating Cost-to-Charge Ratio location (Operating CCR) and Capital Cost-to-Charge location (Capital CCR)	PIF: Operating Cost-to-Charge Ratio location (Operating CCR) and Capital Cost-to-Charge location (Capital CCR)	PIF: Operating Cost-to-Charge Ratio location (Operating CCR) and Capital Cost-to-Charge location (Capital CCR)

	Discharges Occurring On or After 12/01/2011	*Discharges Occurring On or After 03/15/2013*	*Discharges Occurring On or After 03/05/2015*	*Discharges Occurring On or After 03/05/2015 (These 2015 factors are updated by AD Order dated 02/05/2015, and supersedes 2014 factors adopted under the OMFS rulemaking filed with the Secretary of State on 02/04/2015)*
Applicable Payment Impact File (PIF)	FY 2012 Final Rule-IPPS Impact File	FY 13 FR Impact File — updated October 2012	FY 2014 Impact file — updated January 2014 to reflect changes from the September 2013 correction notice and interim final rule with comment	FY 15 Impact File (August 22, 2014 Final Rule and October 3, 2014 Correction Notice)
Capital Geographic Adjustment Factor	FY 2012 GAF	FY 2013 GAF	FY 2014 GAF— Updated September 2013	FY 2015 GAF— Updated October 2014
Capital Disproportionate Share Adjustment Factor	PIF: Capital Disproportionate Share (DSH) adjustment location (DSHCPG)	PIF: Capital Disproportionate Share (DSH) adjustment location (DSHCPG)	PIF: Capital Disproportionate Share (DSH) adjustment location (DSHCPG)	PIF: Capital Disproportionate Share (DSH) adjustment location (DSHCPG)
Capital Indirect Medical Education Adjustment Factor	PIF: IME adjustment factor for capital PPS location (TCHCP)	PIF: IME adjustment factor for capital PPS location (TCHCP)	PIF: IME adjustment factor for capital PPS location (TCHCP)	PIF: IME adjustment factor for capital PPS location (TCHCP)
Operating Wage Index	Tables 4A–C at https://www.cms.gov/AcuteInpatientPPS/01_overview.asp; PIF: FY 2012 Wage Index location	Tables 4A–C at https://www.cms.gov/AcuteInpatientPPS/01_overview.asp; PIF: FY 2013 Wage Index location	Tables 4A–C–CN2 at https://www.cms.gov/AcuteInpatientPPS/01_overview.asp; PIF: FY 2014 Wage Index location	Tables 4A-1 Through 4C-2CN at https://www.cms.gov/Medicare/Medicare-Fee-for-Service-Payment/AcuteInpatientPPS/index.html
Operating Disproportionate Share Adjustment Factor	PIF: Operating Disproportionate Share (DSH) Adjustment Factor location (DSHOPG)	PIF: Operating Disproportionate Share (DSH) Adjustment Factor location (DSHOPG)	PIF: Operating Disproportionate Share Hospital (DSH) Adjustment Factor location (DSHOPG)	PIF: Operating Disproportionate Share Hospital (DSH) Adjustment. Reflects a 75% reduction to the DSH adjustment required under Section 3133 of the Affordable Care Act. Factor location (DSHOPG)
Operating Indirect Medical Education Adjustment	PIF: IME Adjustment Factor for Operating PPS location (TCHOP)	PIF: IME Adjustment Factor for Operating PPS location (TCHOP)	PIF: IME Adjustment Factor for Operating PPS location (TCHOP)	PIF: IME Adjustment Factor for Operating PPS location (TCHOP)

Sole Community Hospital — Hospital Specific Rate	PIF: 82/87/96/06 Hospital Specific Payment (HSP) Rate Updated to FY2012 for SCH Providers location (FY12 HSP Rate)	PIF: 82/87/96/06 Hospital Specific Payment (HSP) Rate Updated to FY2013 for SCH Providers location (FY13 HSP Rate)	PIF: 82/87/96/06 Hospital Specific Payment (HSP) Rate Updated to FY2014 for SCH and MDH Providers with the -0.2% adjustment for presumptive inpatient hospital status policy. Location (FY14 HSP Rate)	PIF: 82/87/96/06 Hospital Specific Payment (HSP) Rate Updated to FY2015 for SCH and MDH Providers. Location (FY14 HSP Rate)
Cost-to-Charge Ratio	PIF: Operating Cost-to-Charge Ratio location (Operating CCR) and Capital Cost-to-Charge location (Capital CCR) *Discharges Occurring On or After 03/01/2016*	PIF: Operating Cost-to-Charge Ratio location (Operating CCR) and Capital Cost-to-Charge location (Capital CCR) *Discharges Occurring On or After 01/01/2017*	PIF: Operating Cost-to-Charge Ratio location (Operating CCR) and Capital Cost-to-Charge location (Capital CCR) *Discharges Occurring On or After 12/01/2017*	PIF: Operating Cost-to-Charge Ratio location (Operating CCR) and Capital Cost-to-Charge location (Capital CCR) *Discharges Occurring On or After 12/01/2018*
Applicable Payment Impact File (PIF)	FY 16 Impact File (August 17, 2015 Final Rule and October 5, 2015 Correction Notice)	FY 17 Impact File (August 22, 2016 Final Rule and October 5, 2016 Correction Notice)	FY 18 Impact File (August 14, 2017 Final Rule and October 4, 2017 Correction Notice)	FY 19 Impact File (August 17, 2018 Final Rule and October 3, 2018 Correction Notice)
Capital Geographic Adjustment Factor	FY 2016 GAF — Updated October 2015	FY 2017 GAF — Updated October 2016	FY 2018 GAF — Updated October 2017	FY 2019 GAF — Updated October 2018
Capital Disproportionate Share Adjustment Factor	PIF: Capital Disproportionate Share (DSH) adjustment location (DSHCPG)	PIF: Capital Disproportionate Share (DSH) adjustment location (DSHCPG)	PIF: FY 2018 Capital Disproportionate Share (DSH) adjustment location (DSHCPG)	PIF: FY 2019 Capital Disproportionate Share Share (DSH) adjustment (DSHCPP)
Capital Indirect Medical Education Adjustment Factor	PIF: IME adjustment factor for capital PPS location (TCHCP)	PIF: IME adjustment factor for capital PPS location (TCHCP)	PIF: IME adjustment factor for capital PPS location (TCHCP)	PIF: IME adjustment factor for capital PPS location (TCHCP)
Operating Wage Index	Table 3 at https://www.csm.gov/Medicare/Medicare-Fee-for-Service-Payment/AcuteInpatientPPS/index.html Note: Table 3 contains information by CBSA and information from the following tables that have been provided in previous fiscal years: Tables 3A, 3B, 4A, 4B, 4C, 4D, and 4F.	Table 3 at https://www.cms.gov/Medicare/Medicare-Fee-for-Service-Payment/AcuteInpatientPPS/index.html	Table 3 at https://www.cms.gov/Medicare/Medicare-Fee-for-Service-Payment/AcuteInpatientPPS/index.html	Table 3 at https://www.cms.gov/Medicare/Medicare-Fee-for-Service-Payment/AcuteInpatientPPS/index.html

Operating Disproportionate Share Adjustment Factor	PIF: Operating Disproportionate Share Hospital (DSH) Adjustment. Reflects a 75% reduction to the DSH adjustment required under section 3133 of the Affordable Care Act. Factor location (DSHOPG)	PIF: Operating Disproportionate Share Hospital (DSH) Adjustment. Reflects a 75% reduction to the DSH adjustment required under Section 3133 of the Affordable Care Act. Factor location (DSHOPG)	PIF: Estimated FY 2018 Operating Disproportionate Share Hospital (DSH) adjustment. Reflects a 75% reduction to the DSH adjustment required under Section 3333 of the Affordable Care Act (DSHOPP)	PIF: Estimated FY 2019 Operating Disproportionate Share Hospital (DSH) adjustment. Reflects a 75% reduction to the DSH adjustment required under Section 3333 of the Affordable Care Act (DSHOPP)
Operating Indirect Medical Education Adjustment	PIF: IME Adjustment Factor for Operating PPS location (TCHOP)	PIF: IME Adjustment Factor for Operating PPS location (TCHOP)	PIF: IME Adjustment Factor for Operating IPPS location (TCHOP)	PIF: IME Adjustment Factor for Operating IPPS location (TCHOP)
Sole Community Hospital — Hospital Specific Rate	PIF: Hospital Specific Payment (HSP) Rate updated to FY 2016 for SCH and MDH providers. HSP Rate is based on the March 2015 update of the Provider Specific File (PSF). Location (HSP Rate)	PIF: Hospital Specific Payment (HSP) Rate updated to FY 2017 for SCH and MDH providers. HSP Rate is based on the March 2016 update of the Provider Specific File (PSF). Location (HSP Rate)	PIF: Hospital Specific Payment (HSP) Rate updated to FY 2018 for SCH providers. HSP Rate is based on the March 2017 update of the Provider Specific File (PSF). Location (HSP Rate)	PIF: Hospital Specific Payment (HSP) Rate updated to FY 2019 for SCH providers. HSP Rate is based on the March 2018 update of the Provider Specific File (PSF). Location (HSP Rate)
Cost-to-Charge Ratio	PIF: Operating Cost-to-Charge Ratio location (Operating CCR) and Capital Cost-to-Charge location (Capital CCR)	PIF: Operating Cost-to-Charge Ratio location (Operating CCR) and Capital Cost-to-Charge location (Captial CCR)	PIF: Operating Cost-to-Charge Ratio location (Operating CCR) and Capital Cost-to-Charge location (Capital CCR)	PIF: Operating Cost-to-Charge Ratio location (Operating CCR) and Capital Cost-to-Charge location (Capital CCR)

Discharges Occurring On or After 11/01/2019

Applicable Payment Impact File (PIF)	FY 20 Impact File (Final Rule and Correction Notice)
Capital Geographic Adjustment Factor	FY 2020 GAF — Updated October 2019
Capital Disproportionate Share Adjustment Factor	PIF: Capital Disproportionate Share (DSH) adjustment location (DSHCPP)
Capital Indirect Medical Education Adjustment Factor	PIF: IME adjustment factor for capital PPS location (TCHCP)

Operating Wage Index	Table 3 (CN) at https:// www.csm.gov/ Medicare/Medicare-Fee-for-Service-Payment/ AcuteInpatientPPS/ index.html
Operating Disproportionate Share Adjustment Factor	PIF: Estimated FY 2020 Operating Disproportionate Share Hospital (DSH) adjustment. Reflects a 75% reduction to the DSH adjustment required under Section 3333 of the Affordable Care Act (DSHOPP)
Operating Indirect Medical Education Adjustment	PIF: IME Adjustment Factor for Operating IPPS location (TCHOP)
Sole Community Hospital — Hospital Specific Rate	PIF: Hospital Specific Payment (HSP) Rate updated to FY 2020 for SCH providers. HSP Rate is based on the March 2019 update of the Provider Specific File (PSF). Location (HSP Rate)
Cost-to-Charge Ratio	PIF: Operating Cost-to-Charge Ratio location (Operating CCR) and Capital Cost-to-Charge location (Capital CCR)

Note: Authority cited: Sections 133, 4603.5, 5307.1, 5307.3 and 5318, Labor Code. Reference: Sections 4600, 4603.2, 5307.1 and 5318, Labor Code.

History: 1. New section filed 12-27-2012; operative 1-1-2013 as a file and print only pursuant to Government Code section 11340.9(g) (Register 2012, No. 52).

2. Amendment filed 3-13-2013; operative 3-15-2013. Submitted to OAL for filing and printing only pursuant to Labor Code section 5307.1(g)(2) (Register 2013, No. 11).

3. Amendment filed 2-4-2015; operative 3-5-2015. Submitted to OAL for printing only pursuant to Government Code section 11340.9 (Register 2015, No. 6).

4. Amendment filed 2-25-2015; operative 3-5-2015 pursuant to Labor Code section 5307.1(g)(2). Submit-ted to OAL for printing only pursuant to Labor Code section 5307.1(g)(2) (Register 2015, No. 9).

5. Amendment filed 3-14-2016; operative 3-1-2016 pursuant to Labor Code section 5307.1(g)(2). Submit-ted to OAL for filing and printing only pursuant to Labor Code section 5307.1(g)(2) (Register 2016, No. 12).

6. Editorial correction of subsection (b) (Register 2016, No. 49).

7. Amendment of subsections (a)(1), (b)(1) and (c)(1) filed 1-19-2017; operative 1-1-2017 pursuant to Labor Code section 5307.1(g)(2). Submitted to OAL for printing only pursuant to Labor Code section 5307.1(g)(2) (Register 2017, No. 3).

8. Amendment filed 11-28-2017; operative 12-1-2017 pursuant to Labor Code section 5307.1(g)(2). Submit-

ted to OAL for filing and printing only pursuant to Labor Code section 5307.1(g)(2) (Register 2017, No. 48).

9. Editorial correction of formatting (Register 2018, No. 15).

10. Nonsubstantive action without change filed 4-27-2018 pursuant to section 100, title 1, California Code of Regulations to correct errors in 11-28-2017 filing (Register 2018, No. 17).

11. Editorial correction of subsections (b)(1) and (c)(1) (Register 2018, No. 48).

12. Amendment filed 11-26-2018; operative 12-1-2018 pursuant to Labor Code section 5307.1(g)(2). Submitted to OAL for filing and printing only pursuant to Labor Code section 5307.1(g)(2) (Register 2018, No. 48).

13. Amendment filed 10-16-2019; operative 11-1-2019 pursuant to Labor Code section 5307.1(g)(2). Submitted to OAL for filing and printing only pursuant to Labor Code section 5307.1(g)(2) (Register 2019, No. 42).

14. Amendment of subsections (b)(1) and (c)(1) filed 12-12-2019; operative 11-1-2019 pursuant to Labor Code section 5307.1(g)(2). Submitted to OAL for filing and printing only pursuant to Labor Code section 5307.1(g)(2) (Register 2019, No. 50).

ARTICLE 5.5.2
Medical Treatment Utilization Schedule

§9792.23.10.   Hip and Groin Disorders Guideline.

The Administrative Director adopts and incorporates by reference the Hip and Groin Disorders Guideline (ACOEM April 24, 2019) into the MTUS from the ACOEM Practice Guidelines.

Note: Authority cited: Sections 133, 4603.5, 5307.3 and 5307.27, Labor Code. Reference: Sections 77.5, 4600, 4604.5 and 5307.27, Labor Code.

History: 1. New section filed 1-11-2018; operative 12-1-2017. Submitted to OAL for filing and printing only pursuant to Labor Code section 5307.27(a) (Register 2018, No. 2).

2. Amendment of section heading, section and Note filed 10-21-2019; operative 10-7-2019. Submitted to OAL for printing only pursuant to Labor Code section 5302.27(a) (Register 2019, No. 43).

SUBCHAPTER 1.7
[Repealed]

§10175.   Definitions. [Repealed]

Note: Authority cited: Sections 133, 4612 and 5307.3, Labor Code. Reference: Section 4612, Labor Code.

History: 1. New subchapter 1.7 and section filed 8-31-93; operative 8-31-93. Submitted to OAL for printing only pursuant to Government Code section 11351 (Register 93, No. 36).

2. Change without regulatory effect repealing subchapter 1.7 (sections 10175-10181) and section filed 11-6-2019 pursuant to section 100, title 1, California Code of Regulations (Register 2019, No. 45).

§10176.   Eligible Employers and Employees. [Repealed]

Note: Authority cited: Sections 133, 4612 and 5307.3, Labor Code. Reference: Section 4612, Labor Code.

History: 1. New section filed 8-31-93; operative 8-31-93. Submitted to OAL for printing only pursuant to Government Code section 11351 (Register 93, No. 36).

2. Change without regulatory effect repealing section filed 11-6-2019 pursuant to section 100, title 1, California Code of Regulations (Register 2019, No. 45).

§10177.   Eligible Applicants. [Repealed]

Note: Authority cited: Sections 133, 4612 and 5307.3, Labor Code. Reference: Section 4612, Labor Code.

History: 1. New section filed 8-31-93; operative 8-31-93. Submitted to OAL for printing only pursuant to Government Code section 11351 (Register 93, No. 36).

2. Change without regulatory effect repealing section filed 11-6-2019 pursuant to section 100, title 1, California Code of Regulations (Register 2019, No. 45).

§10178.   Pilot Project Proposal Requirements. [Repealed]

Note: Authority cited: Sections 133, 4612 and 5307.3, Labor Code. Reference: Section 4612, Labor Code.

History: 1. New section filed 8-31-93; operative 8-31-93. Submitted to OAL for printing only pursuant to Government Code section 11351 (Register 93, No. 36).

2. Change without regulatory effect repealing section filed 11-6-2019 pursuant to section 100, title 1, California Code of Regulations (Register 2019, No. 45).

§10179.   Selection of Proposals; Priorities; Pilot Termination. [Repealed]

Note: Authority cited: Sections 133, 4612 and 5307.3, Labor Code. Reference: Section 4612, Labor Code.

History: 1. New section filed 8-31-93; operative 8-31-93. Submitted to OAL for printing only pursuant to Government Code section 11351 (Register 93, No. 36).

2. Amendment of section heading and subsection (c) filed 10-11-94; operative 10-11-94. Submitted to OAL for printing only pursuant to Government Code section 11351 (Register 94, No. 41).

3. Change without regulatory effect repealing section filed 11-6-2019 pursuant to section 100, title 1, California Code of Regulations (Register 2019, No. 45).

§10180. Employee Choice of Plans. [Repealed]

Note: Authority cited: Sections 133, 4612 and 5307.3, Labor Code. Reference: Section 4612, Labor Code.

History: 1. New section filed 8-31-93; operative 8-31-93. Submitted to OAL for printing only pursuant to Government Code section 11351 (Register 93, No. 36).

2. Change without regulatory effect repealing section filed 11-6-2019 pursuant to section 100, title 1, California Code of Regulations (Register 2019, No. 45).

§10181. Records, Claims Administration, Auditing, and Termination. [Repealed]

Note: Authority cited: Sections 133, 4612 and 5307.3, Labor Code. Reference: Sections 3700, 4612, 5300, 6409 and 6409.1, Labor Code.

History: 1. New section filed 8-31-93; operative 8-31-93. Submitted to OAL for printing only pursuant to Government Code section 11351 (Register 93, No. 36).

2. Change without regulatory effect repealing section filed 11-6-2019 pursuant to section 100, title 1, California Code of Regulations (Register 2019, No. 45).

SUBCHAPTER 2
Workers' Compensation Appeals Board—Rules and Practice Procedure

ARTICLE 1
General

§10300. Construction of Rules.

(a) The provisions of these rules are severable. If any provision of these rules, or the application thereof to any person or circumstances, is held invalid, that invalidity shall not affect other provisions or applications that can be given effect without the invalid provision or application.

(b) Article and section headings shall not be deemed to limit or modify the meaning or intent of the provisions of any rule hereof.

Note: Authority cited: Sections 133, 5307, 5309 and 5708, Labor Code. Reference: Section 5307, Labor Code.

History: 1. Repeal of chap. 4.5 (Industrial Accident Commission—Rules of Practice and Procedure) and new chap. 4.5 filed by Industrial Accident Commission 12-27-65; effective thirtieth day thereafter (Register 65, No. 25). For former chap. 4.5, see Registers 58, No. 14; 59, No. 21; 61, No. 9; 61, No. 12; 62, No. 7; 62, No. 21; 63, No. 2; 65, Nos. 5, 13 and 22.

2. Ratification and adoption by Workmen's Compensation Appeals Board, of regulations filed by Industrial Accident Commission on 12-27-65, filed 1-26-66 (Register 66, No. 3).

3. Repealer of subchapter 2 (articles 1-19, sections 10300-10957, not consecutive and Appendix) and new subchapter 2 (articles 1-20, sections 10300-10958, not consecutive) filed 6-1-81; designated effective 7-1-81 (Register 81, No. 23). For prior history, see Registers 79, No. 1; 78, No. 3; 77, No. 49; 76, No. 3; 75, No. 35; 75, No. 15; 75, No. 11; 74, No. 6; 73, No. 51; 73, No. 36; 73, No. 6; 68, No. 29; 66, No. 8; 66, No. 7; and 65, No. 25.

4. Amendment filed 12-23-93; operative 1-1-94. Submitted to OAL for printing only pursuant to Government Code section 11351 (Register 93, No. 52).

5. Designation of existing section as subsection (a), new subsection (b) and amendment of Note filed 9-23-2013; operative 10-23-2013. Submitted as a file and print by the Workers' Compensation Appeals Board pursuant to Government Code section 11351 (Register 2013, No. 39).

6. Repealer and new section filed 12-17-2019; operative 1-1-2020. Submitted to OAL for printing only pursuant to Government Code section 11351 (Register 2019, No. 51).

§10301. Definitions. [Renumbered]

Note: Authority cited: Sections 133, 5307, 5309 and 5708, Labor Code. Reference: Sections 20, 54, 110, 130, 131, 134, 3201.5 et seq., 4903 et seq., 5300, 5307, 5309, 5310, 5500, 5500.3, 5501, 5501.5, 5501.6, 5502, 5700, 5701 and 5808, Labor Code.

History: 1. Amendment of section and Note filed 12-19-2002; operative 1-1-2003. Submitted to OAL for printing only pursuant to Government Code section 11351 (Register 2002, No. 51).

2. Amendment of section and Note filed 11-17-2008; operative 11-17-2008. Submitted to OAL for printing only (Register 2008, No. 47).

3. Amendment of section and Note filed 9-23-2013; operative 10-23-2013. Submitted as a file and print by the Workers' Compensation Appeals Board pursuant to Government Code section 11351 (Register 2013, No. 39).

4. Renumbering of former section 10301 to section 10305 filed 12-17-2019; operative 1-1-2020. Submitted to OAL for printing only pursuant to Government Code section 11351 (Register 2019, No. 51).

§10302. Rulemaking Notices.

Notices required by Labor Code sections 5307 and 5307.4 shall be served by the Appeals Board by regular mail, fax, electronic mail or any similar technology on those who have filed a written request for notification with the Secretary of the Workers' Compensation Appeals Board.

Note: Authority cited: Sections 133, 5307, 5309 and 5708, Labor Code. Reference: Sections 5307, 5307.4 and 5309, Labor Code.

History: 1. Amendment of section heading, section and Note filed 11-17-2008; operative 11-17-2008. Submitted to OAL for printing only (Register 2008, No. 47).

2. Repealer and new section filed 12-17-2019; operative 1-1-2020. Submitted to OAL for printing only pursuant to Government Code section 11351 (Register 2019, No. 51).

§10304. Article and Section Headings. [Repealed]

Note: Authority cited: Sections 133, 5307, Labor Code. Reference: Sections 133, 5307, Labor Code.

History: 1. Repealer filed 12-17-2019; operative 1-1-2020. Submitted to OAL for printing only pursuant to Government Code section 11351 (Register 2019, No. 51).

§10305. Definitions.

As used in this subchapter:

(a) "Administrative Director" means the Administrative Director of the Division of Workers' Compensation or a designee.

(b) "Appeals Board" means the commissioners and deputy commissioners of the Workers' Compensation Appeals Board acting en banc, in panels or individually.

(c) "Appear" means to act on behalf of any party.

(d) "Applicant" or "injured employee" or "injured worker" or "dependent" means any person asserting a right to relief under the provisions of Labor Code section 5300.

(e) "Claims administrator" means an entity that reviews or adjusts workers' compensation claims on behalf of either (1) an insurer or (2) an employer that has secured a certificate of consent to self-insure from the Department of Industrial Relations, whether employed directly or as a third party.

(f) "Defendant" means any person against whom a right to relief is claimed.

(g) "Director" means the Director of Industrial Relations or a designee.

(h) "District office" means a location of a trial court of the Workers' Compensation Appeals Board and includes a permanently staffed satellite office.

(i) "Electronic Adjudication Management System" or "EAMS" means the computerized case management system used by the Division of Workers' Compensation to electronically store and maintain adjudication files and to perform other case management functions.

(j) "En Banc decision" means a decision of the Appeals Board as a whole, issued in order to achieve uniformity of decision or in a case presenting novel issues, that is binding on panels of the Appeals Board and workers' compensation judges as legal precedent under the principle of stare decisis.

(k) "Entity" means a corporation, limited liability company, limited partnership, general partnership, limited liability partnership, sole proprietorship or any other organizational structure.

(l) "Hearing" means any trial, mandatory settlement conference, status conference, lien conference, lien trial or priority conference at a district office, a remote location or before the Appeals Board.

(m) "Lien claimant" means any person or entity claiming payment under the provisions of Labor Code section 4903 et seq., including a claim of costs filed as a lien.

(n) "Non-attorney representative" means a person who is not licensed to practice law by the State of California who acts on behalf of a party in proceedings before the Workers' Compensation Appeals Board as allowed by Labor Code sections 5700 and 4907.

(o) "Party" means any person or entity joined in a case, including but not limited to:

(1) An applicant;

(2) A defendant; or

(3) A lien claimant.

(p) "Presiding workers' compensation judge" means the presiding workers' compensation judge of any district office and includes workers' compensation judges designated to perform the functions of a presiding workers' compensation judge.

(q) "Section 4903(b) lien" means a lien claim filed in accordance with Labor Code section 4903(b) for medical treatment expenses incurred by or on behalf of the injured employee, as provided by Article 2 (commencing with Labor Code section 4600), including but not limited to expenses for interpreter services, copying and related services and transportation services incurred in connection with medical treatment. It shall not include any amount payable directly to the injured employee.

(r) "Significant panel decision" means a decision of the Appeals Board that has been designated by all members of the Appeals Board as of significant interest and importance to the workers' compensation community. Although not binding precedent, significant panel decisions are intended to augment the body of binding appellate and en banc decisions by providing further guidance to the workers' compensation community.

(s) "Status conference" means a proceeding set for the purpose of ascertaining if there are genuine disputes requiring resolution, of providing assistance to the parties in resolving disputes, of narrowing the issues, and of facilitating preparation for trial if a trial is necessary.

(t) "Submission" means the closing of the record to the receipt of further evidence or argument.

(u) "Walk-through document" means a document that is presented to a workers' compensation judge for immediate action where no notice of hearing has issued.

(v) "Workers' Compensation Appeals Board" means the commissioners and deputy commissioners of the Appeals Board, presiding workers' compensation judges and workers' compensation judges.

(w) "Workers' compensation judge" means "workers' compensation administrative law judge" (formerly, "referee") and includes pro tempore judges appointed pursuant to section 10350.

Note: Authority cited: Sections 133, 5307, 5309 and 5708, Labor Code. Reference: Sections 20, 110(a), 5300, 5307, 5309, 5500, 5500.3, 5501, 5501.5, 5501.6, 5502, 5700 and 5701, Labor Code.

History: 1. Renumbering of former section 10301 to section 10305, including amendment of section and Note, filed 12-17-2019; operative 1-1-2020. Submitted to OAL for printing only pursuant to Government Code section 11351 (Register 2019, No. 51).

ARTICLE 2
Powers, Duties and Responsibilities

§10320. Appeals Board Decisions and Orders.

The following orders, decisions and awards shall be issued only by a panel of the Appeals Board or the Appeals Board acting en banc:

(a) Any order, including a final, interim or interlocutory order, made more than 15 days after a petition for reconsideration is filed unless allowed by rule 10961.

(b) All orders dismissing, denying or granting petitions for reconsideration.

(c) All decisions after reconsideration that terminate proceedings on reconsideration, including, but not limited to, findings, orders, awards, orders approving or disapproving a Compromise and Release, orders allowing or disallowing a lien and orders for dismissal.

(d) All orders dismissing, denying or granting petitions for removal and all orders pertaining to removal.

(e) All orders in disciplinary proceedings pursuant to Labor Code section 4907.

(f) Decisions on remittitur.

(g) Orders disqualifying a workers' compensation judge under Labor Code section 5311.

Note: Authority cited: Sections 133 and 5307, Labor Code. Reference: Sections 115, 4907 and 5311, Labor Code.

History: 1. New article 2 heading and renumbering of former section 10340 to section 10320, including amendment of section and Note, filed 12-17-2019; operative 1-1-2020. Submitted to OAL for printing only pursuant to Government Code section 11351 (Register 2019, No. 51).

§10322. Workers' Compensation Appeals Board Records Not Subject to Subpoena. [Repealed]

Note: Authority cited: Sections 133 and 5307, Labor Code. Reference: Sections 127 and 5811, Labor Code.

History: 1. Amendment filed 12-19-2002; operative 1-1-2003. Submitted to OAL for printing only pursuant to Government Code section 11351 (Register 2002, No. 51).

2. Repealer filed 12-17-2019; operative 1-1-2020. Submitted to OAL for printing only pursuant to Government Code section 11351 (Register 2019, No. 51).

§10324.   Ex Parte Communications. [Renumbered]

Note: Authority cited: Sections 133, 5307, 5309 and 5708, Labor Code. Reference: Sections 5701, 5703.5, 5706, 5708 and 5906, Labor Code.

History: 1. Amendment filed 12-19-2002; operative 1-1-2003. Submitted to OAL for printing only pursuant to Government Code section 11351 (Register 2002, No. 51).

2. Amendment of section and Note filed 11-17-2008; operative 11-17-2008. Submitted to OAL for printing only (Register 2008, No. 47).

3. Renumbering of former section 10324 to section 10410 filed 12-17-2019; operative 1-1-2020. Submitted to OAL for printing only pursuant to Government Code section 11351 (Register 2019, No. 51).

§10325.   En Banc and Significant Panel Decisions.

(a)   En banc decisions of the Appeals Board are assigned by the chairperson on a majority vote of the commissioners and are binding on panels of the Appeals Board and workers' compensation judges as legal precedent under the principle of *stare decisis*.

(b)   Significant panel decisions of the Appeals Board involve an issue of general interest to the workers' compensation community but are not binding precedent.

Note: Authority cited: Sections 133 and 5307, Labor Code. Reference: Section 115, Labor Code.

History: 1. Renumbering of former section 10341 to section 10325, including amendment of section heading and section, filed 12-17-2019; operative 1-1-2020. Submitted to OAL for printing only pursuant to Government Code section 11351 (Register 2019, No. 51).

§10330.   Authority of Workers' Compensation Judges.

In any case that has been regularly assigned to a workers' compensation judge, the workers' compensation judge shall have full power, jurisdiction and authority to hear and determine all issues of fact and law presented and to issue any interim, interlocutory and final orders, findings, decisions and awards as may be necessary to the full adjudication of the case, including the fixing of the amount of the bond required in Labor Code section 3715. Orders, findings, decisions and awards issued by a workers' compensation judge shall be the orders, findings, decisions and awards of the Workers' Compensation Appeals Board unless reconsideration is granted.

Note: Authority cited: Sections 133, 5307, 5309 and 5708, Labor Code. Reference: Sections 3715, 5309 and 5310, Labor Code.

History: 1. Renumbering of former section 10348 to section 10330, including amendment of section and Note, filed 12-17-2019; operative 1-1-2020. Submitted to OAL for printing only pursuant to Government Code section 11351 (Register 2019, No. 51).

§10338.   Authority of Commissioners of the Appeals Board.

The following orders may be issued only by a commissioner:

(a)   Approving undertakings on stays of proceedings on reconsideration and petitions for writ of review; and

(b)   Directing exhumation or autopsy.

Note: Authority cited: Sections 133 and 5307, Labor Code. Reference: Sections 115, 5706, 5707 and 6002, Labor Code.

History: 1. Renumbering of former section 10342 to section 10338, including amendment of section heading, section and Note, filed 12-17-2019; operative 1-1-2020. Submitted to OAL for printing only pursuant to Government Code section 11351 (Register 2019, No. 51).

§10340.   Appeals Board Decisions and Orders. [Renumbered]

Note: Authority cited: Sections 133 and 5307, Labor Code. Reference: Sections 115 and 5311, Labor Code.

History: 1. Amendment of subsections (b) and (d) filed 12-19-2002; operative 1-1-2003. Submitted to OAL for printing only pursuant to Government Code section 11351 (Register 2002, No. 51).

2. Repealer of article 2 heading and renumbering of former section 10340 to section 10320 filed 12-17-2019; operative 1-1-2020. Submitted to OAL for printing only pursuant to Government Code section 11351 (Register 2019, No. 51).

§10341.   En Banc Decisions. [Renumbered]

Note: Authority cited: Sections 133 and 5307, Labor Code. Reference: Section 115, Labor Code.

History: 1. New section filed 12-19-2002; operative 1-1-2003. Submitted to OAL for printing only pursuant to Government Code section 11351 (Register 2002, No. 51).

2. Renumbering of former section 10341 to section 10325 filed 12-17-2019; operative 1-1-2020. Submitted to OAL for printing only pursuant to Government Code section 11351 (Register 2019, No. 51).

§10342.   Appeals Board, Member Orders. [Renumbered]

Note: Authority cited: Sections 133 and 5307, Labor Code. Reference: Sections 115, 5706, 5707 and 6002, Labor Code.

History: 1. Amendment filed 12-23-93; operative 1-1-94. Submitted to OAL for printing only pursuant to Government Code section 11351 (Register 93, No. 52).

2. Renumbering of former section 10342 to section 10338 filed 12-17-2019; operative 1-1-2020. Submitted to OAL for printing only pursuant to Government Code section 11351 (Register 2019, No. 51).

§10344.   Authority of Commissioners, Deputy Commissioners and Presiding Workers' Compensation Judges.

The following orders may be issued only by the Appeals Board, a commissioner, a deputy commissioner or a presiding workers' compensation judge:

(a)   Orders issuing certified copies of orders, decisions or awards except that a certified copy may be issued by a presiding workers' compensation judge only if the time for seeking reconsideration and judicial review has expired, and no proceedings are pending on reconsideration or judicial review;

(b)   Orders staying, quashing and recalling writs of execution and fixing and approving undertaking thereon;

(c)   Orders directing entry of satisfaction of judgment; and

(d)   Orders issuing, recalling, quashing, discharging and staying writs of attachment and fixing and approving undertakings thereon.

Note: Authority cited: Sections 133 and 5307, Labor Code. Reference: Sections 115, 5706, 5707 and 6002, Labor Code.

History: 1. Amendment of section heading, section and Note filed 12-17-2019; operative 1-1-2020. Submitted to OAL for printing only pursuant to Government Code section 11351 (Register 2019, No. 51).

§10346.   Authority of Presiding Workers' Compensation Judge to Assign or Transfer Cases.

(a)   The presiding workers' compensation judge has full responsibility for the assignment of cases to the workers' compensation judges of each office and may utilize EAMS to assign cases.

(b)   In the event of the death, extended absence, unavailability, retirement or disqualification of the workers' compensation judge, the presiding workers' compensation judge may reassign a case to another workers' compensation judge. Where testimony has been received, the new workers' compensation judge shall recommence the proceeding unless the parties agree to waive the requirements of Labor Code section 5700.

(c)   To the extent practicable and fair, supplemental proceedings shall be assigned to the workers' compensation judge who heard the original proceedings.

(d)   Any conflict that may arise between presiding workers' compensation judges of different district offices respecting assignment of a case, venue or priority of hearing where there is conflict in calendar settings will be resolved by a deputy commissioner of the Appeals Board.

(e)   If a Compromise and Release or Stipulations with Request for Award have not been approved, disapproved or noticed for trial on the issue of adequacy and other disputed issues within 45 days after filing, the file shall be transferred to the presiding workers' compensation judge for review.

Note: Authority cited: Sections 133, 5307, 5309 and 5708, Labor Code. Reference: Sections 5309, 5310 and 5700, Labor Code.

History: 1. Amendment of section and Note filed 12-19-2002; operative 1-1-2003. Submitted to OAL for printing only pursuant to Government Code section 11351 (Register 2002, No. 51).

2. Amendment of section and Note filed 11-17-2008; operative 11-17-2008. Submitted to OAL for printing only (Register 2008, No. 47).

3. Amendment of section heading, section and Note filed 12-17-2019; operative 1-1-2020. Submitted to OAL for printing only pursuant to Government Code section 11351 (Register 2019, No. 51).

§10348.   Authority of Workers' Compensation Judges. [Renumbered]

Note: Authority cited: Sections 133 and 5307, Labor Code. Reference: Sections 121, 134, 5309 and 5310, Labor Code.

History: 1. Amendment exempt from OAL review puruant to Government Code section 11351 filed 12-19-90; operative 1-1-91 (Register 91, No. 7).

2. Amendment of first paragraph filed 12-19-2002; operative 1-1-2003. Submitted to OAL for printing only pursuant to Government Code section 11351 (Register 2002, No. 51).

3. Renumbering of former section 10348 to section 10330 filed 12-17-2019; operative 1-1-2020. Submitted to OAL for printing only pursuant to Government Code section 11351 (Register 2019, No. 51).

§10349. Orders Equivalent to Notices of Intention. [Repealed]

Note: Authority cited: Sections 133 and 5307, Labor Code. Reference: Section !, Labor Code.

History: 1. New section filed 12-19-2002; operative 1-1-2003. Submitted to OAL for printing only pursuant to Government Code section 11351 (Register 2002, No. 51). For prior history, see Register 96, No. 43.

2. Repealer filed 12-17-2019; operative 1-1-2020. Submitted to OAL for printing only pursuant to Government Code section 11351 (Register 2019, No. 51).

§10350. Trials: Appointment and Authority of Pro Tempore Workers' Compensation Judges. [Repealed]

Note: Authority cited: Sections 133 and 5307, Labor Code. Reference: Sections 123.7, 5309 and 5310, Labor Code.

History: 1. New section filed 5-25-82; designated effective 7-1-82 (Register 82, No. 22).

2. Amendment of section heading, section and Note filed 12-19-2002; operative 1-1-2003. Submitted to OAL for printing only pursuant to Government Code section 11351 (Register 2002, No. 51).

3. Repealer filed 12-17-2019; operative 1-1-2020. Submitted to OAL for printing only pursuant to Government Code section 11351 (Register 2019, No. 51).

§10351. Conference Hearings: Appointment and Authority of Pro Tempore Workers' Compensation Judges. [Repealed]

Note: Authority cited: Sections 133 and 5307, Labor Code. Reference: Sections 123.7, 5309 and 5310, Labor Code.

History: 1. New section filed 5-25-82; designated effective 7-1-82 (Register 82, No. 22).

2. Amendment of section and Note filed 12-19-2002; operative 1-1-2003. Submitted to OAL for printing only pursuant to Government Code section 11351 (Register 2002, No. 51).

3. Repealer filed 12-17-2019; operative 1-1-2020. Submitted to OAL for printing only pursuant to Government Code section 11351 (Register 2019, No. 51).

§10352. Reconsideration of Pro Tempore Workers' Compensation Judge's Orders, Decisions or Awards. [Repealed]

Note: Authority cited: Sections 133 and 5307, Labor Code. Reference: Sections 121, 123.7, 5309, 5310 and 5900-5911, Labor Code.

History: 1. New section filed 5-25-82; designated effective 7-1-82 (Register 82, No. 22).

2. Editorial correction of NOTE filed 2-2-83 (Register 83, No. 6).

3. Repealer filed 12-17-2019; operative 1-1-2020. Submitted to OAL for printing only pursuant to Government Code section 11351 (Register 2019, No. 51).

§10353. Settlement Conference Authority. [Repealed]

Note: Authority cited: Sections 133, 5307 and 5502, Labor Code. Reference: Sections 5502 and 5502.5, Labor Code.

History: 1. New section exempt from OAL review pursuant to Government Code section 11351, filed 12-19-90; operative 1-1-91 (Register 91, No. 7).

2. Amendment of section heading and text filed 12-23-93; operative 1-1-94. Submitted to OAL for printing only pursuant to Government Code section 11351 (Register 93, No. 52).

3. Amendment of section and Note filed 12-19-2002; operative 1-1-2003. Submitted to OAL for printing only pursuant to Government Code section 11351 (Register 2002, No. 51).

4. Repealer filed 12-17-2019; operative 1-1-2020. Submitted to OAL for printing only pursuant to Government Code section 11351 (Register 2019, No. 51).

§10355. Appointment and Authority of Pro Tempore Workers' Compensation Judges.

A presiding workers' compensation judge may appoint a pro tempore workers' compensation judge to any conference hearing calendar including mandatory settlement conferences or status conferences.

(a) A pro tempore workers' compensation judge shall have the same power as a workers' compensation judge and shall be bound by the Rules of Practice and Procedure of the Workers' Compensation Appeals Board.

(b)   Any order, decision or award filed by a pro tempore workers' compensation judge shall be subject to reconsideration or removal in the same manner as any order, decision, or award filed by a workers' compensation judge.

Note: Authority cited: Sections 133 and 5307, Labor Code. Reference: Sections 121, 123.7, 5309, 5310 and 5900-5911, Labor Code.

History: 1. New section filed 12-17-2019; operative 1-1-2020. Submitted to OAL for printing only pursuant to Government Code section 11351 (Register 2019, No. 51).

§10360.   Testimony of Judicial or Quasi-Judicial Officers.

(a)   No judicial or quasi-judicial officer of the Workers' Compensation Appeals Board or of the Division of Workers' Compensation may be subpoenaed or ordered to testify regarding either:

(1)   The reasons for or basis of any decision or ruling they have made; or

(2)   Their opinion regarding any statements, conduct or events occurring in proceedings before them, except:

(A)   The judicial or quasi-judicial officer may be ordered to testify where their testimony is necessary on an issue of disqualification under Labor Code section 5311 and Code of Civil Procedure section 641.

(B)   The judicial or quasi-judicial officer may be ordered to testify where their testimony is necessary on an issue of an alleged ex parte communication.

(C)   The judicial or quasi-judicial officer may be subpoenaed or ordered to testify as a percipient witness to statements, conduct or events that occurred in the proceedings before them, to the same extent as any other percipient witness.

(b)   The testimony of a judicial or quasi-judicial officer shall be given only on the terms and conditions ordered by the presiding workers' compensation judge of the district office having venue, or by the Appeals Board, after the filing of a "Petition to Compel the Testimony of a Judicial or Quasi-Judicial Officer."

(1)   The petition to compel shall set forth with specificity the facts (or alleged facts) and law that support the petition.

(2)   The petition to compel shall be verified under penalty of perjury.

(3)   The petition to compel shall be served on all other parties, on all lien claimants whose liens are presently pending in issue in the underlying claim to which the petition relates and on the Legal Unit of the Division of Workers' Compensation (DWC-Legal Unit), together with a proof of service.

(4)   A petition to compel that does not meet all of the foregoing requirements may be summarily dismissed or denied.

(c)   The other parties, lien claimants, and the DWC-Legal Unit shall have 15 days within which to file any objection to the petition to compel.

(d)   The petition to compel shall be determined:

(1)   By the presiding workers' compensation judge of the district office having venue; or

(2)   By a deputy commissioner of the Appeals Board, if the petition to compel relates to the presiding workers' compensation judge of the district office having venue; or

(3)   By the Appeals Board, if the petition to compel relates to a petition for reconsideration, removal or disqualification.

(e)   The petition may be determined on the pleadings submitted or, in the discretion of the presiding workers' compensation judge, the deputy commissioner or the Appeals Board, the petition may be set for a hearing. In determining whether to grant the petition to compel, the presiding workers' compensation judge, the deputy commissioner or the Appeals Board may consider, among other things:

(1)   Whether the testimony of the judicial or quasi-judicial officer is reasonably necessary, taking into consideration:

(A)   Whether statements in the judicial or quasi-judicial officer's opinion on decision, report on reconsideration, removal or disqualification, or other similar statements are sufficient to resolve any allegation by a party; and

(B)   If not, whether the judicial or quasi-judicial officer's factual statements may be fairly provided by an affidavit or declaration under penalty of perjury.

(2)   Whether the testimony of the judicial or quasi-judicial officer under the "percipient witness" exception would be cumulative to the testimony of other percipient witnesses.

(f)   For purposes of this rule, the term "judicial or quasi-judicial officer of the Workers' Compensation Appeals Board or of the Division of Workers' Compensation" shall include, but shall not be limited to:

(1) Any commissioner;

(2) Any deputy commissioner;

(3) Any presiding workers' compensation judge or workers' compensation judge;

(4) Any pro tempore workers' compensation judge;

(5) Any special master appointed by the Workers' Compensation Appeals Board;

(6) The Administrative Director and the Administrative Director's designee;

(7) Any workers' compensation consultant of the Retraining and Return to Work Unit; and

(8) Any arbitrator or mediator; and

(9) The Director of Industrial Relations and the Director of Industrial Relations' designee.

(g) For the purposes of this rule, the term "testify" shall include testimony in either oral or written form (e.g., affidavits, declarations or interrogatories) and shall include all testimony, whether given at a deposition or a hearing.

(h) This rule shall apply solely to testimony sought in connection with a matter within the jurisdiction of the Workers' Compensation Appeals Board, and it shall not apply to testimony sought pursuant to the authority of any other forum.

Note: Authority cited: Sections 133, 5307, 5309 and 5708, Labor Code. Reference: Sections 5300, 5301, 5309, 5311, 5700, 5701 and 5708, Labor Code; Section 641, Code of Civil Procedure; and Section 703.5, Evidence Code.

History: 1. Amendment of section and Note filed 12-19-2002; operative 1-1-2003. Submitted to OAL for printing only pursuant to Government Code section 11351 (Register 2002, No. 51).
2. Repealer of article 3 heading, renumbering of former section 10360 to section 10380 and renumbering of former section 10593 to section 10360, including amendment of section and Note, filed 12-17-2019; operative 1-1-2020. Submitted to OAL for printing only pursuant to Government Code section 11351 (Register 2019, No. 51).

§10364. Parties Applicant. [Repealed]

Note: Authority cited: Sections 133 and 5307, Labor Code. Reference: Sections 5300, 5303, 5307.5, 5500 and 5503, Labor Code.

History: 1. New subsection (a) designator and new subsections (b) and (c) filed 10-21-96; operative 11-1-96. Submitted to OAL for printing only pursuant to Government Code section 11351 (Register 96, No. 43).
2. Amendment of subsection (a) filed 12-19-2002; operative 1-1-2003. Submitted to OAL for printing

only pursuant to Government Code section 11351 (Register 2002, No. 51).
3. Repealer filed 12-17-2019; operative 1-1-2020. Submitted to OAL for printing only pursuant to Government Code section 11351 (Register 2019, No. 51).

§10370. Extensions Of Time During Public Emergencies.

(a) Notwithstanding rule 10390 or any other rule in this title, in the event of a public emergency, including but not limited to an earthquake, fire or the destruction of or danger to a district office, the chief workers' compensation judge, the designee of the chief workers' compensation judge or the Appeals Board may:

(1) Extend by no more than 14 additional days the time to perform any act required or permitted under these rules, except for those acts subject to a statute of limitations or a jurisdictional time limitation, including but not limited to the filing of Petitions for Reconsideration or Removal, Petitions to Reopen, Applications for Adjudication of Claim or lien claim forms; or

(2) Authorize the presiding workers' compensation judge of a specific district office to extend by no more than 30 additional days the time to perform any act required or permitted under these rules, except for those acts subject to a statute of limitations or a jurisdictional time limitation, including but not limited to the filing of Petitions for Reconsideration or Removal, Petitions to Reopen, Applications for Adjudication of Claim or lien claim forms; or

(3) Authorize any district office to accept for filing, including by fax, those documents required by statute or regulation to be filed in a district office that is closed due to a public emergency.

(b) Any order under (a)(1), (a)(2) or (a)(3) must specify the nature of the emergency and the district office or offices to which it applies. Any order under (a)(2) must also specify the length of the authorized extension and the reason for the extension.

(c) If made necessary by the nature or extent of the public emergency, the chief workers' compensation judge, the designee of the chief workers' compensation judge or the Appeals Board may extend or renew an order issued under (a)(1) or (a)(2) for no more than 30 days.

Note: Authority cited: Sections 133, 5307 and 5309, Labor Code. Reference: Sections 5301 and 5307, Labor Code.

History: 1. New section filed 12-17-2019; operative 1-1-2020. Submitted to OAL for printing only pursuant to Government Code section 11351 (Register 2019, No. 51).

ARTICLE 3
Parties, Joinder and Consolidation

§10380.　Necessary Parties.

Any applicant other than the injured employee shall join the injured employee as a party. In such instances the Application for Adjudication of Claim shall include the injured employee's address or, if not known, a statement of that fact.

Note: Authority cited: Sections 133 and 5307, Labor Code. Reference: Sections 126, 5307.5 and 5503, Labor Code.

History: 1. Amendment exempt from OAL review pursuant to Government Code section 11351, filed 12-19-90; operative 1-1-91 (Register 91, No. 7).
2. Amendment filed 12-19-2002; operative 1-1-2003. Submitted to OAL for printing only pursuant to Government Code section 11351 (Register 2002, No. 51).
3. New article 3 heading, repealer of former section 10380 and renumbering and amendment of former section 10360 to section 10380 filed 12-17-2019; operative 1-1-2020. Submitted to OAL for printing only pursuant to Government Code section 11351 (Register 2019, No. 51).

§10382.　Joinder of Parties.

The Appeals Board or a workers' compensation judge may order the joinder of additional parties not named in the Application for Adjudication of Claim, whose presence is necessary for the full adjudication of the case. A party shall not be joined until 10 days after service of either a petition for joinder by a party or a notice of intention to order joinder issued by a workers' compensation judge, unless the party to be joined waives its right to this notice period. The Workers' Compensation Appeals Board may designate the party or parties who are to make service.

(a)　Any person in whom any right to relief is alleged to exist may appear, or be joined, as an applicant in any case or controversy before the Workers' Compensation Appeals Board.

(b)　Any person against whom any right to relief is alleged to exist may be joined as a defendant.

(c)　In death cases, all persons who may be dependents shall either join or be joined as applicants so that the entire liability of the employer or the insurer may be determined in one proceeding.

(d)　If an objection is received within 10 days of service of a petition for joinder or a notice of intention to order joinder, the workers' compensation judge shall consider the objection before joining the party and, if requested in the objection, shall provide the objector the opportunity to be heard before ordering joinder.

Note: Authority cited: Sections 133 and 5307, Labor Code. Reference: Sections 5300, 5303, 5307.5, 5316, 5500 and 5503, Labor Code.

History: 1. New section filed 12-17-2019; operative 1-1-2020. Submitted to OAL for printing only pursuant to Government Code section 11351 (Register 2019, No. 51).

§10390.　Proper Identification of Parties.

Any party that appears at a hearing or files a pleading, document or lien shall:

(a)　Set forth the party's full legal name on the record of proceedings, pleading, document or lien;

(b)　File a notice of representation if a party is represented and the attorney or non-attorney representative has not previously filed a notice of representation or an Application for Adjudication of Claim; and

(c)　Identify the insurer and/or employer as the party or parties and not identify a third party administrator as a party. The third party administrator shall be included on the official address record and case caption if identified as such.

Note: Authority cited: Sections 133, 5307, 5309 and 5708, Labor Code. Reference: Sections 3755-3759, 4903.1(c), 5001, 5002, 5003, 5004, 5500, 5502, 5503, 5505, 5702 and 5709, Labor Code.

History: 1. New section filed 10-15-2014; operative 1-1-2015. Submitted to OAL for printing only pursuant to Government Code section 11351 (Register 2014, No. 42). For prior history, see Register 2008, No. 47.
2. Editorial correction of History 1 (Register 2017, No. 8).
3. Repealer of article 4 heading, repealer of former section 10390 and renumbering of former section 10550 to section 10390, including amendment of

section heading and section, filed 12-17-2019; operative 1-1-2020. Submitted to OAL for printing only pursuant to Government Code section 11351 (Register 2019, No. 51).

§10391. Filing of Documentary Evidence. [Repealed]

Note: Authority cited: Sections 133, 5307, 5309 and 5708, Labor Code. Reference: Sections 126 and 5500.3, Labor Code.

History: 1. New section filed 10-15-2014; operative 1-1-2015. Submitted to OAL for printing only pursuant to Government Code section 11351 (Register 2014, No. 42). For prior history, see Register 2008, No. 47.

2. Editorial correction of History 1 (Register 2017, No. 8).

3. Repealer filed 12-17-2019; operative 1-1-2020. Submitted to OAL for printing only pursuant to Government Code section 11351 (Register 2019, No. 51).

§10392. Time of Filing Documents. [Repealed]

Note: Authority cited: Sections 133, 5307, 5309 and 5708, Labor Code. Reference: Sections 126 and 5500.3, Labor Code.

History: 1. New section filed 10-15-2014; operative 1-1-2015. Submitted to OAL for printing only pursuant to Government Code section 11351 (Register 2014, No. 42). For prior history, see Register 2008, No. 47.

2. Editorial correction of History 1 (Register 2017, No. 8).

3. Repealer filed 12-17-2019; operative 1-1-2020. Submitted to OAL for printing only pursuant to Government Code section 11351 (Register 2019, No. 51).

§10393. Filing of Medical Reports, Medical-Legal Reports, and Various Records. [Repealed]

Note: Authority cited: Sections 133, 5307, 5309 and 5708, Labor Code. Reference: Sections 126, 5316, 5500, 5501 and 5813, Labor Code.

History: 1. New section filed 10-15-2014; operative 1-1-2015. Submitted to OAL for printing only pursuant to Government Code section 11351 (Register 2014, No. 42).

2. Editorial correction of History 1 (Register 2017, No. 8).

3. Repealer filed 12-17-2019; operative 1-1-2020. Submitted to OAL for printing only pursuant to Government Code section 11351 (Register 2019, No. 51).

§10396. Consolidation of Cases.

(a) Consolidation of two or more related cases, involving either the same injured employee or multiple injured employees, rests in the sound discretion of the Workers' Compensation Appeals Board. In exercising that discretion, the Workers' Compensation Appeals Board shall take into consideration any relevant factors, including but not limited to the following:

(1) Whether there are common issues of fact or law;

(2) The complexity of the issues involved;

(3) The potential prejudice to any party, including but not limited to whether granting consolidation would significantly delay the trial of any of the cases involved;

(4) The avoidance of duplicate or inconsistent orders; and

(5) The efficient utilization of judicial resources.

Consolidation may be ordered for limited purposes or for all purposes.

(b) Consolidation may be ordered by the Workers' Compensation Appeals Board on its own motion, or may be ordered based upon a petition filed by one of the parties. A petition to consolidate shall:

(1) List all named parties in each case;

(2) Contain the adjudication case numbers of all the cases sought to be consolidated, with the lowest numbered case shown first;

(3) Be filed in each case sought to be consolidated; and

(4) Be served on all attorneys or non-attorney representatives of record and on all non-represented parties in each case sought to be consolidated.

(c) Any order regarding consolidation shall be filed in each case to which the order relates.

(d) If consolidation is ordered, the Workers' Compensation Appeals Board, in its discretion, may designate one case as the master file for exhibits and pleadings. If a master file is designated, any subsequent exhibits and pleadings filed by the parties during the period of consolidation shall be filed only in the master case. However, all pleadings and exhibit cover sheets filed shall include the caption and case number of the master file case, followed by the case numbers of all of the other consolidated cases.

(e) All relevant documentary evidence previously received in an individual case shall be deemed admitted in evidence in the consolidated proceedings and shall be deemed part of the record of each of the several consolidated cases.

(f) When cases are consolidated, joint minutes of hearing, summaries of evidence, opinions, decisions, orders, findings or awards may be used; however, copies shall be filed in the record of proceedings of each case.

Note: Authority cited: Sections 133, 5307, 5309 and 5708, Labor Code. Reference: Sections 5300, 5301, 5303 and 5708, Labor Code.

History: 1. Renumbering and amendment of former section 10589 to section 10396 filed 12-17-2019; operative 1-1-2020. Submitted to OAL for printing only pursuant to Government Code section 11351 (Register 2019, No. 51). For prior history of section 10396, see Register 208, No. 47.

§10397. Restrictions on the Rejection for Filing of Documents Subject to a Statute of Limitations or a Jurisdictional Time Limitation. [Renumbered]

Note: Authority cited: Article XIV, Section 4, California Constitution; and Sections 133, 5307, 5309 and 5708, Labor Code. Reference: Sections 126, 5316, 5500, 5501 and 5813, Labor Code.

History: 1. New section filed 11-17-2008; operative 11-17-2008. Submitted to OAL for printing only (Register 2008, No. 47).

2. Amendment of subsection (b), redesignation of former subsections (d)–(f) as subsections (c)–(e), amendment of newly designated subsections (d) and (e) and amendment of Note filed 10-15-2014; operative 1-1-2015. Submitted to OAL for printing only pursuant to Government Code section 11351 (Register 2014, No. 42).

3. Editorial correction of History 2 (Register 2017, No. 8).

4. Renumbering of former section 10397 to section 10617 filed 12-17-2019; operative 1-1-2020. Submitted to OAL for printing only pursuant to Government Code section 11351 (Register 2019, No. 51).

§10398. Assignment of Consolidated Cases.

(a) Any request or petition to consolidate cases that are assigned to different workers' compensation judges in the same district office, or that have not been assigned but are venued at the same district office, shall be referred to the presiding workers' compensation judge of that office, whether the cases involve the same injured worker or multiple injured workers.

(b) Any request or petition to consolidate cases involving the same injured worker that are assigned to workers' compensation judges at different district offices, or that have not been assigned but are venued at different district offices, shall first be referred to the presiding workers' compensation judges of the district offices to which the cases are assigned. If the presiding workers' compensation judges are unable to agree on where the cases will be assigned for hearing, the conflict shall be resolved by the chief workers' compensation judge of the Division of Workers' Compensation or by their designee upon referral by one of the presiding workers' compensation judges.

(c) Any request or petition to consolidate cases involving multiple injured workers that are assigned to workers' compensation judges at different district offices, or that have not been assigned but are venued at different district offices, shall be referred to the chief workers' compensation judge or their designee.

(d) In resolving any request or petition to consolidate cases under subdivision (b) or (c), the chief workers' compensation judge or their designee shall set the request or petition for a conference regarding the place of hearing. At or after the conference, the chief workers' compensation judge or their designee shall determine the place of hearing and may determine the workers' compensation judge to whom the cases will be assigned, giving consideration to the factors set forth in rule 10396. In reaching any determination, the chief workers' compensation judge or their designee may assign a workers' compensation judge to hear any discovery motions and disputes in the action and to report their findings and recommendations to the chief workers' compensation judge or their designee.

(e) Any party aggrieved by the determination of the chief workers' compensation judge or their designee may request proceedings pursuant to Labor Code section 5310, except that an assignment to a particular workers' compensation judge shall be challenged only in accordance with the provisions of rules 10788 and 10960.

Note: Authority cited: Sections 133, 5307, 5309 and 5708, Labor Code. Reference: Sections 5300, 5301, 5303, 5310 and 5708, Labor Code.

History: 1. Renumbering of former section 10592 to section 10398, including amendment of section and Note, filed 12-17-2019; operative 1-1-2020. Submitted to OAL for printing only pursuant to Government Code section 11351 (Register 2019, No. 51).

ARTICLE 4
Conduct of Parties, Attorneys and Non-Attorney Representatives

§10400.   Attorney Representatives.

(a)   An attorney representative shall file and serve a notice of representation before filing a document or appearing on behalf of a party unless the information required to be included in the notice of representation is set forth on an opening document.

(b)   The notice of representation or opening document shall comply with rule 10390 and shall include:

(1)   The name of the represented party;

(2)   The legal name and State Bar number of the attorney;

(3)   The name-address, and telephone number of the law firm or other entity's agent for service of process;

(c)   The name of the attorney representative and law firm or other entity shall be set forth on the record of proceedings at all appearances and on any pleading, document or lien prepared or filed by an attorney representative.

(d)   Attorney representatives of lien claimants shall also comply with the requirements set forth in rule 10868.

Note: Authority cited: Sections 133, 5307, 5309 and 5708, Labor Code. Reference: Sections 3755-3759, 4903.1(c), 5001, 5002, 5003, 5004, 5500, 5502, 5503, 5505, 5702 and 5709, Labor Code.

History: 1. Repealer and new section exempt from OAL review pursuant to Government Code section 11351 filed 12-19-90; operative 1-1-91 (Register 91, No. 7).

2. Amendment of section filed 6-11-92 with Secretary of State by Workers' Compensation Appeals Board; operative 6-11-92. Submitted to OAL for printing only pursuant to Government Code section 11351 (Register 92, No. 24).

3. Amendment filed 12-23-93; operative 1-1-94. Submitted to OAL for printing only pursuant to Government Code section 11351 (Register 93, No. 52).

4. Editorial correction of article heading (Register 93, No. 53).

5. Amendment of section and Note filed 12-19-2002; operative 1-1-2003. Submitted to OAL for printing only pursuant to Government Code section 11351 (Register 2002, No. 51).

6. Amendment of section heading, section and Note filed 11-17-2008; operative 11-17-2008. Submitted to OAL for printing only (Register 2008, No. 47).

7. Amendment of article 5 heading filed 9-23-2013; operative 10-23-2013. Submitted as a file and print by the Workers' Compensation Appeals Board pursuant to Government Code section 11351 (Register 2013, No. 39).

8. Repealer of article 5 heading, new article 4 heading and repealer and new section filed 12-17-2019; operative 1-1-2020. Submitted to OAL for printing only pursuant to Government Code section 11351 (Register 2019, No. 51).

§10401.   Non-Attorney Representatives.

(a)   Except as prohibited by rule 10445, a non-attorney representative may act on behalf of a party in proceedings before the Workers' Compensation Appeals Board if the party has been informed that the non-attorney representative is not licensed to practice law by the State of California.

(b)   A non-attorney representative shall be held to the same professional standards of conduct as an attorney.

(c)   A non-attorney representative shall file and serve a notice of representation before filing a document or appearing on behalf of a party unless the information required to be included in the notice of representation is set forth on an opening document.

(1)   If the non-attorney representative is appearing pursuant to an agreement between a law firm or other entity that provides non-attorney representatives and a party, the notice of representation shall include:

(A)   The name of the represented party;

(B)   The legal name, address, telephone number and form of the law firm or other entity;

(C)   The name and address of the law firm or other entity's agent for service of process;

(D)   The name of the person who entered into an agreement on behalf of the law firm or other entity with the party to provide non-attorney representatives; and

(E)   The name of the non-attorney representative responsible for assuring that appearances are made on behalf of the party.

(2)   If a non-attorney representative is appearing as an individual pursuant to an agreement between the non-attorney representative and a party, the notice of representation shall include the name of the represented party and

the non-attorney representative's name, address and telephone number.

(d) The name of the non-attorney representative and any entity responsible for providing a party with the non-attorney representative shall be set forth on the record of proceedings at all appearances and on any pleading, document or lien prepared or filed by a non-attorney representative.

(e) If an attorney is responsible for supervising a non-attorney representative, the attorney shall be identified in all documents. The supervising attorney's specific written authorization must be included with all Compromise and Release agreements and Stipulations with Request for Award.

(f) A non-attorney representative whose name is not on the notice of representation must file a notice of appearance as provided in rule 10751 before appearing before the Workers' Compensation Appeals Board.

(g) Non-attorney representatives of lien claimants shall also comply with the requirements set forth in rule 10868.

Note: Authority cited: Sections 133, 5307 and 5700 Labor Code. Reference: Section 4907, Labor Code; and Section 6126, Business and Professions Code.

History: 1. Repealer and new section filed 12-17-2019; operative 1-1-2020. Submitted to OAL for printing only pursuant to Government Code section 11351 (Register 2019, No. 51).

§10402. Substitution or Dismissal of Attorneys and Non-Attorney Representatives.

(a) Substitution or dismissal of attorneys must be made in the manner provided by Code of Civil Procedure sections 284, 285 and 286.

(b) A non-attorney representative or entity providing non-attorney representatives pursuant to an agreement with a party shall continue to provide representation until the party consents to termination of representation or withdrawal is permitted by the Workers' Compensation Appeals Board.

(1) A party that consents to termination of representation shall serve and file a fully executed "Substitution of Non-attorney Representative" that includes the information required for a notice of representation filed pursuant to rules 10400 and 10401 or that identifies the party as self-represented and the name, address, telephone number and signature of the person au-

thorized to consent to the substitution on behalf of the party.

(2) If a party does not consent to termination of representation, representation shall continue until the Appeals Board or the worker's compensation judge issues an order allowing withdrawal for good cause.

(c) Any changes in representation of lien claimants shall also comply with the requirements set forth in rule 10868.

Note: Authority cited: Sections 133 and 5307, Labor Code. Reference: Sections 4903 and 4906, Labor Code; and Sections 284, 285 and 286, Code of Civil Procedure.

History: 1. Amendment exempt from OAL review pursuant to Government Code section 11351 filed 12-19-90; operative 1-1-91 (Register 91, No. 7).

2. Repealer of second paragraph filed 12-19-2002; operative 1-1-2003. Submitted to OAL for printing only pursuant to Government Code section 11351 (Register 2002, No. 51).

3. Repealer of former section 10402 and renumbering of former section 10774 to section 10402, including amendment of section heading, section and Note, filed 12-17-2019; operative 1-1-2020. Submitted to OAL for printing only pursuant to Government Code section 11351 (Register 2019, No. 51).

§10403. Complaints Regarding Violations of Labor Code Section 4907.

(a) Any person may submit to the Secretary of the Appeals Board a written complaint that a non-attorney representative has violated the provisions of Labor Code section 4907. The complaint shall not be filed at any district office or in EAMS.

(b) The complaint shall be made under penalty of perjury and shall state in detail the acts and omissions of the non-attorney representative alleged to be in violation of the provisions of Labor Code section 4907, and shall identify relevant case numbers and documents.

(c) Upon receipt of a complaint, the Secretary shall review it for form and content.

(d) The non-attorney representative shall be served with notice of the complaint as part of any investigation by the Secretary and shall be provided with an opportunity to respond.

(e) Upon the conclusion of any investigation, the Secretary shall serve the complainant and the non-attorney representative with a written Notice of Determination.

(f) Nothing in this rule shall preclude the Appeals Board from initiating proceedings under Labor Code section 4907 in the absence of a complaint.

(g)   Information gathered as part of any investigation under this rule and records of deliberation generated as part of any investigation under this rule shall be confidential and not subject to public disclosure under any law of this state pending the issuance of a Notice of Determination.

Note: Authority cited: Sections 4907 and 5307, Labor Code. Reference: Section 4907, Labor Code.

History: 1. New section filed 11-17-2008; operative 11-17-2008. Submitted to OAL for printing only (Register 2008, No. 47). For prior history, see Register 92, No. 24.

2. Repealer and new section filed 12-17-2019; operative 1-1-2020. Submitted to OAL for printing only pursuant to Government Code section 11351 (Register 2019, No. 51).

§10404.   Suspension and Removal of a Non-Attorney Representative's Privilege to Appear Before the Workers' Compensation Appeals Board Under Labor Code Section 4907.

(a)   Upon motion of the Appeals Board, a non-attorney representative may have the privilege to appear before the Workers' Compensation Appeals Board removed or suspended for good cause after a hearing.

(b)   Good cause includes, but is not limited to, serious or repeated violations of these rules, failure to comply with rule 10400 or failure to pay a final order of sanctions, attorney's fees or costs issued under Labor Code section 5813 within 60 days.

(c)   The Appeals Board shall designate a hearing officer to conduct the hearing and make initial rulings on all issues and objections. The hearing officer is subject to disqualification as provided in Labor Code section 5311 and rule 9721.12. A Petition for Disqualification of a Hearing Officer shall be filed with the Appeals Board as provided in rule 10960.

(d)   The Appeals Board shall initiate proceedings by issuing a Notice of Proposed Action setting forth:

(1)   the acts or omissions that constitute good cause for removal or suspension and any statutes and rules that the non-attorney representative is alleged to have violated;

(2)   the intended action, whether removal or suspension, and the length of time of any proposed suspension;

(3)   the date on which the hearing regarding suspension or removal of the non-attorney representative's privilege to appear will take place and the identity of the hearing officer; and

(4)   the right to submit a written response to the Notice of Proposed Action within the time specified in the Notice of Proposed Action.

(e)   The Appeals Board shall serve the non-attorney representative with the Notice of Proposed Action and copies of materials relied upon.

(f)   Any pleadings, response, correspondence, requests and other documents shall be submitted in writing only to the Appeals Board and not filed at any district office or in EAMS.

(g)   All hearings regarding the removal or suspension of a non-attorney representative's privilege to appear shall be held at the office of the Appeals Board, or at a District Office of the Workers' Compensation Appeals Board as designated by the Appeals Board.

(h)   If the non-attorney representative does not testify on their own behalf, their testimony may be taken as if under cross-examination.

(i)   After considering the evidence and any response submitted by the non-attorney representative, the hearing officer shall issue a recommended decision and findings of fact addressing all issues and objections and setting forth the recommended action to be taken. The recommended decision shall be submitted to the Appeals Board.

(j)   The Appeals Board, acting en banc, may (1) adopt and incorporate the recommended decision of the hearing officer as its own in whole or in part; (2) review the record and increase or decrease the recommended action; or (3) take further or other action, including directing the conduct of a new hearing on one or more of the issues presented, as deemed just and appropriate. The Appeals Board shall serve the non-attorney representative and hearing officer with copies of its final decision as well as the hearing officer's recommended decision.

(k)   Once the Appeals Board has served its final decision, any person may request a copy of all or a portion of the record, subject to any assertions of privilege, protective orders or provisions of law prohibiting disclosure. The complete record includes the pleadings, all notices and orders issued by the Appeals Board, any proposed decision by the hearing officer, the final decision, all exhibits whether admitted or rejected, the written evidence and any other papers in the case, except as provided by law.

(*l*) A non-attorney representative whose privilege to appear has been removed or suspended may petition the Appeals Board for reinstatement of the privilege after a period of not less than one year has elapsed from the date on which the decision of the Appeals Board took effect, or from the date of the denial of a similar petition.

Note: Authority cited: Sections 4907 and 5307, Labor Code. Reference: Sections 4907 and 5311, Labor Code.

History: 1. New section filed 12-23-93; operative 1-1-94. Submitted to OAL for printing only pursuant to Government Code section 11351 (Register 93, No. 52). For prior history, see Register 91, No. 7.
2. Amendment filed 12-19-2002; operative 1-1-2003. Submitted to OAL for printing only pursuant to Government Code section 11351 (Register 2002, No. 51).
3. Renumbering of former section 10404 to section 10470 and new section 10404 filed 12-17-2019; operative 1-1-2020. Submitted to OAL for printing only pursuant to Government Code section 11351 (Register 2019, No. 51).

§10405.   Request for Findings of Fact. [Renumbered]

Note: Authority cited: Sections 133 and 5307, Labor Code. Reference: Sections 21164, 21166, 21537, 21538, 21540 and 21540.5, Government Code; and Sections 4800.5(d), 4801, 4804.2, 4807 and 4851, Labor Code.

History: 1. Amendment of section and Note filed 12-19-2002; operative 1-1-2003. Submitted to OAL for printing only pursuant to Government Code section 11351 (Register 2002, No. 51).
2. Renumbering of former section 10405 to section 10460 filed 12-17-2019; operative 1-1-2020. Submitted to OAL for printing only pursuant to Government Code section 11351 (Register 2019, No. 51).

§10408.   Application for Adjudication of Claim Form and Other Forms. [Renumbered]

Note: Authority: Sections 133, 5307, 5309 and 5708, Labor Code. Reference: Sections 3716, 4903.5, 5500, 5500.3, 5501.5 and 5502, Labor Code.

History: 1. Amendment filed 12-23-93; operative 1-1-94. Submitted to OAL for printing only pursuant

to Government Code section 11351 (Register 93, No. 52).
2. Amendment filed 12-19-2002; operative 1-1-2003. Submitted to OAL for printing only pursuant to Government Code section 11351 (Register 2002, No. 51).
3. Amendment of section heading, section and Note filed 9-23-2013; operative 10-23-2013. Submitted as a file and print by the Workers' Compensation Appeals Board pursuant to Government Code section 11351 (Register 2013, No. 39).
4. Renumbering of former section 10408 to section 10500 filed 12-17-2019; operative 1-1-2020. Submitted to OAL for printing only pursuant to Government Code section 11351 (Register 2019, No. 51).

§10409.   Venue. [Renumbered]

Note: Authority cited: Sections 133, 5307, 5309 and 5708, Labor Code. Reference: Sections 5500 and 5501.5, Labor Code.

History: 1. New section filed 11-17-2008; operative 11-17-2008. Submitted to OAL for printing only (Register 2008, No. 47).
2. Renumbering of former section 10409 to section 10480 filed 12-17-2019; operative 1-1-2020. Submitted to OAL for printing only pursuant to Government Code section 11351 (Register 2019, No. 51).

§10410.   Ex Parte Communications.

(a)   No document, including letters or other writings, shall be filed by a party with the Workers' Compensation Appeals Board unless service of a copy thereof is made on all parties together with the filing of a proof of service as provided for in rule 10625.

(b)   When the Appeals Board or a workers' compensation judge receives an ex parte letter or other document from any party in a case pending before the Appeals Board or the workers' compensation judge, the Appeals Board or the workers' compensation judge shall serve copies of the letter or document on all other parties to the case with a cover letter explaining that the letter or document was received ex parte in violation of this rule.

(c)   No party shall discuss with the Appeals Board or a workers' compensation judge the merits of any case pending before the Appeals Board or that workers' compensation judge without the presence of all necessary parties to the proceeding, except when submitting a walk-through document in accordance with rule 10789.

(d)   All correspondence concerning the examination by and the reports of a physician appointed by a workers' compensation judge or the Appeals Board pursuant to Labor Code sections 5701, 5703.5, 5706 or 5906 shall be made, respectively, through the workers' compensation judge or the Appeals Board, and no party, attorney or non-attorney representative shall communicate with that physician regarding the merits of the case unless ordered to do so.

Note: Authority cited: Sections 133, 5307, 5309 and 5708, Labor Code. Reference: Sections 5701, 5703.5, 5706, 5708 and 5906, Labor Code.

History: 1. New section filed 12-19-2002; operative 1-1-2003. Submitted to OAL for printing only pursuant to Government Code section 11351 (Register 2002, No. 51).
2. Amendment of section heading, section and Note filed 11-17-2008; operative 11-17-2008. Submitted to OAL for printing only (Register 2008, No. 47).
3. Renumbering of former section 10410 to section 10488 and renumbering and amendment of former section 10324 to section 10410 filed 12-17-2019; operative 1-1-2020. Submitted to OAL for printing only pursuant to Government Code section 11351 (Register 2019, No. 51).

§10411. Petition for Change of Venue Under Labor Code Section 5501.6. [Renumbered]

Note: Authority cited: Sections 133, 5307, 5309 and 5708, Labor Code. Reference: Section 5501.6, Labor Code.

History: 1. New section filed 12-19-2002; operative 1-1-2003. Submitted to OAL for printing only pursuant to Government Code section 11351 (Register 2002, No. 51).
2. Amendment of section heading, section and Note filed 11-17-2008; operative 11-17-2008. Submitted to OAL for printing only (Register 2008, No. 47).
3. Renumbering of former section 10411 to section 10490 filed 12-17-2019; operative 1-1-2020. Submitted to OAL for printing only pursuant to Government Code section 11351 (Register 2019, No. 51).

§10412. Proceedings and Decisions After Venue Change. [Repealed]

Note: Authority cited: Sections 133, 5307, 5309 and 5708, Labor Code. Reference: Sections 126 and 5501.6, Labor Code.

History: 1. New section filed 12-19-2002; operative 1-1-2003. Submitted to OAL for printing only pursuant to Government Code section 11351 (Register 2002, No. 51). For prior history, see Register 93, No. 52.
2. Amendment of section heading, section and Note filed 11-17-2008; operative 11-17-2008. Submitted to OAL for printing only (Register 2008, No. 47).

3. Repealer filed 12-17-2019; operative 1-1-2020. Submitted to OAL for printing only pursuant to Government Code section 11351 (Register 2019, No. 51).

§10414. Declaration of Readiness to Proceed. [Renumbered]

Note: Authority cited: Sections 133, 5307, 5309 and 5708, Labor Code. Reference: Sections 4903.05, 4903.06, 5500.3, 5502 and 5813, Labor Code.

History: 1. New section filed 10-15-2014; operative 1-1-2015. Submitted to OAL for printing only pursuant to Government Code section 11351 (Register 2014, No. 42). For prior history, see Register 2008, No. 47.
2. Editorial correction of History 1 (Register 2017, No. 8).
3. Renumbering of former section 10414 to section 10742 filed 12-17-2019; operative 1-1-2020. Submitted to OAL for printing only pursuant to Government Code section 11351 (Register 2019, No. 51).

§10416. Objection to Declaration of Readiness to Proceed. [Renumbered]

Note: Authority cited: Sections 133, 5307, 5309 and 5708, Labor Code. Reference: Sections 5500.3, 5502 and 5813, Labor Code.

History: 1. New section filed 10-15-2014; operative 1-1-2015. Submitted to OAL for printing only pursuant to Government Code section 11351 (Register 2014, No. 42). For prior history, see Register 2008, No. 47.
2. Editorial correction of History 1 (Register 2017, No. 8).
3. Renumbering of former section 10416 to section 10744 filed 12-17-2019; operative 1-1-2020. Submitted to OAL for printing only pursuant to Government Code section 11351 (Register 2019, No. 51).

§10417. Walk-Through Documents. [Renumbered]

Note: Authority cited: Sections 133 and 5307, Labor Code. Reference: Sections 4053, 4054, 5001, 5002, 5702 and 5710, Labor Code.

History: 1. New section filed 10-15-2014; operative 1-1-2015. Submitted to OAL for printing only pursuant to Government Code section 11351 (Register 2014, No. 42). For prior history, see Register 2002, No. 51.
2. Editorial correction of History 1 (Register 2017, No. 8).
3. Renumbering of former section 10417 to section 10789 filed 12-17-2019; operative 1-1-2020. Submitted to OAL for printing only pursuant to Government Code section 11351 (Register 2019, No. 51).

§10420.   Setting the Case.
[Renumbered]

Note: Authority cited: Sections 133 and 5307, Labor Code. Reference: Section 5310, Labor Code.

History: 1. Renumbering and amendment of former section 10417 to new section 10420 filed 12-19-2002; operative 1-1-2003. Submitted to OAL for printing only pursuant to Government Code section 11351 (Register 2002, No. 51).

2. Renumbering of former section 10420 to section 10745 filed 12-17-2019; operative 1-1-2020. Submitted to OAL for printing only pursuant to Government Code section 11351 (Register 2019, No. 51).

§10421.   Sanctions.

(a)   On its own motion or upon the filing of a petition pursuant to rule 10510, the Workers' Compensation Appeals Board may order payment of reasonable expenses, including attorney's fees and costs and, in addition, sanctions as provided in Labor Code section 5813. Before issuing such an order, the alleged offending party or attorney must be given notice and an opportunity to be heard. In no event shall the Workers' Compensation Appeals Board impose a monetary sanction pursuant to Labor Code section 5813 where the one subject to the sanction acted with reasonable justification or other circumstances make imposition of the sanction unjust.

(b)   Bad faith actions or tactics that are frivolous or solely intended to cause unnecessary delay include actions or tactics that result from a willful failure to comply with a statutory or regulatory obligation, that result from a willful intent to disrupt or delay the proceedings of the Workers' Compensation Appeals Board, or that are done for an improper motive or are indisputably without merit. Violations subject to the provisions of Labor Code section 5813 shall include but are not limited to the following:

(1)   Failure to appear or appearing late at a conference or trial where a reasonable excuse is not offered or the offending party has demonstrated a pattern of such conduct.

(2)   Filing a pleading, petition or legal document unless there is some reasonable justification for filing the document.

(3)   Failure to timely serve documents (including but not limited to medical reports and medical-legal reports) as required by the rules of the Workers' Compensation Appeals Board, or the Administrative Director, where the documents are within the party's possession or control, unless that failure resulted from mistake, inadvertence or excusable neglect.

(4)   Failing to comply with the Workers' Compensation Appeals Board's Rules of Practice and Procedure, with the regulations of the Administrative Director, or with any award or order of the Workers' Compensation Appeals Board, including an order of discovery, which is not pending on reconsideration, removal or appellate review and which is not subject to a timely petition for reconsideration, removal or appellate review, unless that failure results from mistake, inadvertence, surprise or excusable neglect.

(5)   Executing a declaration or verification to any petition, pleading or other document filed with the Workers' Compensation Appeals Board:

(A)   That:

(i)   Contains false or substantially false statements of fact;

(ii)   Contains statements of fact that are substantially misleading;

(iii)   Contains substantial misrepresentations of fact;

(iv)   Contains statements of fact that are made without any reasonable basis or with reckless indifference as to their truth or falsity;

(v)   Contains statements of fact that are literally true, but are intentionally presented in a manner reasonably calculated to deceive; and/or

(vi)   Conceals or substantially conceals material facts; and

(B)   Where a reasonable excuse is not offered or where the offending party has demonstrated a pattern of such conduct.

(6)   Bringing a claim, conducting a defense or asserting a position:

(A)   That is:

(i)   Indisputably without merit;

(ii)   Done solely or primarily for the purpose of harassing or maliciously injuring any person; and/or

(iii)   Done solely or primarily for the purpose of causing unnecessary delay or a needless increase in the cost of litigation; and

(B)   Where a reasonable excuse is not offered or where the offending party has demonstrated a pattern of such conduct.

(7)   Presenting a claim or a defense, or raising an issue or argument, that is not war-

ranted under existing law—unless it can be supported by a non-frivolous argument for an extension, modification or reversal of the existing law or for the establishment of new law— and where a reasonable excuse is not offered or where the offending party has demonstrated a pattern of such conduct. In determining whether a claim, defense, issue or argument is warranted under existing law, or if there is a reasonable excuse for it, consideration shall be given to:

(A) Whether there are reasonable ambiguities or conflicts in the existing statutory, regulatory or case law, taking into consideration the extent to which a litigant has researched the issues and found some support for its theories; and

(B) Whether the claim, defense, issue or argument is reasonably being asserted to preserve it for reconsideration or appellate review.

This subdivision is specifically intended not to have a "chilling effect" on a party's ability to raise and pursue legal arguments that reasonably can be regarded as not settled.

(8) Asserting a position that misstates or substantially misstates the law, and where a reasonable excuse is not offered or where the offending party has demonstrated a pattern of such conduct.

(9) Using any language or gesture at or in connection with any hearing, or using any language in any pleading or other document:

(A) Where the language or gesture:

(i) Is directed to the Workers' Compensation Appeals Board, to any of its officials or staff or to any party (or the attorney or non-attorney representative for a party); and

(ii) Is patently insulting, offensive, insolent, intemperate, foul, vulgar, obscene, abusive or disrespectful; or

(B) Where the language or gesture impugns the integrity of the Workers' Compensation Appeals Board or its commissioners, judges or staff.

Note: Authority cited: Sections 133, 5307, 5309 and 5708, Labor Code. Reference: Sections 4903.6(c), 5701, 5703.5, 5706, 5708, 5813 and 5906, Labor Code.

History: 1. Renumbering of former section 10561 to section 10421, including amendment of section and Note, filed 12-17-2019; operative 1-1-2020. Submitted to OAL for printing only pursuant to Government Code section 11351 (Register 2019, No. 51).

§10430. Vexatious Litigants.

(a) For purposes of this rule, "vexatious litigant" means:

(1) A party who, while acting in propria persona in proceedings before the Workers' Compensation Appeals Board, repeatedly relitigates, or attempts to relitigate, an issue of law or fact that has been finally determined against that party by the Workers' Compensation Appeals Board or by an appellate court;

(2) A party who, while acting in propria persona in proceedings before the Workers' Compensation Appeals Board, repeatedly files unmeritorious motions, pleadings or other papers, repeatedly conducts or attempts to conduct unnecessary discovery, or repeatedly engages in other tactics that are in bad faith, are frivolous or are solely intended to cause harassment or unnecessary delay; or

(3) A party who has previously been declared to be a vexatious litigant by any state or federal court of record in any action or proceeding based upon the same or substantially similar facts, transaction(s) or occurrence(s) that are the subject, in whole or in substantial part, of the party's workers' compensation case.

For purposes of this rule, the phrase "finally determined" shall mean:

(i) That all appeals have been exhausted or the time for seeking appellate review has expired; and

(ii) The time for reopening under Labor Code sections 5410 or 5803 and 5804 has passed or, although the time for reopening under those sections has not passed, there is no good faith and non-frivolous basis for reopening.

(b) Upon the petition of a party, or upon the motion of any workers' compensation judge or the Appeals Board, a presiding workers' compensation judge of any district office having venue or the Appeals Board may declare a party to be a vexatious litigant.

(c) No party shall be declared a vexatious litigant without being given notice and an opportunity to be heard. If a hearing is requested, the presiding workers' compensation judge or the Appeals Board, in their discretion, either may take and consider both oral and documentary evidence or may take and consider solely documentary evidence, including affidavits or other written declarations of fact made under penalty of perjury.

(d) If a party is declared to be a vexatious litigant, a presiding workers' compensation judge or the Appeals Board may enter a "prefiling order," i.e., an order which prohibits the vexatious litigant from filing, in propria persona, any Application for Adjudication of Claim, Declaration of Readiness to Proceed, petition or other request for action by the Workers' Compensation Appeals Board without first obtaining leave of the presiding workers' compensation judge of the district office where the request for action is proposed to be filed or, if the matter is pending before the Appeals Board on a petition for reconsideration, removal or disqualification, without first obtaining leave from the Appeals Board. For purposes of this rule, a "petition" shall include, but not be limited to, a petition to reopen under Labor Code sections 5410, 5803 and 5804, a petition to enforce a medical treatment award, a penalty petition or any other petition seeking to enforce or expand the vexatious litigant's previously determined rights.

(e) If a vexatious litigant proposes to file, in propria persona, any Application for Adjudication of Claim, Declaration of Readiness to Proceed, petition or other request for action by the Workers' Compensation Appeals Board, the request for action shall be conditionally filed. Thereafter, the presiding workers' compensation judge, or the Appeals Board if the petition is for reconsideration, removal or disqualification, shall deem the request for action to have been properly filed only if it appears that the request for action has not been filed in violation of subdivision (a). In determining whether the vexatious litigant's request for action has not been filed in violation of subdivision (a), the presiding workers' compensation judge, or the Appeals Board, shall consider the contents of the request for action and the Workers' Compensation Appeals Board's existing record of proceedings, as well as any other documentation that, in its discretion, the presiding workers' compensation judge or the Appeals Board asks to be submitted. Among the factors that the presiding workers' compensation judge or the Appeals Board may consider is whether there has been a significant change in circumstances (such as new or newly discovered evidence or a change in the law) that might materially affect an issue of fact or law that was previously finally determined against the vexatious litigant.

(f) If any in propria persona Application for Adjudication of Claim, Declaration of Readiness to proceed, petition or other request for action by the Workers' Compensation Appeals Board from a vexatious litigant subject to a prefiling order is inadvertently accepted for filing (other than conditional filing in accordance with subdivision (e) above), then any other party may file (and shall concurrently serve on the vexatious litigant and any other affected parties) a notice stating that the request for action is being submitted by a vexatious litigant subject to a prefiling order as set forth in subdivision (d). The filing of the notice shall automatically stay the request for action until it is determined, in accordance with subdivision (e), whether the request for action should be deemed to have been properly filed.

(g) A copy of any prefiling order issued by a presiding workers' compensation judge or by the Appeals Board shall be submitted to the Secretary of the Appeals Board, who shall maintain a record of vexatious litigants subject to those prefiling orders and who shall annually disseminate a list of those persons to all presiding workers' compensation judges.

Note: Authority cited: Sections 133, 5307, 5309 and 5708, Labor Code. Reference: Article XIV, section 4, California Constitution; Sections 5410, 5803 and 5804, Labor Code; and Sections 391, 391.2 and 391.7, Code of Civil Procedure.

History: 1. Renumbering and amendment of former section 10418 to new section 10430 filed 12-19-2002; operative 1-1-2003. Submitted to OAL for printing only pursuant to Government Code section 11351 (Register 2002, No. 51).
2. Repealer of former section 10430 and renumbering of former section 10782 to section 10430, including amendment of section and Note, filed 12-17-2019; operative 1-1-2020. Submitted to OAL for printing only pursuant to Government Code section 11351 (Register 2019, No. 51).

§10440. Contempt.

(a) A workers' compensation judge or a deputy commissioner may issue writs or summons, warrants of attachment, warrants of commitment and all necessary process in proceedings for direct and hybrid contempt as defined by Labor Code section 5309(c) in a like manner and to the same extent as courts of record.

(b) The Appeals Board may issue writs or summons, warrants of attachment, warrants of commitment and all necessary process in proceedings for direct, hybrid, or indirect contempt in a like manner and to the same extent as the courts of record.

Note: Authority cited: Sections 133, 134 and 5307, Labor Code. Reference: Sections 4550, 4551, 4552, 4553, 4553.1 and 5309(c), Labor Code; and Sections 1209-1222, Code of Civil Procedure.

History: 1. Amendment of section heading filed 12-19-2002; operative 1-1-2003. Submitted to OAL for printing only pursuant to Government Code section 11351 (Register 2002, No. 51).

2. Repealer and new section filed 12-17-2019; operative 1-1-2020. Submitted to OAL for printing only pursuant to Government Code section 11351 (Register 2019, No. 51).

§10445. Disbarred and Suspended Attorneys.

An attorney who has been disbarred or suspended by the Supreme Court for reasons other than nonpayment of State Bar fees, or who has been placed on involuntary inactive enrollment status by the State Bar or who has resigned while disciplinary action is pending shall be deemed unfit to appear as a non-attorney representative of any party before the Workers' Compensation Appeals Board during the time that the attorney is precluded from practicing law in this state.

Note: Authority cited: Sections 133, 5307, 5309 and 5708, Labor Code. Reference: Section 4907, Labor Code; and Section 6126, Business and Professions Code.

History: 1. Repealer of last paragraph filed 12-19-2002; operative 1-1-2003. Submitted to OAL for printing only pursuant to Government Code section 11351 (Register 2002, No. 51).

2. Repealer of former section 10445 and renumbering and amendment of former section 10779 to section 10445 filed 12-17-2019; operative 1-1-2020. Submitted to OAL for printing only pursuant to Government Code section 11351 (Register 2019, No. 51).

§10447. Pleadings—Discrimination. [Renumbered]

Note: Authority cited: Sections 133 and 5307, Labor Code. Reference: Section 132a, Labor Code.

History: 1. Editorial correction filed 2-2-83 (Register 83, No. 6).

2. Amendment of section heading and repealer of second paragraph filed 12-19-2002; operative 1-1-2003. Submitted to OAL for printing only pursuant to Government Code section 11351 (Register 2002, No. 51).

3. Renumbering of former section 10447 to section 10528 filed 12-17-2019; operative 1-1-2020. Submitted to OAL for printing only pursuant to Government Code section 11351 (Register 2019, No. 51).

ARTICLE 5
Applications and Answers

§10450. Invoking the Jurisdiction of the Workers' Compensation Appeals Board.

(a) Except as provided by rules 10990 and 10590, proceedings for the adjudication of rights and liabilities before the Workers' Compensation Appeals Board shall be initiated and jurisdiction of the Workers' Compensation Appeals Board invoked by the filing of an Application for Adjudication of Claim, a case opening Compromise and Release Agreement, a case opening Stipulations with Request for Award or a Request for Findings of Fact under rule 10460.

(b) Until an application or other case opening document has been filed, the Workers' Compensation Appeals Board may not conduct hearings, issue orders or authorize the commencement of formal, compelled discovery, including the use of subpoenas to obtain records or sworn testimony.

(c) The pre-application assignment of a non-adjudication EAMS case number by any ancillary unit of the Division of Workers' Compensation (e.g., the Disability Evaluation Unit, the Information and Assistance Office):

(1) Does not establish the jurisdiction of the Workers' Compensation Appeals Board and, therefore, does not permit it to conduct any hearings or to issue any orders;

(2) Does not toll the statute of limitations (except as provided in Labor Code section 5454 for submissions to the Information and Assistance Unit); and

(3) Does not authorize the commencement of formal, compelled discovery.

Nothing in this rule shall be construed to preclude any non-compelled pre-application medical evaluations or investigations.

Note: Authority cited: Sections 133, 5307, 5309 and 5708, Labor Code. Reference: Sections 126, 5300, 5301, 5316, 5454, 5500 and 5501, Labor Code.

History: 1. Amendment of section and Note filed 12-19-2002; operative 1-1-2003. Submitted to OAL for printing only pursuant to Government Code section 11351 (Register 2002, No. 51).

2. Amendment of section and Note filed 11-17-2008; operative 11-17-2008. Submitted to OAL for printing only (Register 2008, No. 47).

3. Amendment of section heading, section and Note filed 9-23-2013; operative 10-23-2013. Submitted as a

file and print by the Workers' Compensation Appeals Board pursuant to Government Code section 11351 (Register 2013, No. 39).

4. New article 5 heading, renumbering of former section 10450 to section 10510 and new section 10450 filed 12-17-2019; operative 1-1-2020. Submitted to OAL for printing only pursuant to Government Code section 11351 (Register 2019, No. 51).

§10451.1.   Determination of Medical-Legal Expense Disputes. [Repealed]

Note: Authority cited: Sections 133, 4622(e)(2), 4627, 5307, 5309 and 5708, Labor Code. Reference: Sections 139.5, 4603.3, 4603.6, 4620, 4621, 4622, 4903.05 and 4903.06, Labor Code; and Sections 9792.5.5(b)(2) and 9792.5.7(c)(5), title 8, California Code of Regulations.

History: 1. New section filed 9-23-2013; operative 10-23-2013. Submitted as a file and print by the Workers' Compensation Appeals Board pursuant to Government Code section 11351 (Register 2013, No. 39).

2. Repealer filed 12-17-2019; operative 1-1-2020. Submitted to OAL for printing only pursuant to Government Code section 11351 (Register 2019, No. 51).

§10451.2.   Determination of Medical Treatment Disputes. [Repealed]

Note: Authority cited: Sections 133, 4606.2(f), 4604, 5304, 5307, 5309 and 5708, Labor Code. Reference: Sections 4061, 4601.5, 4062, 4600, 4603.2, 4603.3, 4604.5, 4610, 4610.5, 4610.6, 4616.3, 4616.4 and 4903(b), Labor Code.

History: 1. New section filed 9-23-2013; operative 10-23-2013. Submitted as a file and print by the Workers' Compensation Appeals Board pursuant to Government Code section 11351 (Register 2013, No. 39).

2. Repealer filed 12-17-2019; operative 1-1-2020. Submitted to OAL for printing only pursuant to Government Code section 11351 (Register 2019, No. 51).

§10451.3.   Petition for Costs. [Renumbered]

Note: Authority cited: Sections 133, 5307, 5309 and 5708, Labor Code. Reference: Sections 4600, 4903 et seq., 5710, 5811 and 5813, Labor Code; and Section 10561, title 8, California Code of Regulations.

History: 1. New section filed 9-23-2013; operative 10-23-2013. Submitted as a file and print by the Workers' Compensation Appeals Board pursuant to Government Code section 11351 (Register 2013, No. 39).

2. Renumbering of former section 10451.3 to section 10545 filed 12-17-2019; operative 1-1-2020. Submitted to OAL for printing only pursuant to Government Code section 11351 (Register 2019, No. 51).

§10451.4.   Petition to Enforce Independent Bill Review Determination. [Renumbered]

Note: Authority cited: Sections 133, 5307, 5309 and 5708, Labor Code. Reference: Sections 4603.6, 4622, 4903.05 and 4903.06, Labor Code.

History: 1. New section filed 9-23-2013; operative 10-23-2013. Submitted as a file and print by the Workers' Compensation Appeals Board pursuant to Government Code section 11351 (Register 2013, No. 39).

2. Renumbering of former section 10451.4 to section 10570 filed 12-17-2019; operative 1-1-2020. Submitted to OAL for printing only pursuant to Government Code section 11351 (Register 2019, No. 51).

§10452.   Petition for Disqualification of Judge. [Renumbered]

Note: Authority cited: Section 5307, Labor Code. Reference: Sections 5310 and 5311, Labor Code.

History: 1. Renumbering of former section 10452 to section 10960 filed 12-17-2019; operative 1-1-2020. Submitted to OAL for printing only pursuant to Government Code section 11351 (Register 2019, No. 51).

§10453.   Petition for Automatic Reassignment of Trial or Expedited Hearing to Another Workers' Compensation Judge. [Renumbered]

Note: Authority cited: Section 5307, Labor Code. Reference: Section 5310, Labor Code.

History: 1. Editorial correction filed 2-2-83 (Register 83, No. 6).

2. Amendment of section heading, section and Note filed 12-19-2002; operative 1-1-2003. Submitted to OAL for printing only pursuant to Government Code section 11351 (Register 2002, No. 51).

3. Renumbering of former section 10453 to section 10788 filed 12-17-2019; operative 1-1-2020. Submitted to OAL for printing only pursuant to Government Code section 11351 (Register 2019, No. 51).

§10454.   Automatic Reassignment After Reversal. [Repealed]

Note: Authority cited: Sections 133 and 5307, Labor Code. Reference: Section 5310, Labor Code.

History: 1. Renumbering of former section 10454 to new section 10455 and new section 10454 filed 12-19-2002; operative 1-1-2003. Submitted to OAL for printing only pursuant to Government Code section 11351 (Register 2002, No. 51).

2. Repealer filed 12-17-2019; operative 1-1-2020. Submitted to OAL for printing only pursuant to Government Code section 11351 (Register 2019, No. 51).

§10455.   Applications.

A separate Application for Adjudication of Claim shall be filed for each separate injury for which benefits are claimed. All applications shall conform to the following requirements:

(a)   Only one application shall be filed for each injury. Duplicative applications are subject to summary dismissal.

(b)   Upon filing an Application for Adjudication of Claim, the filing party shall concurrently serve a copy of the application and any accompanying documents on all other parties.

(c)   When filing an amended application, the applicant shall indicate on the box set forth on the application form that it is an amended application.

(d)   If the applicant is a minor or incompetent, the Application for Adjudication of Claim shall be accompanied by a Petition for Appointment of Guardian ad Litem and Trustee.

(e)   An applicant is not required to disclose their social security number. If an applicant discloses their Social Security number on the application, the Social Security number will be used solely for identification and verification purposes in order to administer the workers' compensation system except with the consent of the applicant, or as permitted or required by statute, regulation or judicial order.

(f)   Upon the filing of an initial application, the Workers' Compensation Appeals Board shall assign an adjudication case number and a venue. The case number and venue shall be indicated on a conformed copy of the application.

(1)   If the party filing the application is unrepresented, the Workers' Compensation Appeals Board shall serve a conformed copy of the application on all parties and lien claimants on the proof of service to the application.

(2)   If the party filing the application is represented, the Workers' Compensation Appeals Board shall serve a conformed copy of the application on the filing party or lien claimant. Upon receipt of the conformed copy of the application, the filing party shall forthwith serve a copy of the conformed application on all other parties and lien claimants.

Note: Authority cited: Sections 133, 5307, 5309 and 5708, Labor Code. Reference: Sections 126, 3208.2, 5307.5, 5316, 5500 and 5501, Labor Code.

History: 1. Renumbering of former section 10454 to new section 10455 filed 12-19-2002; operative 1-1-2003. Submitted to OAL for printing only pursuant to Government Code section 11351 (Register 2002, No. 51).

2. Renumbering of former section 10455 to section 10534 and new section 10455 filed 12-17-2019; operative 1-1-2020. Submitted to OAL for printing only pursuant to Government Code section 11351 (Register 2019, No. 51).

§10458.   Petition for New and Further Disability. [Renumbered]

Note: Authority cited: Sections 133 and 5307, Labor Code. Reference: Section 5803, Labor Code.

History: 1. Renumbering of former section 10458 to section 10534 filed 12-17-2019; operative 1-1-2020. Submitted to OAL for printing only pursuant to Government Code section 11351 (Register 2019, No. 51).

§10460.   Request for Findings of Fact.

A request for findings of fact under Government Code sections 21164, 21166, 21537, 21538, 21540 or 21540.5 or under Labor Code sections 4800.5(d), 4801, 4804.2, 4807 or 4851 is a proceeding separate from a claim for workers' compensation benefits even though it arises out of the same incident, injury or exposure. The request for findings of fact shall be filed separately and a separate file folder and record of the proceeding will be maintained, but the request for findings of fact may be consolidated for hearing with a claim for workers' compensation benefits.

Note: Authority cited: Sections 133 and 5307, Labor Code. Reference: Sections 21164, 21166, 21537, 21538, 21540 and 21540.5, Government Code; Sections 4800.5(d), 4801, 4804.2, 4807 and 4851, Labor Code.

History: 1. Renumbering and amendment of former section 10405 to section 10460 filed 12-17-2019; operative 1-1-2020. Submitted to OAL for printing only pursuant to Government Code section 11351 (Register 2019, No. 51).

§10462.   Subsequent Injuries Benefits Trust Fund Application.

(a)   All claims against the Subsequent Injuries Benefits Trust Fund shall be by an application in writing setting forth the date and nature of the industrial injury, together with all factors of disability alleged to have pre-existed the injury.

(b) All such applications shall be filed with the Workers' Compensation Appeals Board district office having venue or in EAMS, and a copy shall be served by mail on the Division of Workers' Compensation, Subsequent Injuries Benefits Trust Fund, in accordance with rules 10530 and 10540. Where joinder of the Subsequent Injuries Benefits Trust Fund has been ordered, the applicant shall forthwith file and serve an application as provided herein.

(c) After such an application is filed, any party who has previously filed medical reports shall serve copies on the Division of Workers' Compensation, Subsequent Injuries Benefits Trust Fund no later than 30 days prior to the mandatory settlement conference or other hearing, unless service is waived by the Division of Workers' Compensation, Subsequent Injuries Benefits Trust Fund.

Note: Authority cited: Sections 133, 5307, 5309 and 5708, Labor Code. Reference: Sections 4750, 4751, 4753, 4753.5 and 4754.5, Labor Code.

History: 1. Amendment filed 12-19-2002; operative 1-1-2003. Submitted to OAL for printing only pursuant to Government Code section 11351 (Register 2002, No. 51).

2. Repealer and new section filed 12-17-2019; operative 1-1-2020. Submitted to OAL for printing only pursuant to Government Code section 11351 (Register 2019, No. 51).

§10464. Contents of Petition to Terminate Liability. [Repealed]

Note: Authority cited: Sections 133 and 5307, Labor Code. Reference: Sections 4650 and 4651.1, Labor Code.

History: 1. Amendment filed 12-19-2002; operative 1-1-2003. Submitted to OAL for printing only pursuant to Government Code section 11351 (Register 2002, No. 51).

2. Repealer filed 12-17-2019; operative 1-1-2020. Submitted to OAL for printing only pursuant to Government Code section 11351 (Register 2019, No. 51).

§10465. Answers.

Any Answer to an Application for Adjudication of Claim shall be filed and served no later than the shorter of either: 10 days after service of a Declaration of Readiness to Proceed, or 90 days after service of the Application for Adjudication of Claim.

(a) The Answer used by the parties shall conform to a form prescribed and approved by the Appeals Board. Additional matters may be pleaded as deemed necessary by the answering party. A general denial is not an answer within this rule.

(b) The Answer shall be accompanied by a proof of service upon the opposing parties.

(c) Evidence upon matters and affirmative defenses not pleaded by Answer will be allowed only upon such terms and conditions as the Appeals Board or workers' compensation judge may impose in the exercise of sound discretion.

Note: Authority cited: Sections 133 and 5307, Labor Code. Reference: Sections 5500 and 5505, Labor Code.

History: 1. New section filed 12-17-2019; operative 1-1-2020. Submitted to OAL for printing only pursuant to Government Code section 11351 (Register 2019, No. 51).

§10466. Objections to Petition, Hearing, Interim Order. [Repealed]

Note: Authority cited: Sections 133 and 5307, Labor Code. Reference: Sections 4650 and 4651.1, Labor Code.

History: 1. Amendment of section and Note filed 12-19-2002; operative 1-1-2003. Submitted to OAL for printing only pursuant to Government Code section 11351 (Register 2002, No. 51).

2. Repealer filed 12-17-2019; operative 1-1-2020. Submitted to OAL for printing only pursuant to Government Code section 11351 (Register 2019, No. 51).

§10470. Labor Code Section 4906(h) Statement.

(a) The employee, insurer, employer and the attorneys for each party shall comply with Labor Code section 4906(h). Failure to file the statement required by Labor Code section 4906(h) shall result in refusal to file that party's Application for Adjudication of Claim or Answer.

(b) If anyone subject to subdivision (a) of this rule is not available, cannot be located or is unwilling to sign, a declaration under penalty of perjury setting forth in specific detail the reasons and describing good faith efforts made to comply with this rule may be filed with the Application for Adjudication of Claim or Answer. If the presiding workers' compensation judge determines from the facts set forth in the declaration that good cause has been established, the presiding workers' compensation judge may accept the Application for Adjudication of Claim or Answer for filing. For the purpose of this rule, a Compromise and Release agreement or Stipulations with Request for Award shall not be treated as an Application for Adjudication of Claim.

Note: Authority cited: Sections 133 and 5307, Labor Code. Reference: Section 4906(h), Labor Code.

History: 1. New section filed 10-15-2014; operative 1-1-2015. Submitted to OAL for printing only pursuant to Government Code section 11351 (Register 2014, No. 42). For prior history, see Register 2002, No. 51.

2. Editorial correction of History 1 (Register 2017, No. 8).

3. Renumbering of former section 10470 to section 10530 and renumbering of former section 10404 to section 10470, including amendment of section heading, section and Note, filed 12-17-2019; operative 1-1-2020. Submitted to OAL for printing only pursuant to Government Code section 11351 (Register 2019, No. 51).

ARTICLE 6
Venue

§10480. Venue.

When filing a case opening document, the filer shall designate venue and shall specify the basis for venue in accordance with Labor Code section 5501.5.

Note: Authority cited: Sections 133, 5307, 5309 and 5708, Labor Code. Reference: Sections 5500 and 5501.5, Labor Code.

History: 1. Amendment exempt from OAL review pursuant to Government Code section 11351 filed 12-19-90; operative 1-1-91 (Register 91, No. 7).

2. Amendment filed 12-23-93; operative 1-1-94. Submitted to OAL for printing only pursuant to Government Code section 11351 (Register 93, No. 52).

3. Amendment filed 12-19-2002; operative 1-1-2003. Submitted to OAL for printing only pursuant to Government Code section 11351 (Register 2002, No. 51).

4. New article 6 heading, repealer of former section 10480 and renumbering and amendment of former section 10409 to section 10480 filed 12-17-2019; operative 1-1-2020. Submitted to OAL for printing only pursuant to Government Code section 11351 (Register 2019, No. 51).

§10482. Venue When Applicant is Employee of Division of Workers' Compensation.

When a Division of Workers' Compensation employee files an Application for Adjudication of Claim or other case opening document regardless of the venue designated by the employee, venue shall be determined as follows:

(a) The parties may agree on a venue, subject to the approval of the presiding workers' compensation judge of the agreed-upon venue.

(b) If the parties are unable to agree on a suitable venue, or for any other good cause shown, the presiding workers' compensation judge of the district office designated on the application or other case opening document shall consult with the Secretary or other deputy commissioner of the Appeals Board to determine the appropriate venue, with the secretary or other deputy commissioner issuing the appropriate venue order.

(c) The secretary or other deputy commissioner of the Appeals Board shall assign the case to a workers' compensation judge unfamiliar with the employee. When appropriate, a workers' compensation judge from a region other than the employee's region shall be assigned.

Note: Authority cited: Sections 133, 5307, 5309 and 5708, Labor Code. Reference: Sections 5500 and 5501.5, Labor Code.

History: 1. New section filed 12-17-2019; operative 1-1-2020. Submitted to OAL for printing only pursuant to Government Code section 11351 (Register 2019, No. 51).

§10484. Procedural Requirement. [Repealed]

Note: Authority cited: Sections 133 and 5307, Labor Code. Reference: Sections 5500 and 5505, Labor Code.

History: 1. Amendment filed 12-23-93; operative 1-1-94. Submitted to OAL for printing only pursuant to Government Code section 11351 (Register 93, No. 52).

2. Amendment of second paragraph filed 12-19-2002; operative 1-1-2003. Submitted to OAL for printing only pursuant to Government Code section 11351 (Register 2002, No. 51).

3. Repealer filed 12-17-2019; operative 1-1-2020. Submitted to OAL for printing only pursuant to Government Code section 11351 (Register 2019, No. 51).

§10488. Objection to Venue Based on an Attorney's Principal Place of Business.

Pursuant to Labor Code section 5501.5(c), any employer or insurance carrier listed on an initial Application for Adjudication of Claim may file an objection to a venue selection, based on the employee's attorney's principal place of business under Labor Code section 5501.5(a)(3), within 30 days after notice of the adjudication case number and venue is received by the employer or insurance carrier. The objecting employer or insurance carrier shall state under penalty of perjury the date when the notice of the adjudication case number and venue was received. A timely objection shall result in venue being assigned in accordance with Labor Code section 5501.5(a)(1) or (a)(2).

Note: Authority cited: Sections 133, 5307, 5309 and 5708, Labor Code. Reference: Section 5501.5, Labor Code.

History: 1. Renumbering and amendment of former section 10410 to section 10488 filed 12-17-2019; operative 1-1-2020. Submitted to OAL for printing only pursuant to Government Code section 11351 (Register 2019, No. 51). For prior history of section 10488, see Register 93, No. 52.

§10490. Petition for Change of Venue for Good Cause.

A petition for change of venue pursuant to Labor Code section 5501.6 shall be filed at the district office or permanently staffed satellite office having venue. Any objection to a petition for a change of venue shall be filed within 10 days of the filing of the petition. The presiding workers' compensation judge of the district office having venue, or the workers' compensation judge of the permanently staffed satellite office having venue, shall grant or deny the petition for change of venue, or serve notice of a status conference concerning the petition, within 30 days of the filing of the petition.

Note: Authority cited: Sections 133, 5307, 5309 and 5708, Labor Code. Reference: Section 5501.6, Labor Code.

History: 1. Amendment of section heading and section filed 12-19-2002; operative 1-1-2003. Submitted to OAL for printing only pursuant to Government Code section 11351 (Register 2002, No. 51).
2. Renumbering of former section 10490 to section 10515 and renumbering of former section 10411 to section 10490, including amendment of section heading and section, filed 12-17-2019; operative 1-1-2020.

Submitted to OAL for printing only pursuant to Government Code section 11351 (Register 2019, No. 51).

§10492. When Pleadings Deemed Amended. [Renumbered]

Note: Authority cited: Sections 133 and 5307, Labor Code. Reference: Section 5702, Labor Code.

History: 1. Renumbering of former section 10492 to section 10517 filed 12-17-2019; operative 1-1-2020. Submitted to OAL for printing only pursuant to Government Code section 11351 (Register 2019, No. 51).

§10496. Awards and Orders Without Hearing. [Repealed]

Note: Authority cited: Sections 133 and 5307, Labor Code. Reference: Section 5702, Labor Code.

History: 1. Repealer filed 12-17-2019; operative 1-1-2020. Submitted to OAL for printing only pursuant to Government Code section 11351 (Register 2019, No. 51).

§10497. Rejection of Stipulations. [Repealed]

Note: Authority cited: Sections 133 and 5307, Labor Code. Reference: Section 5702, Labor Code.

History: 1. Repealer filed 12-17-2019; operative 1-1-2020. Submitted to OAL for printing only pursuant to Government Code section 11351 (Register 2019, No. 51).

§10498. Special Requirements for Pleadings Filed or Served by Attorneys or by Non-Attorney Employees of an Attorney or Law Firm. [Renumbered]

Note: Authority: Sections 133, 5307, 5309 and 5708, Labor Code. Reference: Sections 5000, 5501, 5505 and 5900 et seq., Labor Code; Sections 10232(a)(4), 10450 and 10773, title 8, California Code of Regulations; and Rules 2.111(1) and 8.204(b)(10)(D), California Rules of Court.

History: 1. New section filed 9-23-2013; operative 10-23-2013. Submitted as a file and print by the Workers' Compensation Appeals Board pursuant to Government Code section 11351 (Register 2013, No. 39).
2. Renumbering of former section 10498 to section 10520 filed 12-17-2019; operative 1-1-2020. Submitted to OAL for printing only pursuant to Government Code section 11351 (Register 2019, No. 51).

ARTICLE 7
Petitions, Pleadings and Forms

§10500. Form Pleadings.

(a) No workers' compensation judge and no district office of the Workers' Compensation Appeals Board shall require the parties to use a form other than that prescribed and approved by the Appeals Board.

(b) Each of the following documents shall be on a form prescribed and approved by the Appeals Board:

(1) An Application for Adjudication of Claim for compensation benefits or death benefits;

(2) A lien;

(3) A Declaration of Readiness to Proceed;

(4) A Pre-Trial Conference Statement;

(5) Minutes of Hearing except Minutes of Hearing prepared by a court reporter;

(6) A Compromise and Release agreement;

(7) Stipulations with Request for Award;

(8) A petition to terminate liability for temporary disability indemnity;

(9) A special notice of lawsuit; and

(10) Any other form the Appeals Board, in its discretion, determines should be uniform and standardized.

(c) Any form prescribed and approved by the Appeals Board may be printed by the Division of Workers' Compensation for distribution at district offices of the Workers' Compensation Appeals Board. In addition, the Division of Workers' Compensation may create:

(1) Electronic versions of the prescribed and approved forms; and/or

(2) Optical character recognition versions of those forms, either in fillable format or otherwise, for posting on the Division of Workers' Compensation's Forms webpage.

(d) Any form for proceedings before the Workers' Compensation Appeals Board created by the Division of Workers' Compensation shall be presumed to have been prescribed and approved by the Appeals Board unless the Appeals Board issues an order or a formal written statement to the contrary.

Note: Authority cited: Sections 133, 5307, 5309 and 5708, Labor Code. Reference: Sections 3716, 4903.5, 5500, 5500.3, 5501.5 and 5502, Labor Code.

History: 1. Repealer and new section exempt from OAL review pursuant to Government Code section 11351 filed 12-19-90; operative 1-1-91 (Register 91, No. 7).

2. Amendment filed 12-16-92; operative 2-1-93 and exempt from OAL review pursuant to Government Code section 11351 (Register 92, No. 51).

3. Amendment of section and Note filed 12-23-93; operative 1-1-94. Submitted to OAL for printing only pursuant to Government Code section 11351 (Register 93, No. 52).

4. Amendment filed 12-19-2002; operative 1-1-2003. Submitted to OAL for printing only pursuant to Government Code section 11351 (Register 2002, No. 51).

5. Amendment of section heading, section and Note filed 11-17-2008; operative 11-17-2008. Submitted to OAL for printing only (Register 2008, No. 47).

6. Repealer of article 6 heading, new article 7 heading, repealer of former section 10500 and renumbering of former section 10408 to section 10500, including amendment of section heading and section, filed 12-17-2019; operative 1-1-2020. Submitted to OAL for printing only pursuant to Government Code section 11351 (Register 2019, No. 51).

§10501. Service in Death Cases. [Repealed]

Note: Authority cited: Sections 133 and 5307, Labor Code. Reference: Section 4706.5, Labor Code.

History: 1. Amendment of section heading and section filed 12-19-2002; operative 1-1-2003. Submitted to OAL for printing only pursuant to Government Code section 11351 (Register 2002, No. 51).

2. Repealer filed 12-17-2019; operative 1-1-2020. Submitted to OAL for printing only pursuant to Government Code section 11351 (Register 2019, No. 51).

§10505. Service by the Parties or Lien Claimants. [Repealed]

Note: Authority cited: Sections 133, 5307, 5309 and 5708, Labor Code. Reference: Section 5316, Labor Code.

History: 1. Amendment of section heading and text filed 12-23-93; operative 1-1-94. Submitted to OAL for printing pursuant to Government Code section 11351 (Register 93, No. 52).

2. Amendment filed 12-19-2002; operative 1-1-2003. Submitted to OAL for printing only pursuant to Government Code section 11351 (Register 2002, No. 51).

3. Amendment of section heading, section and Note filed 11-17-2008; operative 11-17-2008. Submitted to OAL for printing only (Register 2008, No. 47).

4. Repealer filed 12-17-2019; operative 1-1-2020. Submitted to OAL for printing only pursuant to Government Code section 11351 (Register 2019, No. 51).

§10506. Service: Mailbox. [Repealed]

Note: Authority cited: Sections 133 and 5307, Labor Code. Reference: Section 5316, Labor Code.

History: 1. New section filed 12-19-2002; operative 1-1-2003. Submitted to OAL for printing only pursuant to Government Code section 11351 (Register 2002, No. 51).

2. Repealer filed 12-17-2019; operative 1-1-2020. Submitted to OAL for printing only pursuant to Government Code section 11351 (Register 2019, No. 51).

§10507. Time Within Which to Act When a Document is Served by Mail, Fax, or E-Mail. [Renumbered]

Note: Authority cited: Sections 133, 5307, 5309 and 5708, Labor Code. Reference: Section 5316, Labor Code.

History: 1. Amendment of section heading and section filed 12-19-2002; operative 1-1-2003. Submitted to OAL for printing only pursuant to Government Code section 11351 (Register 2002, No. 51).

2. Amendment of section heading, section and Note filed 11-17-2008; operative 11-17-2008. Submitted to OAL for printing only (Register 2008, No. 47).

3. Renumbering of former section 10507 to section 10605 filed 12-17-2019; operative 1-1-2020. Submitted to OAL for printing only pursuant to Government Code section 11351 (Register 2019, No. 51).

§10508. Extension of Time for Weekends and Holidays. [Renumbered]

Note: Authority cited: Sections 133, 5307, 5309 and 5708, Labor Code. Reference: Section 5316, Labor Code; Sections 6700, 6701 and 6707, Government Code; and Sections 10, 12, 12a, 12b, 13 and 135, Code of Civil Procedure.

History: 1. New section filed 11-17-2008; operative 11-17-2008. Submitted to OAL for printing only (Register 2008, No. 47).

2. Renumbering of former section 10508 to section 10600 filed 12-17-2019; operative 1-1-2020. Submitted to OAL for printing only pursuant to Government Code section 11351 (Register 2019, No. 51).

§10510. Petitions and Answers to Petitions.

(a) After jurisdiction of the Workers' Compensation Appeals Board is invoked pursuant to rule 10450, a request for action by the Workers' Compensation Appeals Board, other than a rule 10500 form pleading, shall be made by petition. The caption of each petition shall contain the case title and adjudication case number and shall indicate the type of relief sought.

(b) All petitions and answers shall be filed in accordance with rule 10615 and served on all parties in accordance with rule 10625. A failure to concurrently file a proof of service with a petition or answer constitutes a valid ground for summarily dismissing or denying the petition or summarily rejecting the answer.

(c) An answer may be filed within 10 days after the service of a petition unless otherwise provided. The time limit for filing any shall be extended in accordance with rule 10605 unless otherwise provided.

(d) All petitions and answers shall be verified under penalty of perjury in the manner required for verified pleadings in courts of record. A failure to comply with the verification requirement constitutes a valid ground for summarily dismissing or denying a petition or summarily rejecting an answer.

(e) A document cover sheet and a document separator sheet shall be filed with each petition or answer. The appropriate title for the petition or answer shall be entered into the document title field of the document separator sheet.

(f) Any previously filed document shall not be attached to a petition or answer; any such document attached to a petition or answer may be discarded.

Note: Authority cited: Sections 133, 5307, 5309 and 5708, Labor Code. Reference: Sections 126 and 5905, Labor Code.

History: 1. Amendment filed 12-23-93; operative 1-1-94. Submitted to OAL for printing only pursuant to Government Code section 11351 (Register 93, No. 52).

2. Amendment of section heading, section and Note filed 11-17-2008; operative 11-17-2008. Submitted to OAL for printing only (Register 2008, No. 47).

3. Repealer of former section 10510 and renumbering of former section 10450 to section 10510, including amendment of section heading and section, filed 12-17-2019; operative 1-1-2020. Submitted to OAL for printing only pursuant to Government Code section 11351 (Register 2019, No. 51).

§10515. Demurrer, Judgment on the Pleadings and Summary Judgment Not Permitted.

Demurrers, petitions for judgment on the pleadings and petitions for summary judgment are not permitted.

Note: Authority cited: Sections 133 and 5307, Labor Code. Reference: Sections 5500 and 5708, Labor Code.

History: 1. Renumbering of former section 10490 to section 10515, including amendment of section heading and section, filed 12-17-2019; operative 1-1-2020. Submitted to OAL for printing only pursuant to Government Code section 11351 (Register 2019, No. 51).

§10517. When Pleadings Deemed Amended.

Pleadings shall be deemed amended to conform to the stipulations and statement of issues agreed to by the parties on the record. Pleadings may be amended by the Workers' Compensation Appeals Board to conform to proof.

Note: Authority cited: Sections 133 and 5307, Labor Code. Reference: Section 5702, Labor Code.

History: 1. Renumbering and amendment of former section 10492 to section 10517 filed 12-17-2019; operative 1-1-2020. Submitted to OAL for printing only pursuant to Government Code section 11351 (Register 2019, No. 51).

§10520. Special Requirements for Pleadings Filed or Served by Representatives.

(a)   Where a party is represented by an attorney, all pleadings filed with the Workers' Compensation Appeals Board or served on any party or other person shall include the name, State Bar number, law firm, if any, business address and business telephone number of the attorney.

(b)   If a non-attorney employee of an attorney or law firm is executing the pleading being filed or served, the pleading shall include a heading containing the non-attorney's name and the name, State Bar number, law firm, if any, business address and business telephone number of the attorney primarily responsible for supervising the non-attorney.

(c)   If a non-attorney representative who is not an employee of an attorney or law firm is executing the pleading being filed or served, the pleading shall include a heading containing the non-attorney representative's name followed by the words "Non-Attorney Representative," the name of the entity, if any, that employs the non-attorney representative, business address and business telephone number.

Note: Authority cited: Sections 133, 5307, 5309 and 5708, Labor Code. Reference: Sections 5000, 5501, 5505 and 5900 et seq., Labor Code; and Rules 2.111(1) and 8.204(b)(10)(D), California Rules of Court.

History: 1. Renumbering of former section 10498 to section 10520, including amendment of section heading, section and Note, filed 12-17-2019; operative 1-1-2020. Submitted to OAL for printing only pursuant to Government Code section 11351 (Register 2019, No. 51). For prior history of section 10520, see Register 2008, No. 47.

§10525. Petition for Increased or Decreased Compensation — Serious and Willful Misconduct.

(a)   Any claim(s) that an injury was caused by either the serious and willful misconduct of the employee or of the employer must be separately pleaded and must set out in sufficient detail the specific basis upon which a claim is founded. When a claim of serious and willful misconduct is based on more than one theory, the petition shall set forth each theory separately.

(b)   Whenever a claim of serious and willful misconduct is predicated upon the violation of a particular safety order, the petition shall set forth the correct citation or reference and all of the particulars required by Labor Code section 4553.1.

Note: Authority cited: Sections 133 and 5307, Labor Code. Reference: Sections 4550, 4551, 4552, 4553 and 4553.1, Labor Code.

History: 1. New section filed 12-17-2019; operative 1-1-2020. Submitted to OAL for printing only pursuant to Government Code section 11351 (Register 2019, No. 51).

§10528. Petition for Increased Compensation — Discrimination Under Labor Code Section 132a.

Any person seeking to initiate proceedings under Labor Code section 132a other than prosecution for misdemeanor must file a petition setting forth specifically and in detail the nature of each violation alleged, facts relied upon and the relief sought. Each alleged violation must be separately pleaded.

The Workers' Compensation Appeals Board may refer, or any worker may complain of, suspected violations of the criminal misdemeanor provisions of Labor Code section 132a to the Division of Labor Standards Enforcement or directly to the Office of the Public Prosecutor.

Note: Authority cited: Sections 133 and 5307, Labor Code. Reference: Section 132a, Labor Code.

History: 1. Renumbering of former section 10447 to section 10528, including amendment of section heading and section, filed 12-17-2019; operative 1-1-2020. Submitted to OAL for printing only pursuant to Government Code section 11351 (Register 2019, No. 51).

§10530.　Emergency Petition for Stay.

(a)　A party may present to the presiding workers' compensation judge of the district office having venue or the workers' compensation judge of the permanently staffed satellite office having venue a petition to stay an action by another party pending a hearing. Each district office will have a designee of the presiding workers' compensation judge available to assign petitions for stay from 8:00 a.m. to 11:00 a.m. and 1:00 p.m. to 4:00 p.m. on court days.

(b)　A party who walks through a petition to stay an action shall provide notice by fax or e-mail to the opposing party or parties no later than 10:00 a.m. of the immediately preceding court day. This notice shall state with specificity the nature of the relief to be requested by the petition to stay and state the date, time and place that the petition to stay will be presented. A copy of the petition to stay shall be attached to the notice. If notice by fax or e-mail fails, or if an opposing party's fax number or e-mail address are unknown, notice shall be given in the manner best calculated to expeditiously provide the party or parties with notice including notice by phone or by overnight mail or delivery service. First-class mail shall not be utilized for notice of a petition to stay an action.

(c)　A petition to stay an action shall be accompanied by a declaration regarding notice stating under penalty of perjury:

(1)　The notice given, including the date, time, manner and name of the party informed;

(2)　The relief sought; and

(3)　Whether opposition is expected. In addition, if the petitioner was unable to give timely notice to the opposing party, the declaration under penalty of perjury shall state that the petitioner in good faith attempted to inform the opposing party but was unable to do so, and shall specify the efforts made to inform the opposing party.

(d)　Upon the receipt of a proper petition to stay an action, the presiding workers' compensation judge shall, in their discretion, either:

(1)　Deny the petition;

(2)　Grant a temporary stay and set the petition for a hearing; or

(3)　Set the petition for a hearing, without either denying the petition or granting a temporary stay.

Note: Authority cited: Sections 133 and 5307, Labor Code. Reference: Sections 4053, 4054, 4902, 5001, 5002, 5702 and 5710, Labor Code.

History: 1. Amendment exempt from OAL review pursuant to Government Code section 11351 filed 12-19-90; operative 1-1-91 (Register 91, No. 7).

2. Repealer of article 7 heading, renumbering of former section 10530 to section 10640 and renumbering and amendment of former section 10470 to section 10530 filed 12-17-2019; operative 1-1-2020. Submitted to OAL for printing only pursuant to Government Code section 11351 (Register 2019, No. 51).

§10532.　Notice to Appear or Produce. [Renumbered]

Note: Authority cited: Sections 133, 5307, Labor Code. Reference: Section 132, Labor Code.

History: 1. Renumbering of former section 10532 to section 10642 filed 12-17-2019; operative 1-1-2020. Submitted to OAL for printing only pursuant to Government Code section 11351 (Register 2019, No. 51).

§10534.　Petition to Reopen.

Petitions invoking the continuing jurisdiction of the Workers' Compensation Appeals Board under Labor Code section 5803 shall set forth specifically and in detail the facts relied upon to establish good cause for reopening.

Note: Authority cited: Sections 133 and 5307, Labor Code. Reference: Section 5803, Labor Code.

History: 1. Amendment of section and Note filed 12-19-2002; operative 1-1-2003. Submitted to OAL for printing only pursuant to Government Code section 11351 (Register 2002, No. 51).

2. Renumbering of former section 10534 to section 10644 and renumbering of former section 10455 to section 10534 filed 12-17-2019; operative 1-1-2020. Submitted to OAL for printing only pursuant to Government Code section 11351 (Register 2019, No. 51).

§10536.　Petition for New and Further Disability.

The jurisdiction of the Workers' Compensation Appeals Board under Labor Code section 5410 shall be invoked by a petition setting forth specifically and in detail the facts relied upon to establish new and further disability.

If no prior Application for Adjudication of Claim has been filed, jurisdiction shall be invoked by the filing of an original Application for Adjudication of Claim.

Note: Authority cited: Sections 133 and 5307, Labor Code. Reference: Sections 5410 and 5803, Labor Code.

History: 1. Repealer and new section exempt from OAL review pursuant to Government Code section 11351 filed 12-19-90; operative 1-1-91 (Register 91, No. 7).

2. Amendment of section and Note filed 12-19-2002; operative 1-1-2003. Submitted to OAL for printing only pursuant to Government Code section 11351 (Register 2002, No. 51).

3. Renumbering of former section 10536 to section 10647 and renumbering and amendment of former section 10458 to section 10536 filed 12-17-2019; operative 1-1-2020. Submitted to OAL for printing only pursuant to Government Code section 11351 (Register 2019, No. 51).

§10537.   Subpoena for Medical Witness. [Renumbered]

Note: Authority cited: Sections 133, 5307, Labor Code. Reference: Section 132, Labor Code.

History: 1. Renumbering of former section 10537 to section 10650 filed 12-17-2019; operative 1-1-2020. Submitted to OAL for printing only pursuant to Government Code section 11351 (Register 2019, No. 51).

§10538.   Subpoenas for Medical Information by Non-Physician Lien Claimants. [Renumbered]

Note: Authority cited: Sections 133, 4903.6(d), 5307, 5309 and 5708, Labor Code. Reference: Sections 130, 4903.6(d) and 5710(a), Labor Code; and Sections 56.05 and 56.10, Civil Code.

History: 1. New section filed 9-23-2013; operative 10-23-2013. Submitted as a file and print by the Workers' Compensation Appeals Board pursuant to Government Code section 11351 (Register 2013, No. 39).

2. Renumbering of former section 10538 to section 10655 filed 12-17-2019; operative 1-1-2020. Submitted to OAL for printing only pursuant to Government Code section 11351 (Register 2019, No. 51).

§10540.   Petition to Terminate Liability for Continuing Temporary Disability.

(a)   Any petition to terminate liability for temporary total disability indemnity awarded under a findings and award, decision or order of the Workers' Compensation Appeals Board shall include:

(1)   A statement, in capital letters, that an order terminating liability for temporary total disability indemnity may issue unless objection thereto is served and filed on behalf of the employee within 14 days after service and filing of the petition, and

(2)   All medical reports in the possession of the petitioner that have not previously been served and filed;

(b)   If written objection to the petition to terminate is not served and filed within 14 days of the petition's service and filing, the Workers' Compensation Appeals Board may order temporary disability compensation terminated, in accordance with the facts as stated in the petition or in such other manner as may appear appropriate on the record. If the petition to terminate is not properly completed or executed in accordance with this rule, the Workers' Compensation Appeals Board may summarily deny or dismiss the petition.

(c)   Written objection to the petition by the employee shall be served and filed within 14 days of service and filing of the petition, and shall state the facts in support of the employee's contention that the petition should be denied, and shall be accompanied by a Declaration of Readiness to Proceed to Expedited Hearing. All supporting medical reports shall be attached to the objection. The objection shall also show that service of the objection and the reports attached thereto has been made upon petitioner or counsel and a proof of service showing service of the objection upon petitioner.

(d)   Upon the filing of a timely objection, where it appears that the employee is not or may not be working and is not or may not be receiving disability indemnity, the petition to terminate shall be set for expedited hearing not less than 10 nor more than 30 days from the date of the receipt of the objection.

(e)   If complete disposition of the petition to terminate cannot be made at the hearing, the workers' compensation judge assigned thereto, based on the record, including the allegations of the petition, the objection thereto and the evidence (if any) at said hearing, shall forthwith issue an interim order directing whether temporary disability indemnity shall or shall not continue during the pendency of proceedings on the petition to terminate. Said interim order shall not be considered a final order, and will not preclude a complete adjudication of the petition to terminate or the issue of temporary disability or any other issue after full hearing of the issues.

Note: Authority cited: Sections 133 and 5307, Labor Code. Reference: Sections 4650 and 4651.1, Labor Code.

History: 1. New section filed 12-17-2019; operative 1-1-2020. Submitted to OAL for printing only pursuant to Government Code section 11351 (Register 2019, No. 51).

§10541. Submission at Conference. [Renumbered]

Note: Authority cited: Sections 133, 5307, 5309 and 5708, Labor Code. Reference: Sections 5708 and 5709, Labor Code.

History: 1. Amendment filed 12-23-93; operative 1-1-94. Submitted to OAL for printing only pursuant to Government Code section 11351 (Register 93, No. 52).

2. Amendment of section heading, section and Note filed 12-19-2002; operative 1-1-2003. Submitted to OAL for printing only pursuant to Government Code section 11351 (Register 2002, No. 51).

3. Amendment of section and Note filed 11-17-2008; operative 11-17-2008. Submitted to OAL for printing only (Register 2008, No. 47).

4. Repealer of article 8 heading and renumbering of former section 10541 to section 10761 filed 12-17-2019; operative 1-1-2020. Submitted to OAL for printing only pursuant to Government Code section 11351 (Register 2019, No. 51).

§10544. Notice of Hearing. [Renumbered]

Note: Authority cited: Sections 133 and 5307, Labor Code. Reference: Section 5504, Labor Code.

History: 1. Amendment filed 12-23-93; operative 1-1-94. Submitted to OAL for printing only pursuant to Government Code section 11351 (Register 93, No. 52).

2. Amendment of section and Note filed 12-19-2002; operative 1-1-2003. Submitted to OAL for printing only pursuant to Government Code section 11351 (Register 2002, No. 51).

3. Renumbering of former section 10544 to section 10750 filed 12-17-2019; operative 1-1-2020. Submitted to OAL for printing only pursuant to Government Code section 11351 (Register 2019, No. 51).

§10545. Petition for Costs.

(a) A petition for costs is a petition seeking reimbursement of an expense or payment for service that is not allowable as a lien against compensation under Labor Code section 4903. A petition for costs may be filed only by:

(1) An employee or the dependent of a deceased employee;

(2) A defendant; or

(3) An interpreter for services other than those rendered at a medical treatment appointment or medical-legal examination.

(b) The caption of the petition shall identify it as a "Petition for Costs."

(c) A petition for costs filed by an employee or a dependent may include, but is not limited to, a claim for reimbursement of payment(s) previously made directly to a provider for medical-legal goods or services, subject to any applicable official fee schedule.

(d) A petition for costs filed by an interpreter shall contain, in addition to the general factual allegations of the petition:

(1) A statement of the name(s) of any interpreter(s) who performed the services;

(2) A statement that the services were actually performed; and

(3) Either:

(A) A statement of the certification number of the interpreter(s); or

(B) If not certified, a statement that specifies why a certified interpreter was not used and that sets forth the qualifications of the interpreter, including any qualifications for a non-certified interpreter established by the rules of the Administrative Director.

(e) A petition for costs shall not be filed or served until at least 60 days after a written demand for the costs has been served on the defendant or the person or entity from whom the costs are claimed. The petition shall append:

(1) A copy of the written demand, together with a copy of its proof of service; and

(2) A copy of the response, if any.

A petition that fails to comply with these provisions may be dismissed.

(f) A petition for costs submitted by any person or entity not listed in subdivision (a) shall be deemed dismissed by operation of law and shall not toll or extend any statute of limitations.

(g) The Workers' Compensation Appeals Board may, at any time, issue a notice of intention to allow or disallow the costs sought by the petition, in whole or in part. The notice of intention shall give the petitioner and any adverse party no less than 15 calendar days to file written objection showing good cause to the contrary. If no timely objection is filed, or if the objection on its face fails to show good cause, the Workers' Compensation Appeals Board, in its discretion, may:

(1)   Issue an order regarding the petition for costs, consistent with the notice of intention; or

(2)   Set the matter for hearing.

(h)   If the filing of a petition for costs, or the failure to promptly make good faith payments on the costs sought by the petition, was the result of bad faith actions or tactics, the Workers' Compensation Appeals Board may impose monetary sanctions and allow reasonable attorney's fees and costs under Labor Code section 5813 and rule 10421. The amount of the attorney's fees, costs and sanctions payable shall be determined by the Workers' Compensation Appeals Board; however, for bad faith actions or tactics occurring on or after the effective date of this rule, the monetary sanctions shall not be less than $500.00.

Note: Authority cited: Sections 133, 5307, 5309 and 5708, Labor Code. Reference: Sections 4600, 4903 et seq., 5710, 5811 and 5813, Labor Code.

History: 1. Renumbering of former section 10451.3 to section 10545, including amendment of section and Note, filed 12-17-2019; operative 1-1-2020. Submitted to OAL for printing only pursuant to Government Code section 11351 (Register 2019, No. 51).

§10547.   Petition for Labor Code Section 5710 Attorney's Fees.

(a)   A petition for attorney's fees pursuant to Labor Code section 5710 is a petition seeking attorney fees for representation of the applicant at a deposition allowable under Labor Code section 5710(b) as well as any other benefits listed under Labor Code section 5710(b)(1)-(5).

(b)   The caption of the petition shall identify it as a "Petition for Attorney's Fees Pursuant to Labor Code Section 5710."

(c)   A petition for attorney's fees pursuant to Labor Code section 5710 shall be verified upon oath in the manner required for verified pleadings in courts of record.

(d)   A petition for attorney's fees pursuant to Labor Code section 5710 shall not be filed or served until at least 30 days after a written demand for the fees has been served on the defendant(s). The petition shall append:

(1)   A copy of the written demand, together with a copy of the proof of service;

(2)   A copy of the response, if any;

(3)   A proof of service showing service on the injured worker and the defendant alleged to be liable for paying the fees; and

(e)   Failure to comply with subdivisions (c) and (d)(1)-(3) of this rule shall constitute a valid ground for dismissing the petition.

(f)   The petition shall contain the name of the attorney who attended the deposition along with the attorney's State Bar number.

Note: Authority cited: Sections 133, 5307, 5309 and 5708, Labor Code. Reference: Sections 4600, 4903 et seq., 5710, 5811 and 5813, Labor Code.

History: 1. New section filed 12-17-2019; operative 1-1-2020. Submitted to OAL for printing only pursuant to Government Code section 11351 (Register 2019, No. 51).

§10548.   Continuances. [Renumbered]

Note: Authority cited: Sections 133 and 5307, Labor Code. Reference: Article XIV, Section 4, California Constitution; and Sections 5502 and 5502.5, Labor Code.

History: 1. New section filed 10-15-2014; operative 1-1-2015. Submitted to OAL for printing only pursuant to Government Code section 11351 (Register 2014, No. 42). For prior history, see Register 2008, No. 47.

2. Editorial correction of History 1 (Register 2017, No. 8).

3. Renumbering of former section 10548 to section 10748 filed 12-17-2019; operative 1-1-2020. Submitted to OAL for printing only pursuant to Government Code section 11351 (Register 2019, No. 51).

§10549.   Appearances in Settled Cases. [Renumbered]

Note: Authority cited: Sections 133 and 5307, Labor Code. Reference: Article XIV, Section 4, California Constitution; and Sections 5502 and 5502.5, Labor Code.

History: 1. New section filed 10-15-2014; operative 1-1-2015. Submitted to OAL for printing only pursuant to Government Code section 11351 (Register 2014, No. 42).

2. Editorial correction of History 1 (Register 2017, No. 8).

3. Renumbering of former section 10549 to section 10757 filed 12-17-2019; operative 1-1-2020. Submitted to OAL for printing only pursuant to Government Code section 11351 (Register 2019, No. 51).

§10550.   Petition to Dismiss Inactive Cases.

(a)   Unless a case is activated for hearing within one year after the filing of the Application for Adjudication of Claim or the entry of an order taking off calendar, the case may be dismissed after notice and opportunity to be heard. Such dismissals may be entered at the request of an interested party or upon the Workers' Compensation Appeals Board's own motion for lack of prosecution.

(b)   At least 30 days before filing a petition to dismiss, the defendant seeking to dismiss the case shall send a letter to the applicant and, if represented, to the applicant's attorney or nonattorney representative, stating the defendant's intention to file a "Petition to Dismiss Inactive Case" 30 days after the date of that letter, unless the applicant or applicant's attorney or nonattorney representative objects in writing, demonstrating good cause for not dismissing the case.

(c)   A petition to dismiss shall be filed with the district office having venue or in EAMS and the petition shall be served on all parties and all lien claimants pursuant to Rule 10625.

(d)   A petition to dismiss shall be captioned "Petition to Dismiss Inactive Case [assigned ADJ number]."

(e)   The following documents shall be filed with a petition to dismiss:

(1)   A copy of the letter required by subdivision (a) of this rule; and

(2)   Any reply to the letter required by subdivision (a) of this rule.

(f)   A case may be dismissed after issuance of a 10-day notice of intention to dismiss and an opportunity to be heard, but not by an order with a clause rendering the order null and void if an objection showing good cause is filed.

Note: Authority cited: Sections 133 and 5307, Labor Code. Reference: Sections 5405 and 5406, Labor Code.

History: 1. New section filed 11-17-2008; operative 11-17-2008. Submitted to OAL for printing only (Register 2008, No. 47).

2. Renumbering of former section 10550 to section 10390 and renumbering of former section 10582 to section 10550, including amendment of section heading and section, filed 12-17-2019; operative 1-1-2020. Submitted to OAL for printing only pursuant to Government Code section 11351 (Register 2019, No. 51).

§10552.   Expedited Hearing Calendar. [Renumbered]

Note: Authority cited: Sections 133, 5307 and 5502, Labor Code. Reference: Section 5202, Labor Code.

History: 1. New section filed 10-15-2014; operative 1-1-2015. Submitted to OAL for printing only

pursuant to Government Code section 11351 (Register 2014, No. 42).

2. Editorial correction of History 1 (Register 2017, No. 8).

3. Renumbering of former section 10552 to section 10782 filed 12-17-2019; operative 1-1-2020. Submitted to OAL for printing only pursuant to Government Code section 11351 (Register 2019, No. 51).

§10555.   Petition for Credit.

(a)   When a dispute arises as to a credit for any payments or overpayments of benefits pursuant to Labor Code section 4909, any petition for credit shall include:

(1)   A description of the payments made by the employer;

(2)   A description of the benefits against which the employer seeks a credit; and

(3)   The amount of the claimed credit.

(b)   When a dispute arises as to a credit for an employee's third party recovery pursuant to Labor Code section 3861, any petition for credit shall include:

(1)   A copy of the settlement or judgment, if available; and

(2)   An itemization of any credit applied to expenses and attorneys' fees pursuant to Labor Code sections 3856, 3858 and 3860.

(c)   Where a copy of the settlement or judgment required under subdivision (b)(1) of this rule is not available, a workers' compensation judge may order its production for purposes of adjudicating a petition for credit under Labor Code section 3861.

Note: Authority cited: Sections 133 and 5307, Labor Code. Reference: Sections 3856, 3858, 3860, 3861 and 4909, Labor Code.

History: 1. New section filed 10-15-2014; operative 1-1-2015. Submitted to OAL for printing only pursuant to Government Code section 11351 (Register 2014, No. 42). For prior history, see Register 2008, No. 47.

2. Editorial correction of History 1 (Register 2017, No. 8).

3. Renumbering former section 10555 to section 10785 and new section 10555 filed 12-17-2019; operative 1-1-2020. Submitted to OAL for printing only pursuant to Government Code section 11351 (Register 2019, No. 51).

ARTICLE 8
Petitions Related to Administrative Orders

§10560.   Petitions Related to Orders Issued by the Division of Workers' Compensation Administrative Director or the Director of Industrial Relations.

(a)   Where the Labor Code provides that the

Workers' Compensation Appeals Board has jurisdiction over appeals from or enforcement of an order, any aggrieved party may appeal or seek to enforce an order issued by the Division of Workers' Compensation Administrative Director or the Director of Industrial Relations by filing a petition, and an Application for Adjudication of Claim if one has not already been filed.

(b) Any petition that fails to comply with any of the following requirements may be subject to summary dismissal:

(1) The petition must be timely filed with the Workers' Compensation Appeals Board within the timeframe set forth in the applicable statutes and rules.

(2) The petition shall be filed in accordance with rule 10615.

(3) The petition shall be served on all adverse parties, the employee and the Administrative Director or the Director as specified in the relevant rule.

(c) The petition shall set forth specifically and in full detail the factual and/or legal grounds upon which the petitioner considers the determination of the Administrative Director or the Director to be unjust or unlawful, and every issue to be considered. The petitioner shall be deemed to have finally waived all objections, irregularities and illegalities concerning the determination other than those set forth in the petition.

(d) The petition shall be adjudicated by a workers' compensation judge at the trial level of the Workers' Compensation Appeals Board utilizing the same procedures applicable to claims for ordinary benefits, including but not limited to the setting of a mandatory settlement conference and trial.

(e) Where a workers' compensation judge has issued a final decision, order or award, any aggrieved party may file a petition for reconsideration with the Workers' Compensation Appeals Board.

Note: Authority cited: Sections 133, 5307, 5309 and 5708, Labor Code. Reference: Sections 129, 4603, 4604, 5300, 5301 and 5302, Labor Code.

History: 1. Repealer and new section heading and section and amendment of Note filed 12-19-2002; operative 1-1-2003. Submitted to OAL for printing only pursuant to Government Code section 11351 (Register 2002, No. 51).
2. New article 8 heading and repealer and new section filed 12-17-2019; operative 1-1-2020. Submitted to OAL for printing only pursuant to Government Code section 11351 (Register 2019, No. 51).

§10561. Sanctions. [Renumbered]

Note: Authority cited: Sections 133, 5307, 5309 and 5708, Labor Code. Reference: Sections 4903.6(c) and 5813, Labor Code.

History: 1. New section filed 12-23-93; operative 1-1-94. Submitted to OAL for printing only pursuant to Government Code section 11351 (Register 93, No. 52).
2. Amendment filed 12-19-2002; operative 1-1-2003. Submitted to OAL for printing only pursuant to Government Code section 11351 (Register 2002, No. 51).
3. Amendment of section and Note filed 11-17-2008; operative 11-17-2008. Submitted to OAL for printing only (Register 2008, No. 47).
4. Amendment of subsections (b)(3)-(4) filed 10-15-2014; operative 1-1-2015. Submitted to OAL for printing only pursuant to Government Code section 11351 (Register 2014, No. 42).
5. Editorial correction of History 4 (Register 2017, No. 8).
6. Renumbering of former section 10561 to section 10421 filed 12-17-2019; operative 1-1-2020. Submitted to OAL for printing only pursuant to Government Code section 11351 (Register 2019, No. 51).

§10562. Failure to Appear. [Repealed]

Note: Authority cited: Sections 133 and 5307, Labor Code. Reference: Article XIV, Section 4, California Constitution; and Sections 5502(e) and 5708, Labor Code.

History: 1. Repealer and new section filed 12-23-93; operative 1-1-94. Submitted to OAL for printing only pursuant to Government Code section 11351 (Register 93, No. 52). For prior history, see Register 91, No. 7.
2. Amendment of section and Note filed 12-19-2002; operative 1-1-2003. Submitted to OAL for printing only pursuant to Government Code section 11351 (Register 2002, No. 51).
3. Repealer filed 12-17-2019; operative 1-1-2020. Submitted to OAL for printing only pursuant to Government Code section 11351 (Register 2019, No. 51).

§10563. Appearances Required of Parties to Case-in-Chief. [Repealed]

Note: Authority cited: Sections 133, 5307, 5309 and 5708, Labor Code. Reference: Sections 5502 and 5700, Labor Code.

History: 1. New section filed 10-15-2014; operative 1-1-2015. Submitted to OAL for printing only pursuant to Government Code section 11351 (Register

2014, No. 42). For prior history, see Register 2008, No. 47.

2. Editorial correction of History 1 (Register 2017, No. 8).

3. Repealer filed 12-17-2019; operative 1-1-2020. Submitted to OAL for printing only pursuant to Government Code section 11351 (Register 2019, No. 51).

§10563.1. Other Appearances Required. [Repealed]

Note: Authority cited: Sections 133, 5307, 5309 and 5708, Labor Code. Reference: Sections 5502 and 5700, Labor Code.

History: 1. New section filed 10-15-2014; operative 1-1-2015. Submitted to OAL for printing only pursuant to Government Code section 11351 (Register 2014, No. 42).

2. Editorial correction of History 1 (Register 2017, No. 8).

3. Repealer filed 12-17-2019; operative 1-1-2020. Submitted to OAL for printing only pursuant to Government Code section 11351 (Register 2019, No. 51).

§10564. Interpreters. [Renumbered]

Note: Authority cited: Sections 133 and 5307, Labor Code. Reference: Sections 4600, 4621, 5710 and 5811, Labor Code.

History: 1. Amendment of section and Note filed 12-23-93; operative 1-1-94. Submitted to OAL for printing only pursuant to Government Code section 11351 (Register 93, No. 52).

2. Amendment of section and Note filed 12-19-2002; operative 1-1-2003. Submitted to OAL for printing only pursuant to Government Code section 11351 (Register 2002, No. 51).

3. Renumbering of former section 10564 to section 10790 filed 12-17-2019; operative 1-1-2020. Submitted to OAL for printing only pursuant to Government Code section 11351 (Register 2019, No. 51).

§10565. Petition Appealing Denial of Return-to-Work Supplement.

(a) An injured worker may file a "Petition Appealing Denial of Return-to-Work Supplement" with the district office having venue or in EAMS.

(b) The petition shall be filed within 20 days of service of the decision denying the return-to-work supplement, in accordance with rule 10615 and rule 17309.

(c) The petition and any additional documents or pleadings related to the petition shall be served on the Department of Industrial Rela-

tions Return-to-Work Supplement Program in accordance with rule 10632.

(d) The petition shall be captioned "Petition Appealing Denial of Return-to-Work Supplement" and shall include the assigned ADJ number.

(e) The petition shall be based upon one or more of the grounds as prescribed for petitions for reconsideration in Labor Code section 5903.

(f) The Director may file an answer to the petition within 20 days of the date of service of the petition. A document cover sheet and a document separator sheet shall be filed with the answer, and "Return-to-Work Supplement Program Answer to Appeal" shall be entered into the document title field of the document separator sheet.

(g) The petition shall not be placed on calendar unless a Declaration of Readiness to Proceed is filed. The Declaration of Readiness to Proceed may not be filed until 30 days have elapsed from the service of the petition.

(h) If the Director of Industrial Relations acts under rule 17309 to amend, modify or rescind the decision being appealed, the resulting order by the Director shall be served on the parties within 15 days following the date the appeal was filed and shall be filed with the district office having venue or in EAMS.

Note: Authority cited: Sections 133, 139.48, 5307, 5309 and 5708, Labor Code. Reference: Section 5903, Labor Code.

History: 1. New section filed 12-17-2019; operative 1-1-2020. Submitted to OAL for printing only pursuant to Government Code section 11351 (Register 2019, No. 51).

§10566. Minutes of Hearing and Summary of Evidence. [Repealed]

Note: Authority cited: Sections 133 and 5307, Labor Code. Reference: Section 5313, Labor Code.

History: 1. Amendment of subsection (d) filed 12-19-2002; operative 1-1-2003. Submitted to OAL for printing only pursuant to Government Code section 11351 (Register 2002, No. 51).

2. Repealer filed 12-17-2019; operative 1-1-2020. Submitted to OAL for printing only pursuant to Government Code section 11351 (Register 2019, No. 51).

§10567. Petition Appealing Independent Bill Review Determination.

(a) An aggrieved party may file a petition appealing an independent bill review (IBR) determination of the Administrative Director (AD). For purposes of this section, a "determination" includes a decision regarding the amount payable to the provider, if any, and/or a decision that a dispute is not subject to independent bill review.

(b) The petition shall comply with each of the following provisions:

(1) The petition shall be limited to raising one or more of the five grounds specified in Labor Code section 4603.6(f).

(2) The petition shall set forth specifically and in full detail the factual and/or legal grounds upon which the petitioner considers the IBR determination to be unjust or unlawful, and every issue to be considered by the Workers' Compensation Appeals Board. The petitioner shall be deemed to have finally waived all objections, irregularities, and illegalities concerning the IBR determination other than those set forth in the petition appealing.

(c) The petition shall be filed in accordance with rule 10615 no later than 20 days after service of the IBR determination.

(d) In addition to service as required by rule 10625, the petition and any additional documents or pleadings related to the petition shall be served on the IBR Unit in accordance with rule 10632.

(e) The petition shall be captioned "Petition Appealing Administrative Director's Independent Bill Review Determination" and shall include the assigned ADJ number and the IBR case number assigned by the Administrative director.

(f) The petition shall include a copy of the IBR determination and proof of service of that determination.

(g) Upon receiving notice of the petition, the IBR Unit may download the record of the independent bill review organization into EAMS, in whole or in part. The Workers' Compensation Appeals Board, in its discretion, may:

(1) Admit all or any part of the downloaded IBR record into evidence; and/or

(2) Permit the parties to offer in evidence documents that are duplicates of ones already existing in the downloaded IBR record.

(h) The petition shall not be placed on calendar unless a Declaration of Readiness to Proceed is filed and served on the Administrative Director, all adverse parties and the applicant.

(i) If the IBR determination is not affirmed by the workers' compensation judge or the Appeals Board, it shall be rescinded and the dispute returned to the Administrative Director with an order specifying the basis for the rescission, and an order to resubmit the dispute to IBR in accordance with Labor Code section 4603.6(g).

(j) If a final decision of the Workers' Compensation Appeals Board affirms the Administrative Director's IBR determination and results in the defendant being liable for any payment to the provider, the amount for which the defendant is liable shall be paid to the provider forthwith. If the defendant fails to pay forthwith, the provider need not file a lien claim and may file a petition to enforce under rule 10570.

Note: Authority cited: Sections 133, 5307, 5309 and 5708, Labor Code. Reference: Sections 4603.6, 5500, 5501, 5502, 5700 et seq., 5800 et seq. and 5900 et seq., Labor Code.

History: 1. Renumbering of former section 10957 to section 10567, including amendment of section heading, section and Note, filed 12-17-2019; operative 1-1-2020. Submitted to OAL for printing only pursuant to Government Code section 11351 (Register 2019, No. 51).

§10570. Petition to Enforce an Administrative Director Determination.

(a) An aggrieved party may file a "Petition to Enforce an Administrative Director Determination" after the Workers' Compensation Appeals Board has issued a final order affirming an IBR, IMR or other determination issued by the administrative director or after the time to appeal the determination to the Workers' Compensation Appeals Board has expired.

(b) The petition shall be captioned as a "Petition to Enforce an Administrative Director Determination" and shall include the assigned ADJ number and shall append a copy of the Administrative Director's determination.

(c) The petition shall be served on all parties in accordance with rule 10628.

(d) Within 15 days of the filing of the petition to enforce, the Workers' Compensation Appeals Board shall issue a notice of intention to grant or deny the petition, in whole or in part. The notice of intention shall give the petitioner and any adverse party no fewer than 15 calendar days to file written objection showing good cause to the contrary. If no timely written objection is filed, or if the written objection on its face fails to show good cause, the Workers' Compensation Appeals Board, in its discretion, may:

(1) Issue an order regarding the petition to enforce, consistent with the notice of intention; or

(2) Set the matter for hearing.

Note: Authority cited: Sections 133, 5307, 5309 and 5708, Labor Code. Reference: Sections 4603.6, 4622, 4903.05 and 4903.06, Labor Code.

History: 1. Renumbering of former section 10570 to section 10833 and renumbering of former section 10451.4 to section 10570, including amendment of section heading and section, filed 12-17-2019; operative 1-1-2020. Submitted to OAL for printing only pursuant to Government Code section 11351 (Register 2019, No. 51).

§10575. Petition Appealing Independent Medical Review Determination.

(a) An aggrieved party may file a petition appealing the Administrative Director's independent medical review (IMR) determination. For purposes of this rule, a "determination" includes a decision regarding medical necessity and/or a decision that a dispute is not eligible for independent medical review.

(b) The petition shall set forth specifically and in full detail the factual and/or legal grounds upon which the petitioner considers the IMR determination to be incorrect, and every issue to be considered by the Workers' Compensation Appeals Board. The petitioner shall be deemed to have finally waived all objections, irregularities and illegalities concerning the IMR determination other than those set forth in the petition. Any petition that fails to comply with any of the following requirements may be subject to summary dismissal.

(c) The petition shall be filed in accordance with rule 10615 no later than 30 days after service of the IMR determination.

(d) The petition and any additional documents or pleadings related to the petition shall be served on the IMR Unit in accordance with rule 10632.

(e) The petition shall be captioned "Petition Appealing Administrative Director's Independent Medical Review Determination" and shall include the assigned ADJ number and the IMR

case number assigned by the Administrative Director.

(f) The petition shall include a copy of the IMR determination and proof of service of that determination.

(g) Upon receiving notice of the petition, the IMR Unit may download the record of the independent medical review organization into EAMS, in whole or in part. The Workers' Compensation Appeals Board, in its discretion, may:

(1) Admit all or any part of the downloaded IMR record into evidence; and/or

(2) Permit the parties to offer in evidence documents that are duplicates of ones already existing in the downloaded IMR record.

(h)(1) The petition shall not be placed on calendar unless a Declaration of Readiness to Proceed is filed.

(2) Notwithstanding the filing of a Declaration of Readiness to Proceed, a petition appealing an IMR determination shall be deferred if at the time of the determination the defendant is also disputing liability for the treatment for any reason besides medical necessity.

(i) If the IMR determination is rescinded by the workers' compensation judge or the Appeals Board, the medical treatment dispute shall be returned to the Administrative Director with an order specifying the basis for the rescission and an order to submit the dispute to IMR in accordance with Labor Code section 4610.6(i).

Note: Authority cited: Sections 133, 5307, 5309 and 5708, Labor Code. Reference: Sections 4610.6, 5500, 5501, 5502, 5700 et seq., 5800 et seq. and 5900 et seq., Labor Code.

History: 1. Renumbering of former section 10957.1 to section 10575, including amendment of section heading, section and Note, filed 12-17-2019; operative 1-1-2020. Submitted to OAL for printing only pursuant to Government Code section 11351 (Register 2019, No. 51).

§10578. Waiver of Summary of Evidence. [Repealed]

Note: Authority cited: Sections 133 and 5307, Labor Code. Reference: Section 5702, Labor Code.

History: 1. Amendment filed 12-19-2002; operative 1-1-2003. Submitted to OAL for printing only pursuant to Government Code section 11351 (Register 2002, No. 51).

2. Repealer filed 12-17-2019; operative 1-1-2020. Submitted to OAL for printing only pursuant to

Government Code section 11351 (Register 2019, No. 51).

§10580. Petition Appealing Medical Provider Network Determination of the Administrative Director.

(a)   Any aggrieved person or entity may file a petition appealing a determination of the Administrative Director to:

(1)   Deny a medical provider network (MPN) application;

(2)   Revoke or suspend an MPN plan;

(3)   Place an MPN plan on probation;

(4)   Deny a petition to revoke or suspend an MPN plan; or

(5)   Impose administrative penalties relating to an MPN.

(b)   The petition shall be filed only as follows:

(1)   The petition shall be filed no later than 20 days after the date of service of the Administrative Director's determination. An untimely petition may be summarily dismissed.

(2)   Notwithstanding any other provision of these rules or of Administrative Director rules 9767.8(i), 9767.13(f) and 9767.14(f), the petition shall be filed solely in paper form directly with the Office of the Commissioners of the Workers' Compensation Appeals Board.

(3)   The petition shall not be submitted to any district office of the Workers' Compensation Appeals Board, including the San Francisco District Office, and it shall not be submitted electronically.

(4)   A petition submitted in violation of this subdivision shall neither be accepted for filing nor deemed filed and shall not be acknowledged or returned to the submitting party.

(c)   The caption of the petition shall identify it as a "Petition Appealing Administrative Director's Medical Provider Network Determination."

(d)   The caption of the petition shall include:

(1)   The name of the MPN or MPN applicant;

(2)   The identity of the petitioner; and

(3)   The case number assigned by the Administrative Director to the MPN determination.

(e)   The petition shall include a copy of the Administrative Director's determination and proof of service of that determination.

(f)   The petition shall comply with each of the following provisions:

(1)   The petition may appeal the Administrative Director's determination upon one or more of the following grounds and no other:

(A)   The determination was without or in excess of the Administrative Director's powers;

(B)   The determination was procured by fraud;

(C)   The evidence does not justify the determination;

(D)   The petitioner has discovered new material evidence, which the petitioner could not, with reasonable diligence, have discovered and presented to the Administrative Director prior to the determination; and/or

(E)   The Administrative Director's findings of fact do not support the determination.

(2)   The petition shall set forth specifically and in full detail the factual and/or legal grounds upon which the petitioner considers the determination of the Administrative Director to be unjust or unlawful, and every issue to be considered by the Workers' Compensation Appeals Board. The petitioner shall be deemed to have finally waived all objections, irregularities and illegalities concerning the Administrative Director's determination other than those set forth in the petition appealing.

(3)   The petition shall comply with the requirements of rules 10945(a) and (c), and 10972. It shall also comply with the provisions of rule 10940, including but not limited to the 25-page restriction.

(4)   Any failure to comply with the provisions of this subdivision shall constitute valid ground for summarily dismissing or denying the petition.

(g)   A copy of the petition shall be concurrently served on the Division of Workers' Compensation, Medical Provider Network Unit (MPN Unit).

(h)   The petition shall be assigned to a panel of the Appeals Board in accordance with Labor Code section 115.

(i)   Within 30 days after the filing of an answer or the lapse of the time allowed for filing one, the Appeals Board shall issue a notice for an evidentiary hearing regarding the petition. The evidentiary hearing shall be set for the purposes of specifying the issue(s) in dispute and any stipulations, taking testimony, and listing and identifying any documentary evidence offered. The proceedings shall be transcribed by a court reporter, which the Appeals Board in its discretion may order the petitioner to provide. The Appeals Board also may order the petitioner to pay the costs of the transcript(s) of the evidentiary hearing.

(j) In its discretion, the Appeals Board may provide that the evidentiary hearing shall be conducted by:

(1) One or more commissioners of the Appeals Board; or

(2) A workers' compensation judge appointed under Labor Code section 5309(b) for the sole purpose of holding hearings and ascertaining facts necessary to enable the Appeals Board to render a decision on the petition; a workers' compensation judge appointed for this purpose shall not render any factual determinations, but may make a recommendation regarding the credibility of any witness(es) presented.

The time, date, length and place of the evidentiary hearing shall be determined by the Appeals Board in its discretion.

(k) The assigned panel of the Appeals Board shall determine when the petition is submitted for decision. Within 60 days after submission, the panel shall render a decision on the petition unless, within that time, the panel orders that the time be extended so that it may further study the facts and relevant law.

(*l*) Where a timely request to the Administrative Director for a re-evaluation of an initial determination is filed in accordance with rules 9767.8(f), 9767.13(c), and 9767.14(c), the following procedures shall apply:

(1) If a request for re-evaluation is made to the Administrative Director prior to filing a petition with the Office of the Commissioners of the Appeals Board, the time for filing such a petition shall be tolled until the Administrative Director files and serves a decision and order regarding the request for re-evaluation.

(2) If a request for re-evaluation is made to the Administrative Director after a petition appealing the Administrative Director's initial determination is filed with the Office of the Commissioners of the Appeals Board, the petitioner shall file a copy of the re-evaluation request with the Office of the Commissioners in accordance with subdivisions (b)(2) and (b)(3), together with a cover letter requesting that its petition be dismissed without prejudice. A copy of the cover letter and request for re-evaluation shall be concurrently served on the Division of Workers' Compensation MPN Unit.

Note: Authority cited: Sections 133, 5307, 5309 and 5708, Labor Code. Reference: Sections 4616 et seq., 5300(f), 5309 and 5900 et seq., Labor Code.

History: 1. Amendment filed 12-19-2002; operative 1-1-2003. Submitted to OAL for printing only pursuant to Government Code section 11351 (Register 2002, No. 51).

2. Renumbering of former section 10580 to section 10672 and renumbering and amendment of former section 10959 to section 10580 filed 12-17-2019; operative 1-1-2020. Submitted to OAL for printing only pursuant to Government Code section 11351 (Register 2019, No. 51).

§10582. Inactive Cases, Procedure, Subsequent Action. [Renumbered]

Note: Authority cited: Sections 133 and 5307, Labor Code. Reference: Section 5405 and 5406, Labor Code.

History: 1. Amendment exempt from OAL review pursuant to Government Code section 11351 filed 12-19-90; operative 1-1-91 (Register 91, No. 7).

2. Amendment of first paragraph filed 12-23-93; operative 1-1-94. Submitted to OAL for printing only pursuant to Government Code section 11351 (Register 93, No. 52).

3. Amendment of second and third paragraphs and amendment of Note filed 12-19-2002; operative 1-1-2003. Submitted to OAL for printing only pursuant to Government Code section 11351 (Register 2002, No. 51).

4. Renumbering of former section 10582 to section 10550 filed 12-17-2019; operative 1-1-2020. Submitted to OAL for printing only pursuant to Government Code section 11351 (Register 2019, No. 51).

§10582.5. Dismissal of Inactive Lien Claims for Lack of Prosecution. [Repealed]

Note: Authority cited: Sections 133, 5307, 5309 and 5708, Labor Code. Reference: Sections 4903, 4903.5, 4903.6 and 5404.5, Labor Code.

History: 1. New section filed 5-21-2012; operative 5-21-2012 pursuant to Government Code section 11343.4. Submitted to OAL for printing only pursuant to Government Code 11351 (Register 2012, No. 21).

2. Amendment of subsections (a)(1), (c)(2)(B)(i), (c)(2)(C), (d)(1), (d)(2) and (k) filed 9-23-2013; operative 10-23-2013. Submitted as a file and print by the Workers' Compensation Appeals Board pursuant to Government Code section 11351 (Register 2013, No. 39).

3. Repealer filed 12-17-2019; operative 1-1-2020. Submitted to OAL for printing only pursuant to

Government Code section 11351 (Register 2019, No. 51).

§10583. Dismissal of Claim Form — Labor Code Section 5404.5. [Repealed]

Note: Authority cited: Sections 133 and 5307, Labor Code. Reference: Section 5404.5, Labor Code.

History: 1. Renumbering of former section 10407 to new section 10583 filed 12-19-2002; operative 1-1-2003. Submitted to OAL for printing only pursuant to Government Code section 11351 (Register 2002, No. 51).

2. Repealer filed 12-17-2019; operative 1-1-2020. Submitted to OAL for printing only pursuant to Government Code section 11351 (Register 2019, No. 51).

§10589. Consolidation of Cases. [Renumbered]

Note: Authority cited: Sections 133, 5307, 5309 and 5708, Labor Code. Reference: Sections 5300, 5301, 5303 and 5708, Labor Code.

History: 1. Renumbering of former section 10590 to new section 10589, including amendment of section and Note, filed 12-19-2002; operative 1-1-2003. Submitted to OAL for printing only pursuant to Government Code section 11351 (Register 2002, No. 51).

2. Amendment of section heading, section and Note filed 11-17-2008; operative 11-17-2008. Submitted to OAL for printing only (Register 2008, No. 47).

3. Renumbering of former section 10589 to section 10396 filed 12-17-2019; operative 1-1-2020. Submitted to OAL for printing only pursuant to Government Code section 11351 (Register 2019, No. 51).

§10590. Petition Appealing Audit Penalty Assessment — Labor Code Section 129.5(g).

(a) An insurer, self-insured employer or third-party administrator may appeal a civil penalty assessment issued pursuant to subdivision (g) of Labor Code section 129.5 by filing a petition only with the Office of the Commissioners of the Workers' Compensation Appeals Board in the same time and manner as a petition for reconsideration, except that a copy of the petition shall be served on the Administrative Director. The petition shall be accompanied by a completed document cover sheet.

(b) The Administrative Director may answer the petition in the same time and manner provided for the filing of an answer to a petition for reconsideration.

(c) After the filing of a petition appealing a civil penalty assessment issued pursuant to La-

bor Code section 129.5(g), an adjudication case will be created and an adjudication case number will be assigned. The adjudication case number will be served by the Appeals Board on the Administrative Director and on the parties and attorneys listed on the proof of service to the petition.

(d) Within 15 days after the Administrative Director receives a copy of petition appealing a civil penalty assessment issued pursuant to Labor Code section 129.5(g), the Administrative Director shall submit to the Appeals Board a certified copy of the complete record of proceedings created by the Administrative Director in accordance with Article 6 of the Administrative Director's rules (Cal. Code Regs., tit. 8, § 10113 et seq.) The certified copy of the record shall include, but shall not necessarily be limited to:

(1) The Order to Show Cause Re: Assessment of Civil Penalty and Notice of Hearing;

(2) The answer to the Order to Show Cause;

(3) Any amended complaint or supplemental Order to Show Cause that may have been issued, and any Amended Answer filed in response thereto;

(4) Any pre-hearing written statement filed by the claims administrator;

(5) Any pre-hearing Minutes and pre-hearing Orders;

(6) The Minutes of any Hearing, a transcript or summary of any oral testimony offered at the hearing, any documentary evidence or affidavits offered at the hearing; and

(7) The Administrative Director's written Determination and statement of the basis for the Determination. The original record of the proceedings conducted pursuant to Labor Code section 129.5(g) shall not be filed.

(e) The Appeals Board may scan the appeal, any answer and the photocopied record of the Administrative Director's proceedings into the adjudication file within EAMS. Upon scanning, the paper documents may be destroyed.

(f) The Appeals Board shall determine the appeal using the record created by the Administrative Director in accordance with Article 6 of the Administrative Director's rules (Cal. Code Regs., tit. 8, § 10113 et seq.). The Administrative Director's record shall be deemed part of the Workers' Compensation Appeals Board's record of proceedings.

Note: Authority cited: Sections 133, 5307, 5309 and 5708, Labor Code. Reference: Section 129.5(g), Labor Code.

History: 1. Renumbering and amendment of former section 10953 to section 10590 filed 12-17-2019; operative 1-1-2020. Submitted to OAL for printing only pursuant to Government Code section 11351 (Register 2019, No. 51). For prior history of section 10590, see Register 2008, No. 47.

§10592.   Assignment of Consolidated Cases. [Renumbered]

Note: Authority cited: Sections 133, 5307, 5309 and 5708, Labor Code. Reference: Sections 5300, 5301, 5303 and 5708, Labor Code.

History: 1. New section filed 10-15-2014; operative 1-1-2015. Submitted to OAL for printing only pursuant to Government Code section 11351 (Register 2014, No. 42). For prior history, see Register 2008, No. 47.

2. Editorial correction of History 1 (Register 2017, No. 8).

3. Renumbering of former section 10592 to section 10398 filed 12-17-2019; operative 1-1-2020. Submitted to OAL for printing only pursuant to Government Code section 11351 (Register 2019, No. 51).

§10593.   Testimony of Judicial or Quasi-Judicial Officers. [Renumbered]

Note: Authority cited: Sections 133, 5307, 5309 and 5708, Labor Code. Reference: Sections 5300, 5301, 5309, 5700, 5701 and 5708, Labor Code; and Section 703.5, Evidence Code.

History: 1. New section filed 11-17-2008; operative 11-17-2008. Submitted to OAL for printing only (Register 2008, No. 47).

2. Amendment of section heading, repealer of subsection (f)(7), subsection renumbering, amendment of newly designated subsections (f)(7)-(8) and new subsection (f)(9) filed 10-15-2014; operative 1-1-2015. Submitted to OAL for printing only pursuant to Government Code section 11351 (Register 2014, No. 42).

3. Editorial correction of History 2 (Register 2017, No. 8).

4. Renumbering of former section 10593 to section 10360 filed 12-17-2019; operative 1-1-2020. Submitted to OAL for printing only pursuant to Government Code section 11351 (Register 2019, No. 51).

ARTICLE 9
Filing and Service of Documents

§10600.   Time for Actions.

(a)   The time in which any act provided by these rules is to be performed is computed by excluding the first day and including the last.

(b)   Unless otherwise provided by law, if the last day for exercising or performing any right or duty to act or respond falls on a weekend, or on a holiday for which the offices of the Workers' Compensation Appeals Board are closed, the act or response may be performed or exercised upon the next business day.

Note: Authority cited: Sections 133, 5307, 5309 and 5708, Labor Code. Reference: Section 5316, Labor Code; Sections 6700, 6701 and 6707, Government Code; and Sections 10, 12, 12a, 12b, 13 and 135, Code of Civil Procedure.

History: 1. Amendment of section and Note filed 12-19-2002; operative 1-1-2003. Submitted to OAL for printing only pursuant to Government Code section 11351 (Register 2002, No. 51).

2. Amendment of article 9 heading, repealer of former section 10600 and renumbering of former section 10508 to section 10600, including amendment of section heading and section, filed 12-17-2019; operative 1-1-2020. Submitted to OAL for printing only pursuant to Government Code section 11351 (Register 2019, No. 51).

§10601.   Copies of Reports and Records. [Repealed]

Note: Authority cited: Sections 133 and 5307, Labor Code. Reference: Section 5502(e), Labor Code.

History: 1. Amendment of section heading, section and Note filed 12-19-2002; operative 1-1-2003. Submitted to OAL for printing only pursuant to Government Code section 11351 (Register 2002, No. 51).

2. Repealer filed 12-17-2019; operative 1-1-2020. Submitted to OAL for printing only pursuant to Government Code section 11351 (Register 2019, No. 51).

§10602.   Formal Permanent Disability Rating Determinations. [Renumbered]

Note: Authority cited: Sections 133 and 5307, Labor Code. Reference: Sections 4660 and 5708, Labor Code.

History: 1. Amendment of section heading, section and Note filed 12-19-2002; operative 1-1-2003. Submitted to OAL for printing only pursuant to Government Code section 11351 (Register 2002, No. 51).

2. Renumbering of former section 10602 to section 10675 filed 12-17-2019; operative 1-1-2020. Submitted to OAL for printing only pursuant to Government Code section 11351 (Register 2019, No. 51).

§10603.   Oversized Exhibits, Diagnostic Imaging, Physical Exhibits, and Exhibits on Media. [Renumbered]

Note: Authority cited: Sections 133, 5307, 5309

and 5708, Labor Code. Reference: Sections 5309, 5701, 5703, 5704 and 5708, Labor Code

History: 1. New section filed 11-17-2008; operative 11-17-2008. Submitted to OAL for printing only (Register 2008, No. 47).

2. Renumbering of former section 10603 to section 10677 filed 12-17-2019; operative 1-1-2020. Submitted to OAL for printing only pursuant to Government Code section 11351 (Register 2019, No. 51).

§10604. Certified Copies. [Repealed]

Note: Authority cited: Sections 133 and 5307, Labor Code. Reference: Sections 5703 and 5708, Labor Code.

History: 1. Amendment of section and Note filed 12-19-2002; operative 1-1-2003. Submitted to OAL for printing only pursuant to Government Code section 11351 (Register 2002, No. 51).

2. Repealer filed 12-17-2019; operative 1-1-2020. Submitted to OAL for printing only pursuant to Government Code section 11351 (Register 2019, No. 51).

§10605. Time Within Which to Act When a Document is Served by Mail, Fax or E-Mail.

(a) When any document is served by mail, fax, e-mail or any method other than personal service, the period of time for exercising or performing any right or duty to act or respond shall be extended by:

(1) Five calendar days from the date of service, if the place of address and the place of mailing of the party, attorney or other agent of record being served is within California;

(2) Ten calendar days from the date of service, if the place of address and the place of mailing of the party, attorney or other agent of record being served is outside of California but within the United States; and

(3) Twenty calendar days from the date of service, if the place of address and the place of mailing of the party, attorney or other agent of record being served is outside the United States.

(b) For purposes of this rule, "place of address and the place of mailing" means the street address or Post Office Box of the party, attorney or other agent of record being served, as reflected in the Official Address Record at the time of service, even if the method of service actually used was fax, e-mail or other agreed-upon method of service.

Note: Authority cited: Sections 133, 5307, 5309 and 5708, Labor Code. Reference: Section 5316, Labor Code.

History: 1. New section filed 12-19-2002; operative 1-1-2003. Submitted to OAL for printing only pursuant to Government Code section 11351 (Register 2002, No. 51).

2. Renumbering of former section 10605 to section 10680 and renumbering and amendment of former section 10507 to section 10605 filed 12-17-2019; operative 1-1-2020. Submitted to OAL for printing only pursuant to Government Code section 11351 (Register 2019, No. 51).

§10606. Physicians' Reports as Evidence. [Renumbered]

Note: Authority cited: Sections 133, 5307, 5309 and 5708, Labor Code. Reference: Sections 4061, 4603.2, 4603.3, 4603.6, 4610.5, 4610.6, 4616.3, 4616.4, 4628, 5703, 5708 and 5709, Labor Code.

History: 1. New subsections (i), (j) and (k) filed 5-25-82; designated effective 7-1-82 (Register 82, No. 22).

2. Editorial correction of subsection (h) filed 2-2-83 (Register 83, No. 6).

3. Amendment filed 12-23-93; operative 1-1-94. Submitted to OAL for printing only pursuant to Government Code section 11351 (Register 93, No. 52).

4. Amendment of section and Note filed 12-19-2002; operative 1-1-2003. Submitted to OAL for printing only pursuant to Government Code section 11351 (Register 2002, No. 51).

5. Amendment of section and Note filed 9-23-2013; operative 10-23-2013. Submitted as a file and print by the Workers' Compensation Appeals Board pursuant to Government Code section 11351 (Register 2013, No. 39).

6. Renumbering of former section 10606 to section 10682 filed 12-17-2019; operative 1-1-2020. Submitted to OAL for printing only pursuant to Government Code section 11351 (Register 2019, No. 51).

§10606.5. Vocational Experts' Reports as Evidence. [Renumbered]

Note: Authority cited: Sections 133, 5307, 5309 and 5708, Labor Code. Reference: Sections 139.32, 4628, 5502(d)(3) and 5703(j), Labor Code.

History: 1. New section filed 9-23-2013; operative 10-23-2013. Submitted as a file and print by the Workers' Compensation Appeals Board pursuant to Government Code section 11351 (Register 2013, No. 39).

2. Renumbering of former section 10606.5 to section 10685 filed 12-17-2019; operative 1-1-2020. Submitted to OAL for printing only pursuant to Government Code section 11351 (Register 2019, No. 51).

§10607.   Computer Printouts of Benefits Paid. [Repealed]

Note: Authority cited: Sections 133 and 5307, Labor Code. Reference: Sections 5502(e) and 5708, Labor Code.

History: 1. New section filed 12-19-2002; operative 1-1-2003. Submitted to OAL for printing only pursuant to Government Code section 11351 (Register 2002, No. 51).
2. Repealer filed 12-17-2019; operative 1-1-2020. Submitted to OAL for printing only pursuant to Government Code section 11351 (Register 2019, No. 51).

§10608.   Service of Medical Reports, Medical-Legal Reports, and Other Medical Information. [Repealed]

Note: Authority cited: Sections 133, 4903.6(d), 5307, 5309 and 5708, Labor Code. Reference: Sections 4903.6(d), 5001, 5502, 5703 and 5708, Labor Code; and Sections 56.05 and 56.10, Civil Code.

History: 1. Repealer and new section filed 12-23-93; operative 1-1-94. Submitted to OAL for printing only pursuant to Government Code section 11351 (Register 93, No. 52).
2. Amendment of section heading, section and Note filed 12-19-2002; operative 1-1-2003. Submitted to OAL for printing only pursuant to Government Code section 11351 (Register 2002, No. 51).
3. Amendment of section heading, section and Note filed 11-17-2008; operative 11-17-2008. Submitted to OAL for printing only (Register 2008, No. 47).
4. Amendment of section heading, section and Note filed 9-23-2013; operative 10-23-2013. Submitted as a file and print by the Workers' Compensation Appeals Board pursuant to Government Code section 11351 (Register 2013, No. 39).
5. Repealer filed 12-17-2019; operative 1-1-2020. Submitted to OAL for printing only pursuant to Government Code section 11351 (Register 2019, No. 51).

§10608.5.   Service by Parties and Lien Claimants of Reports and Records on Other Parties and Lien Claimants. [Repealed]

Note: Authority cited: Sections 133, 5307, 5309 and 5708, Labor Code. Reference: Art. XIV, § 4, Cal. Const.; Section 5307.9, Labor Code; and Section 250, Evidence Code.

History: 1. New section filed 9-23-2013; operative 10-23-2013. Submitted as a file and print by the Workers' Compensation Appeals Board pursuant to Government Code section 11351 (Register 2013, No. 39).

2. Repealer filed 12-17-2019; operative 1-1-2020. Submitted to OAL for printing only pursuant to Government Code section 11351 (Register 2019, No. 51).

§10610.   Filing and Service of Documents.

Unless a statute or rule provides for a different method for filing or service, a requirement to "file and serve" a document means that a copy of the document must be served on the attorney or non-attorney representative for each party separately represented, on each self-represented party and on any other person or entity when required by statute, rule or court order, and that the document and a proof of service of the document must be filed with the Workers' Compensation Appeals Board.

Note: Authority cited: Sections 133, 5307, 5309 and 5708, Labor Code. Reference: Section 5500.3, Labor Code.

History: 1. New section filed 12-17-2019; operative 1-1-2020. Submitted to OAL for printing only pursuant to Government Code section 11351 (Register 2019, No. 51). For prior history, see Register 2002, No. 51.

§10615.   Filing of Documents.

Except as otherwise provided by these rules or ordered by the Workers' Compensation Appeals Board, after the filing and processing of an initial Application for Adjudication of Claim or other case opening document, all documents required or permitted to be filed under the rules of the Workers' Compensation Appeals Board shall be filed only in EAMS or with the district office having venue.

(a)   Except as provided by rule 10677(a), no "original" business records, medical records or other documentary evidence shall be filed with the Workers' Compensation Appeals Board. Only a photocopy or other reproduction of an original document shall be filed. All paper documents that are scanned into EAMS are destroyed after filing pursuant to rule 10205.10.

(b)   A document is deemed filed on the date it is received, if received prior to 5:00 p.m. on a court day (i.e., Monday through Friday, except designated State holidays). An electronically transmitted document shall be deemed to have been received by EAMS when the electronic transmission of the document into EAMS is complete. A document received after 5:00 p.m.

of a court day shall be deemed filed as of the next court day.

(c)   When a paper document is filed by mail or by personal service, the Workers' Compensation Appeals Board shall affix on it an appropriate endorsement as evidence of receipt. The endorsement may be made by handwriting, hand-stamp, electronic date stamp or by other means. The endorsement shall serve as confirmation of successful filing unless the Administrative Director returns the document to the filer and notifies the filer, through the service of a Notice of Document Discrepancy, that the document has not been accepted for filing and the filer fails to correct the discrepancy within 15 days.

(d)   When a document is filed electronically, confirmation of successful filing shall be made in the manner described by rule 10206.3.

Note: Authority cited: Sections 133, 5307, 5309 and 5708, Labor Code. Reference: Sections 126, 5500.3, 5501.5 and 5501.6, Labor Code.

History: 1. Repealer and new section filed 12-23-93; operative 1-1-94. Submitted to OAL for printing only pursuant to Government Code section 11351 (Register 93, No. 52).

2. Editorial correction of first sentence (Register 96, No. 5).

3. Amendment of section heading, repealer and new section and new Note filed 12-19-2002; operative 1-1-2003. Submitted to OAL for printing only pursuant to Government Code section 11351 (Register 2002, No. 51).

4. Repealer and new section filed 12-17-2019; operative 1-1-2020. Submitted to OAL for printing only pursuant to Government Code section 11351 (Register 2019, No. 51).

§10616.   Employer-Maintained Medical Records. [Repealed]

Note: Authority cited: Sections 133, 5307, 5309 and 5708, Labor Code. Reference: Sections 4600, 5703 and 5708, Labor Code.

History: 1. Amendment of section and Note filed 12-19-2002; operative 1-1-2003. Submitted to OAL for printing only pursuant to Government Code section 11351 (Register 2002, No. 51).

2. Amendment of section heading, section and Note filed 11-17-2008; operative 11-17-2008. Submitted to OAL for printing only (Register 2008, No. 47).

3. Repealer filed 12-17-2019; operative 1-1-2020. Submitted to OAL for printing only pursuant to Government Code section 11351 (Register 2019, No. 51).

§10617.   Restrictions on the Rejection for Filing of Documents Subject to a Statute of Limitations or a Jurisdictional Time Limitation.

(a)   An Application for Adjudication of Claim, a petition for reconsideration, a petition to reopen or any other petition or other document that is subject to a statute of limitations or a jurisdictional time limitation shall not be rejected for filing solely on the basis that:

(1)   The document is not filed in the proper office of the Workers' Compensation Appeals Board;

(2)   The document has been submitted without the proper form, or it has been submitted with a form that is either incomplete or contains inaccurate information; or

(3)   The document has not been submitted with the required document cover sheet and/or document separator sheet(s), or it has been submitted with a document cover sheet and/or document separator sheet(s) not containing all of the required information.

(b)   A document that is subject to a statute of limitations or a jurisdictional time limitation may be rejected for filing if it does not contain a combination of information sufficient to establish the case or cases to which the document relates or, if it is a case opening document, sufficient information to open an adjudication file. If a document is rejected in accordance with this subdivision, the Administrative Director shall return the document to the filer and shall notify the filer, through the service of a Notice of Document Discrepancy, that the document has not been accepted for filing. The Notice of Document Discrepancy shall specify the nature of the discrepancy(ies) and the date of the attempted filing, and it shall state that the filer shall have 15 days from the service of the Notice within which to correct the discrepancy(ies) and resubmit the document for filing. If the document is corrected and resubmitted for filing within 15 days, or at a later date upon a showing of good cause, it shall be deemed filed as of the original date the document was submitted.

(c)   Nothing in this rule shall preclude the discretionary or conditional acceptance for the filing of a document that is subject to a statute of limitations or a jurisdictional time limitation, even if it does not contain a combination of information sufficient to establish the case or cases to which the document relates or, if it is a case opening document, sufficient information to open an adjudication file.

(d)   Where a document that is subject to a statute of limitations or a jurisdictional time limitation has been accepted for filing in accordance with this rule, but the document nevertheless cannot be processed by EAMS, the Administrative Director may serve a copy of the filed document on the filing party, together with a Notice of Document Discrepancy. The notice may specify the nature of the discrepancy(ies) and request that the party correct the discrepancy(ies) within 15 days after service of the Notice, however, a failure to timely correct the discrepancy(ies) shall not nullify the acceptance of the document for filing.

(e)   Nothing in this rule shall be deemed to excuse non-compliance with any of other provisions of the rules of the Workers' Compensation Appeals Board or non-compliance with the rules of the Administrative Director. Any such non-compliance may still give rise to monetary sanctions, attorney's fees and costs under Labor Code section 5813 and rule 10421.

Note: Authority cited: Article XIV, Section 4, California Constitution; and Sections 133, 5307, 5309 and 5708, Labor Code. Reference: Sections 126, 5316, 5500, 5501 and 5813, Labor Code.

History: 1. Renumbering and amendment of former section 10397 to section 10617 filed 12-17-2019; operative 1-1-2020. Submitted to OAL for printing only pursuant to Government Code section 11351 (Register 2019, No. 51).

§10618.   X-Rays. [Renumbered]

Note: Authority cited: Sections 133 and 5307, Labor Code. Reference: Sections 4600 and 5708, Labor Code.

History: 1. Amendment of section heading, section and Note filed 12-19-2002; operative 1-1-2003. Submitted to OAL for printing only pursuant to Government Code section 11351 (Register 2002, No. 51).

2. Renumbering of former section 10618 to section 10660 filed 12-17-2019; operative 1-1-2020. Submitted to OAL for printing only pursuant to Government Code section 11351 (Register 2019, No. 51).

§10620.   Filing Proposed Exhibits.

Any document that a party proposes to offer into evidence at a trial shall be filed with the Workers' Compensation Appeals Board at least 20 days prior to the trial unless otherwise ordered by the Workers' Compensation Appeals Board.

Note: Authority cited: Sections 133, 5307, 5309 and 5708, Labor Code. Reference: Sections 126, 5316, 5500, 5501 and 5813, Labor Code.

History: 1. New section filed 12-17-2019; operative 1-1-2020. Submitted to OAL for printing only pursuant to Government Code section 11351 (Register 2019, No. 51). For prior history, see Register 2002, No. 51.

§10622.   Failure to Comply. [Repealed]

Note: Authority cited: Sections 133 and 5307, Labor Code. Reference: Sections 5703 and 5708, Labor Code.

History: 1. Amendment of section and Note filed 12-19-2002; operative 1-1-2003. Submitted to OAL for printing only pursuant to Government Code section 11351 (Register 2002, No. 51).

2. Amendment of section and Note filed 9-23-2013; operative 10-23-2013. Submitted as a file and print by the Workers' Compensation Appeals Board pursuant to Government Code section 11351 (Register 2013, No. 39).

3. Repealer filed 12-17-2019; operative 1-1-2020. Submitted to OAL for printing only pursuant to Government Code section 11351 (Register 2019, No. 51).

§10625.   Service.

(a)   Except as otherwise provided by these rules at 10300 et seq., service shall be made on the attorney or agent of record of each affected party unless that party is unrepresented, in which event service shall be made directly on the party.

(b)   A document may be served using the following methods:

(1)   Personal service;

(2)   First class mail; or

(3)   An alternative method that will effect service that is equivalent to or more expeditious than first class mail, limited to either:

(A)   The use of express (overnight) or priority mail; or

(B)   The use of a bona fide commercial delivery service or attorney service promising delivery within two business days, as shown on the service's invoice or receipt; or

(4)   A party's preferred method of service if a method has been designated in accordance with rule 10205.6; or

(5)   Another method if the serving and receiving parties have previously agreed to some other method of service.

(c) "Proof of service" means a dated and verified declaration identifying the document(s) served and the parties who were served, and stating that service has been made and the method by which it has been made. If the proof of service names attorneys for separately represented parties, it must also state which party or parties each of the attorneys served represents.

(d) Where a party receives notification that the service to one or more parties failed, the server shall promptly re-serve the document on the intended recipient(s) and execute a new proof of service.

Note: Authority cited: Sections 133, 5307, 5309 and 5708, Labor Code. Reference: Article XIV, Section 4, California Constitution; Sections 4906, 5307.9 and 5316, Labor Code; and Section 250, Evidence Code.

History: 1. New section filed 12-17-2019; operative 1-1-2020. Submitted to OAL for printing only pursuant to Government Code section 11351 (Register 2019, No. 51).

§10626. Examining and Copying Hospital and Physicians' Records. [Repealed]

Note: Authority cited: Sections 133, 5307, 5309 and 5708, Labor Code. Reference: Section 4600, Labor Code.

History: 1. Amendment filed 12-19-2002; operative 1-1-2003. Submitted to OAL for printing only pursuant to Government Code section 11351 (Register 2002, No. 51).
2. Amendment of section heading, section and Note filed 11-17-2008; operative 11-17-2008. Submitted to OAL for printing only (Register 2008, No. 47).
3. Repealer filed 12-17-2019; operative 1-1-2020. Submitted to OAL for printing only pursuant to Government Code section 11351 (Register 2019, No. 51).

§10628. Service by the Workers' Compensation Appeals Board.

(a) The Workers' Compensation Appeals Board shall serve the injured employee or any dependent(s) of a deceased employee, whether or not the employee or dependent is represented, and all parties of record with any final order, decision or award issued by it on a disputed issue after submission. The Workers' Compensation Appeals Board shall not designate a party, or their attorney or agent of record, to serve any final order, decision or award relating to a submitted issue.

(b) If the Workers' Compensation Appeals Board effects personal service of a document at a hearing or at a walk-through proceeding, the proof of personal service shall be made by endorsement on the document, setting forth legibly the name(s) of the person(s) served, the date of service and the fact of personal service. The endorsement shall bear the legibly printed name and signature of the person making the service.

(c) If the Workers' Compensation Appeals Board serves a document by mail, the proof of mail service shall be made by endorsement on the document, setting forth the fact of mail service on the persons or entities listed on the Official Address Record who have not designated e-mail or fax as their preferred method of service. The endorsement shall state the date of mail service and it shall bear the legibly printed name and the signature of the person making the service.

(d) If the Workers' Compensation Appeals Board electronically serves a document through EAMS on persons or entities listed on the official address record who have designated e-mail or fax as their preferred method of service, the proof of e-mail or fax service shall be made by endorsement on the document, setting forth the fact of e-mail or fax service on the persons or entities listed.

(e) Where a district office of the Workers' Compensation Appeals Board maintains mailboxes for outgoing documents and allows consenting parties, lien claimants and attorneys to obtain their documents from their mailboxes, documents so obtained shall be deemed to have been served on the party, lien claimant or attorney by mail on the date of service specified on the document.

Note: Authority cited: Sections 133, 5307, 5309 and 5708, Labor Code. Reference: Sections 5316 and 5504, Labor Code.

History: 1. New section filed 12-17-2019; operative 1-1-2020. Submitted to OAL for printing only pursuant to Government Code section 11351 (Register 2019, No. 51).

§10629. Designated Service.

(a) The Workers' Compensation Appeals Board may, in its discretion, designate a party or their attorney or agent of record to serve any order that is not required to be served by the Workers' Compensation Appeals Board in accordance with rule 10628.

(b)   When a party or their attorney or agent of record is designated to serve an order, the workers' compensation judge shall indicate which parties to serve.

(c)   In addition to the service required by rule 10625, service shall also be made on the injured employee or any dependent of a deceased employee, whether or not the employee or dependent is represented.

(d)   Within 10 days from the date on which designated service is ordered, the person designated to make service shall serve the document and shall file the proof of service.

Note: Authority cited: Sections 133, 5307, 5309 and 5708, Labor Code. Reference: Sections 5316 and 5504, Labor Code.

History: 1. New section filed 11-17-2008; operative 11-17-2008. Submitted to OAL for printing only (Register 2008, No. 47).

2. Repealer and new section filed 12-17-2019; operative 1-1-2020. Submitted to OAL for printing only pursuant to Government Code section 11351 (Register 2019, No. 51).

§10631.   Specific Finding of Fact — Labor Code Section 139.2(d)(2). [Renumbered]

Note: Authority cited: Sections 133 and 5307, Labor Code. Reference: Section 139.2(d)(2), Labor Code.

History: 1. New section filed 12-23-93; operative 1-1-94. Submitted to OAL for printing only pursuant to Government Code section 11351 (Register 93, No. 52).

2. Amendment of first paragraph filed 12-19-2002; operative 1-1-2003. Submitted to OAL for printing only pursuant to Government Code section 11351 (Register 2002, No. 51).

3. Renumbering of former section 10631 to section 10683 filed 12-17-2019; operative 1-1-2020. Submitted to OAL for printing only pursuant to Government Code section 11351 (Register 2019, No. 51).

§10632.   Service on the Division of Workers' Compensation and the Director of Industrial Relations.

(a)   When an Application for Adjudication of Claim, Stipulations with Request for Award or Compromise and Release is filed in a death case in which there is a bona fide issue as to partial or total dependency, the filing party shall serve copies of the documents on the Department of Industrial Relations. Death Without Dependents Unit.

(b)   Service of all documents on the Subsequent Injuries Benefits Trust Fund shall be made on the Division of Workers' Compensation, Subsequent Injuries Benefits Trust Fund.

(c)   Service of documents on the Uninsured Employers Benefits Trust Fund shall be made as follows:

(1)   Service shall be made on the Division of Workers' Compensation. Uninsured Employers Benefits Trust Fund — Oakland if the employee's case is venued in one of the following District Offices: Bakersfield, Eureka, Fresno, Oakland, Oxnard, Redding, Riverside, Sacramento, Salinas, San Diego, San Francisco, San Jose, San Luis Obispo, Santa Ana, Santa Rosa, Stockton or Van Nuys.

(2)   Service shall be made on the Division of Workers' Compensation, Uninsured Employers Benefits Trust Fund — Los Angeles if the employee's case is venued in one of the following District Offices: Anaheim, Los Angeles, Long Beach, Marina del Rey, Pomona or San Bernardino.

(d)   Service of all documents on the Return-to-Work Supplement Program shall be made on the Director of Industrial Relations, Return-to-Work Supplement Program.

(e)   Service of all documents on the Independent Bill Review Unit shall be made on the Division of Workers' Compensation, Independent Bill Review Unit.

(f)   Service of all documents on the Independent Medical Review Unit shall be made on the Division of Workers' Compensation, Independent Medical Review Unit.

Note: Authority cited: Sections 133 and 5307, Labor Code. Reference: Sections 4706.5 and 5501.5, Labor Code.

History: 1. New section filed 12-23-93; operative 1-1-94. Submitted to OAL for printing only pursuant to Government Code section 11351 (Register 93, No. 52).

2. Amendment filed 12-19-2002; operative 1-1-2003. Submitted to OAL for printing only pursuant to Government Code section 11351 (Register 2002, No. 51).

3. Repealer and new section filed 12-17-2019; operative 1-1-2020. Submitted to OAL for printing only pursuant to Government Code section 11351 (Register 2019, No. 51).

§10633.   Proposed Rating — Labor Code Section 4065. [Repealed]

Note: Authority cited: Sections 133 and 5307, Labor Code. Reference: Section 4065, Labor Code.

History: 1. New section filed 12-23-93; operative 1-1-94. Submitted to OAL for printing only pursuant to Government Code section 11351 (Register 93, No. 52).

2. Amendment of first paragraph filed 12-19-2002; operative 1-1-2003. Submitted to OAL for printing only pursuant to Government Code section 11351 (Register 2002, No. 51).

3. Repealer filed 12-17-2019; operative 1-1-2020. Submitted to OAL for printing only pursuant to Government Code section 11351 (Register 2019, No. 51).

§10634. Labor Code Section 4628(k) Requests. [Repealed]

Note: Authority cited: Sections 133 and 5307, Labor Code. Reference: Section 4628(k), Labor Code.

History: 1. New section filed 12-23-93; operative 1-1-94. Submitted to OAL for printing only pursuant to Government Code section 11351 (Register 93, No. 52).

2. Repealer filed 12-17-2019; operative 1-1-2020. Submitted to OAL for printing only pursuant to Government Code section 11351 (Register 2019, No. 51).

§10635. Duty to Serve Documents.

(a) Where documents, including electronic media, are to be offered into evidence, copies shall be served on all adverse parties no later than the mandatory settlement conference, unless good cause is shown.

(b) If a party requests that a defendant provide a computer printout of benefits paid, the defendant shall provide the requesting party with a current computer printout of benefits paid within 20 days. The printout shall include the date and amount of each payment of temporary disability indemnity, permanent disability indemnity, the period covered by each payment, and the date, payee and amount of each payment for medical treatment. After receipt of a printout of benefits, another such request may not be made more frequently than once in a 120-day period unless there is a change in indemnity payments or a new dispute requiring updated payment periods.

(c) During the continuing jurisdiction of the Workers' Compensation Appeals Board, the parties have an ongoing duty to serve within 10 calendar days of receipt:

(1) Each other with any medical reports received; and

(2) A lien claimant who has requested service of medical reports with any medical reports

received unless the lien claimant is not defined as a "physician" by Labor Code section 3209.3 and is not an entity described in Labor Code sections 4903.05(c)(7) and 4903.06(b); and

(3) Any written communication from a physician containing information listed in rule 10682 that is maintained in the employer's capacity as an employer. Records from an employee assistance program are not required to be filed or served unless ordered by the Workers' Compensation Appeals Board.

Note: Authority cited: Sections 133, 4903.6(d), 5307, 5309 and 5708, Labor Code. Reference: Sections 3209.3, 4600, 4903.05, 4903.06, 4903.6(d), 5001, 5502, 5502(e), 5703 and 5708, Labor Code.

History: 1. New section filed 12-17-2019; operative 1-1-2020. Submitted to OAL for printing only pursuant to Government Code section 11351 (Register 2019, No. 51). For prior history, see Register 91, No. 7.

§10637. Service of Medical Reports, Medical-Legal Reports, and other Medical Information on a Non-Physician Lien Claimant.

The provisions of this rule shall apply to the service of medical reports, medical-legal reports, or other medical information on a non-physician lien claimant.

(a) If a party is requested by a non-physician lien claimant to serve a copy of any medical report, medical-legal report, or other medical information relating to the claim, the party receiving the request shall not serve a copy on the non-physician lien claimant unless ordered to do so by the Workers' Compensation Appeals Board.

(b) A non-physician lien claimant shall not subpoena any medical information. Any subpoena that, in whole or in part, requests medical information shall be deemed quashed in its entirety by operation of law.

(c) A non-physician lien claimant shall not seek to obtain any medical information using a waiver, release, or other authorization signed by the employee. Any such waiver, release, or other authorization shall be deemed invalid by operation of law.

(d) A non-physician lien claimant may petition the Workers' Compensation Appeals Board for an order directing a party or other lien claimant in possession or control of any medical report, medical-legal report, or other medical information to serve a copy of that report or information, or a particular portion thereof, on the non-physician lien claimant.

(e) For each document, or a portion thereof, containing medical information that is sought, the petition shall specify each of the following:

(1) The name of the issuing physician, medical organization (e.g., a group medical practice or hospital), or other entity and the date of the document containing medical information, if known, or if not known, sufficient information that the party from whom it is sought may reasonably be expected to identify it; and

(2) The specific reason(s) why the non-physician lien claimant believes that the document containing medical information, or a portion thereof, is or is reasonably likely to be relevant to its burden of proof on its lien claim or its petition for costs.

(f) When the petition is filed, a copy shall be concurrently served on the injured employee (or the dependent(s) of a deceased injured employee) and the defendant(s) or, if represented, their attorney or non-attorney of record. In addition, if the medical information is alleged to be in the possession or control of a non-party or another lien claimant, a copy of the petition shall be concurrently served on that non-party or other lien claimant or, if represented, its attorney or non-attorney of record.

(g) The caption of the petition shall identify it as a "Petition by Non-Physician Lien Claimant for Medical Information."

Note: Authority cited: Sections 133, 4903.6(d), 5307, 5309 and 5708, Labor Code. Reference: Sections 4903.6(d), 5001, 5502, 5703 and 5708, Labor Code; and Sections 56.05 and 56.10, Civil Code.

History: 1. New section filed 12-17-2019; operative 1-1-2020. Submitted to OAL for printing only pursuant to Government Code section 11351 (Register 2019, No. 51).

ARTICLE 10
Subpoenas

§10640. Subpoenas.

The Workers' Compensation Appeals Board shall issue subpoenas and subpoenas duces tecum upon request in accordance with the provisions of Code of Civil Procedure sections 1985 and 1987.5 and Government Code section 68097.1. Subpoenas and subpoenas duces tecum shall be on forms prescribed and approved by the Workers' Compensation Appeals Board and shall contain an ADJ number.

Note: Authority cited: Sections 133 and 5307, Labor Code. Reference: Sections 130 and 5401, Labor Code; Sections 1985 and 1987.5, Code of Civil Procedure; and Section 68097.1, Government Code.

History: 1. New article 10 (sections 10640-10660) and renumbering and amendment of former section 10953 to section 10640 filed 12-17-2019; operative 1-1-2020. Submitted to OAL for printing only pursuant to Government Code section 11351 (Register 2019, No. 51). For prior history of article 10 (sections 10700-10727), see Register 2002, No. 51.

§10642. Notice to Appear or Produce.

A notice to appear or produce in accordance with Code of Civil Procedure section 1987 is permissible in proceedings before the Workers' Compensation Appeals Board.

Note: Authority cited: Sections 133 and 5307, Labor Code. Reference: Section 132, Labor Code; and Section 1987, Code of Civil Procedure.

History: 1. Renumbering of former section 10532 to section 10642, including amendment of Note, filed 12-17-2019; operative 1-1-2020. Submitted to OAL for printing only pursuant to Government Code section 11351 (Register 2019, No. 51).

§10644. Subpoenas of Electronic Records.

Where records or other documentary evidence have been recorded or reproduced using the methods described in section 1551 of the Evidence Code and the original records destroyed, the film, legible print thereof or electronic recording shall be produced in response to a subpoena duces tecum. A party offering a film or electronic recording in evidence may be required to provide legible prints thereof or reproductions from the electronic recording.

Note: Authority cited: Sections 133 and 5307, Labor Code. Reference: Section 130, Labor Code; and Section 1551, Evidence Code.

History: 1. Renumbering of former section 10534 to section 10644, including amendment of section heading, section and Note, filed 12-17-2019; operative 1-1-2020. Submitted to OAL for printing only pursuant to Government Code section 11351 (Register 2019, No. 51).

§10647. Witness Fees and Subpoenas.

Medical examiners appointed by the Workers' Compensation Appeals Board or agreed to by the parties when subpoenaed for cross-examination at the Workers' Compensation Appeals Board or deposition shall be paid by the party requiring the attendance of the witness in accordance with the rules of the Administrative Director.

Failure to serve the subpoena and tender the fee in advance based on the estimated time of the trial or deposition may be treated by the Workers' Compensation Appeals Board as a waiver of the right to examine the witness. Service and payment of the fee may be made by mail if the witness so agrees.

Note: Authority cited: Sections 133 and 5307, Labor Code. Reference: Sections 130, 131, 4621 and 5710, Labor Code; and Section 2034.430, 2034.440 and 2034.450, Code of Civil Procedure.

History: 1. Renumbering of former section 10536 to section 10647, including amendment of Note, filed 12-17-2019; operative 1-1-2020. Submitted to OAL for printing only pursuant to Government Code section 11351 (Register 2019, No. 51).

§10650. Subpoena for Medical Witness.

A subpoena requiring the appearance of a medical witness before the Workers' Compensation Appeals Board must be served no fewer than 10 days before the time the witness is required to appear and testify.

Note: Authority cited: Sections 133 and 5307, Labor Code. Reference: Section 132, Labor Code.

History: 1. Renumbering and amendment of former section 10537 to section 10650 filed 12-17-2019; operative 1-1-2020. Submitted to OAL for printing only pursuant to Government Code section 11351 (Register 2019, No. 51).

§10655. Subpoenas for Medical Information by Non-Physician Lien Claimants.

A lien claimant that is not either a "physician" as defined in Labor Code section 3209.3 or an entity described in Labor Code sections 4903.05(c)(7) and 4903.06(b) shall not issue any subpoena or subpoena duces tecum that seeks to obtain any medical information about an injured worker, but shall instead follow the procedure set forth in rule 10637.

Note: Authority cited: Sections 133, 4903.6(d), 5307, 5309 and 5708, Labor Code. Reference: Sections 130, 4903.6(d) and 5710(a), Labor Code; and Sections 56.05 and 56.10, Civil Code.

History: 1. Renumbering and amendment of former section 10538 to section 10655 filed 12-17-2019;

operative 1-1-2020. Submitted to OAL for printing only pursuant to Government Code section 11351 (Register 2019, No. 51).

§10660. X-Rays.

Upon reasonable request of a party, X-rays in the possession of, or subject to the control of, an adverse party shall be made available for examination by the requesting party or persons designated by that party at a time or place convenient to the persons to make the examination.

Note: Authority cited: Sections 133 and 5307, Labor Code. Reference: Sections 4600 and 5708, Labor Code.

History: 1. Renumbering and amendment of former section 10618 to section 10660 filed 12-17-2019; operative 1-1-2020. Submitted to OAL for printing only pursuant to Government Code section 11351 (Register 2019, No. 51).

ARTICLE 11
Evidence

§10670. Documentary Evidence.

The filing of a document does not signify its receipt in evidence and, except for the documents listed in rule 10803, only those documents that have been received in evidence shall be included in the record of proceedings on the case.

(a) Certified copies of reports or records of any governmental agency, division or bureau shall be admissible in evidence in lieu of the original reports or records.

(b) The Workers' Compensation Appeals Board may decline to receive in evidence:

(1) Any document not listed on the Pre-Trial Conference Statement.

(2) Any document not served at or prior to the mandatory settlement conference, unless good cause is shown.

(3) Any document not filed 20 days prior to trial, unless otherwise ordered by a workers' compensation judge or good cause is shown.

(4) Any physician's report that does not comply with Labor Code section 4628 unless good cause has been shown for the failure to comply and, after notice of non-compliance, compliance takes place within a reasonable period of time or within a time prescribed by the workers' compensation judge.

(5) Any report that does not comply with the verification requirements of Labor Code section 5703(a)(2)or 5703(j)(2).

(c) Where a willful suppression of evidence is shown to exist, it shall be presumed that the evidence would be adverse, if produced.

(d) The remedies in this rule are cumulative to others authorized by law.

Note: Authority cited: Sections 133, 5307, 5309 and 5708, Labor Code. Reference: Sections 126, 4628, 5316, 5500, 5501, 5703, 5708 and 5813, Labor Code.

History: 1. New article 11 heading and new section filed 12-17-2019; operative 1-1-2020. Submitted to OAL for printing only pursuant to Government Code section 11351 (Register 2019, No. 51).

§10672. Evidence Taken Without Notice.

Transcripts or summaries of testimony taken without notice and copies of all reports and other matters added to the record, otherwise than during the course of an open hearing, shall be served upon the parties to the proceeding. Unless it is otherwise expressly provided, the parties shall be allowed 10 days after service of the testimony and reports within which to produce evidence in explanation or rebuttal or to request further proceedings before the case shall be deemed submitted for decision.

Note: Authority cited: Sections 133 and 5307, Labor Code. Reference: Section 5704, Labor Code.

History: 1. Renumbering of former section 10580 to section 10672 filed 12-17-2019; operative 1-1-2020. Submitted to OAL for printing only pursuant to Government Code section 11351 (Register 2019, No. 51).

§10675. Formal Permanent Disability Rating Determinations.

The Workers' Compensation Appeals Board may request the Disability Evaluation Unit to prepare a formal rating determination on a form prescribed for that purpose by the Administrative Director. The request may refer to an accompanying medical report or chart for the sole purpose of describing measurable physical elements of the condition that are clearly and exactly identifiable. In every instance the request shall describe the factors of disability in full.

The report of the Disability Evaluation Unit in response to the request shall constitute evidence only as to the percentage of the permanent disability based on the factors described, and the report shall not constitute evidence as to the existence of the permanent disability described.

The report of the Disability Evaluation Unit shall be filed and served on the parties and shall include or be accompanied by a notice that the case shall be submitted for decision 7 days after service unless written objection is made within that time.

Note: Authority cited: Sections 133 and 5307, Labor Code. Reference: Sections 4660 and 5708, Labor Code.

History: 1. Renumbering and amendment of former section 10602 to section 10675 filed 12-17-2019; operative 1-1-2020. Submitted to OAL for printing only pursuant to Government Code section 11351 (Register 2019, No. 51).

§10677. Oversized Exhibits, Diagnostic Imaging, Physical Exhibits and Exhibits on Media.

(a) The following exhibits shall be filed only at the time of trial:

(1) Oversized documents, other than medical reports, that are:

(A) Larger than 11 x 17 inches (e.g., maps, diagrams and schematic drawings); and

(B) Over 25 pages in length;

(2) Diagnostic imaging, including but not limited to any X-ray, computed axial tomography (CAT) scan, magnetic resonance imaging (MRI), nuclear medicine, positron emission tomography (PET) scan, mammography, ultrasound or other similar medical imaging that is stored on digital, film or other non-paper media;

(3) Original business or office records;

(4) Physical objects or other tangible things;

(5) Any CD-ROM, DVD or other digital media, including but not limited to:

(A) Digital photographs;

(B) Digital video recordings; and

(C) Digital audio recordings;

(6) Videotapes, audiotapes, films and other non-digital video and/or audio recordings or images; and

(7) Photographs printed on paper.

(b) Unless otherwise ordered by the Workers' Compensation Appeals Board, any exhibit listed in subdivision (a) that is offered into evidence (whether or not admitted into evidence) shall be retained by the filing party (or an agent of the filing party) until the later of either:

(1) Five years after the filing of the initial Application for Adjudication of Claim (or other case opening document); or

(2) At least six months after all appeals have been exhausted or the time for seeking appellate review has expired with respect to the decision on the issue(s) for which the exhibit was offered in evidence.

After expiration of the later of these two time periods, the party may destroy the exhibit, unless the Workers' Compensation Appeals Board has ordered that the exhibit be preserved for a longer period.

(c) Before and during the period of retention, the filing party shall:

(1) Maintain the exhibit under conditions that will protect it against loss, destruction or tampering, and that will preserve its quality and integrity as far as practicable;

(2) At the request of any other party to the action, promptly permit the party to inspect or view the exhibit; and

(3) At the request of any other party to the action, and if practicable, promptly furnish the party a copy of the exhibit or promptly permit the party to make a copy.

For purposes of subsection (c), the term "exhibit" shall include any item listed in subsection (a), whether or not the party in possession or control of that item intends to offer it in evidence.

(d) Any disputes regarding subdivision (c), including but not limited to issues of timing and costs, may be submitted for determination to the Workers' Compensation Appeals Board.

Note: Authority cited: Sections 133, 5307, 5309 and 5708, Labor Code. Reference: Sections 5309, 5701, 5703, 5704 and 5708, Labor Code.

History: 1. Renumbering and amendment of former section 10603 to section 10677 filed 12-17-2019; operative 1-1-2020. Submitted to OAL for printing only pursuant to Government Code section 11351 (Register 2019, No. 51).

§10680. Reproductions of Documents.

(a) It is presumed a filed photocopy is an accurate representation of the original document. If a party alleges that a filed photocopy is inaccurate or unreliable, the party alleging the document is inaccurate or unreliable shall state the basis for the objection. The filing party must establish that the document is an accurate representation of the original document.

(b) A nonerasable optical image reproduction provided that additions, deletions or changes to the original document are not permitted by the technology, a photostatic, microfilm, microcard, miniature photographic or other photographic copy or reproduction, or an enlargement thereof, of a writing is admissible as the writing itself if the copy or reproduction was made and preserved as a part of the records of a business (as defined by Evidence Code section 1270) in the regular course of that business. The introduction of the copy, reproduction or enlargement does not preclude admission of the original writing if it is still in existence. The Workers' Compensation Appeals Board may require the introduction of a hard copy printout of the document.

(c) A printed representation of images stored on a video or digital medium is presumed to be an accurate representation of the images it purports to represent. This presumption is a presumption affecting the burden of producing evidence. If a party to an action introduces evidence that a printed representation of images stored on a video or digital medium is inaccurate or unreliable, the party introducing the printed representation into evidence has the burden of proving by a preponderance of the evidence that the printed representation is an accurate representation of the existence and content of the images that it purports to represent.

Note: Authority cited: Sections 133 and 5307, Labor Code. Reference: Section 5708, Labor Code; and Section 1270, Evidence Code.

History: 1. Renumbering of former section 10605 to section 10680, including amendment of section and Note, filed 12-17-2019; operative 1-1-2020. Submitted to OAL for printing only pursuant to Government Code section 11351 (Register 2019, No. 51).

§10682. Physicians' Reports as Evidence.

(a) The Workers' Compensation Appeals Board favors the production of medical evidence in the form of written reports. Direct examination of a medical witness will not be received at a trial except upon a showing of good cause. A continuance may be granted for rebuttal medical testimony subject to Labor Code section 5502.5.

(b) Medical reports should include where applicable:

(1) The date of the examination;

(2) The history of the injury;

(3)   The patient's complaints;

(4)   A listing of all information received in preparation of the report or relied upon for the formulation of the physician's opinion;

(5)   The patient's medical history, including injuries and conditions, and residuals thereof, if any;

(6)   Findings on examination;

(7)   A diagnosis;

(8)   Opinion as to the nature, extent and duration of disability and work limitations, if any;

(9)   Cause of the disability;

(10)   Treatment indicated, including past, continuing and future medical care;

(11)   Opinion as to whether or not permanent disability has resulted from the injury and whether or not it is stationary. If stationary, a description of the disability with a complete evaluation;

(12)   Apportionment of disability, if any;

(13)   A determination of the percent of the total causation resulting from actual events of employment, if the injury is alleged to be a psychiatric injury;

(14)   The reasons for the opinion; and

(15)   The signature of the physician.

In death cases, the reports of non-examining physicians may be admitted into evidence in lieu of oral testimony.

(c)   All medical-legal reports shall comply with the provisions of Labor Code section 4628. Except as otherwise provided by the Labor Code and the Rules of Practice and Procedure of the Workers' Compensation Appeals Board, failure to comply with the requirements of this rule will not make the report inadmissible but will be considered in weighing the evidence.

Note: Authority cited: Sections 133 and 5307, Labor Code. Reference: Sections 4628, 5502.5, 5703 and 5708, Labor Code.

History: 1. Renumbering of former section 10606 to section 10682, including amendment of section and Note, filed 12-17-2019; operative 1-1-2020. Submitted to OAL for printing only pursuant to Government Code section 11351 (Register 2019, No. 51).

§10683.   Specific Finding of Fact — Labor Code Section 139.2(d)(2).

Where a qualified medical evaluator's report has been considered and rejected pursuant to Labor Code section 139.2(d)(2), the workers' compensation judge or Appeals Board shall

make and serve a specific finding on the qualified medical evaluator and the Division of Workers' Compensation at the time of decision on the regular workers' compensation issues. The specific finding may be included in the decision.

If the Appeals Board, on reconsideration, affirms or sets aside the specific finding of fact filed by a workers' compensation judge, it shall advise the qualified medical evaluator and the Division of Workers' Compensation at the time of service of its decision on the petition for reconsideration. If the workers' compensation judge does not make a specific finding and the Appeals Board, on reconsideration, makes a specific finding of rejection pursuant to Labor Code section 139.2(d)(2), it shall serve its specific finding on the qualified medical evaluator and the Division of Workers' Compensation at the time it serves its decision after reconsideration.

Rejection of a qualified medical evaluator's report pursuant to Labor Code section 139.2(d)(2) shall occur where the qualified medical evaluator's report does not meet the minimum standards prescribed by the provisions of rule 10682 and the regulations of the Division of Workers' Compensation.

This rule shall apply to injuries on or after January 1, 1994.

Note: Authority cited: Sections 133 and 5307, Labor Code. Reference: Section 139.2(d)(2), Labor Code.

History: 1. Renumbering and amendment of former section 10631 to section 10683 filed 12-17-2019; operative 1-1-2020. Submitted to OAL for printing only pursuant to Government Code section 11351 (Register 2019, No. 51).

§10685.   Vocational Experts' Reports as Evidence.

(a)   The Workers' Compensation Appeals Board favors the production of vocational expert evidence in the form of written reports. Direct examination of a vocational expert witness will not be received at a trial except upon a showing of good cause. Good cause shall not be found if the vocational expert witness has not issued a report and the party offering the witness fails to demonstrate that it exercised due diligence in attempting to obtain a report. A continuance may be granted for rebuttal testimony if a report that was not served sufficiently in advance of the close of discovery to permit rebuttal is admitted into evidence.

(b) A vocational expert's written report shall meet the following requirements:

(1) The report shall contain a declaration by the vocational expert signing the report stating: "I declare under penalty of perjury that the information contained in this report and its attachments, if any, is true and correct to the best of my knowledge, except as to information that I have indicated I received from others. As to that information, I declare under penalty of perjury that the information accurately describes the information provided to me and, except as noted herein, that I believe it to be true. I further declare under penalty of perjury that there has not been a violation of Labor Code section 139.32." The foregoing declaration shall be dated and signed by the vocational expert and shall indicate the county wherein it was signed.

(2) The report shall disclose the qualifications of the vocational expert signing the report, which may be satisfied by attaching a curriculum vitae.

(3) Except as provided in subdivision (b)(4), the body of the report shall contain a statement, above the declaration under penalty of perjury, that: "No person, other than the vocational expert signing the report, has participated in the non-clerical preparation of the report, including all of the following:

(i) Taking a history from the employee;

(ii) Reviewing and summarizing medical and/or non-medical records; and

(iii) Composing and drafting the conclusions of the report."

(4) Notwithstanding subdivision (b)(3), it is permissible for a person or persons, other than the vocational expert signing the report, to prepare an initial outline of the employee's history and/or to excerpt prior medical and non-medical records. If this is done, however, the vocational expert signing the report:

(A) Shall review the excerpts and the entire outline and shall make additional inquiries and examinations as are necessary and appropriate to identify and determine the relevant issues;

(B) Shall include in the statement required by subdivision (b)(3) that, as applicable, an initial outline of the employee's history and/or an excerpt of the employee's prior medical and non-medical records were prepared by another person or persons and that the vocational expert signing the report has reviewed any such excerpts and/or outline and has made any additional inquiries and examinations necessary and appropriate to identify and determine the relevant issues; and

(C) Shall comply with subdivision (b)(5), below.

(5) The report shall disclose the name(s) and qualifications of each person who performed any services in connection with the report, including diagnostic studies, other than its clerical preparation.

(c) The vocational expert's report should include, where applicable:

(1) The date(s) of any evaluation(s), interview(s) and test(s);

(2) The history of the injury;

(3) The employee's vocational history;

(4) The injured employee's complaints;

(5) A listing of all information reviewed in preparation of the report or relied upon for the formulation of the vocational expert's opinion;

(6) The injured employee's medical history, including injuries and conditions, and residuals thereof, if any;

(7) Findings and opinion on evaluation;

(8) The reasons for the opinion; and

(9) The signature of the vocational expert.

A failure to comply with the requirements of subdivision (c) will not make the report inadmissible but will be considered in weighing the evidence.

(d) Statements concerning any vocational expert's bill for services are admissible only if they comply with subdivision (b)(1).

Note: Authority cited: Sections 133, 5307, 5309 and 5708, Labor Code. Reference: Sections 139.32, 4628, 5502(d)(3) and 5703(j), Labor Code.

History: 1. Renumbering and amendment of former section 10606.5 to section 10685 filed 12-17-2019; operative 1-1-2020. Submitted to OAL for printing only pursuant to Government Code section 11351 (Register 2019, No. 51).

ARTICLE 12
Settlements

§10700. Approval of Settlements.

(a) When filing a Compromise and Release or a Stipulations with Request for Award, the filing party shall file all agreed medical evaluator reports, qualified medical evaluator reports, treating physician reports, and any other that are relevant to a determination of the adequacy of the Compromise and Release or Stipulations with Request for Award that have not been filed previously.

(b) The Workers' Compensation Appeals Board shall inquire into the adequacy of all Compromise and Release agreements and Stipulations with Request for Award, and may set the matter for hearing to take evidence when necessary to determine whether the agreement should be approved or disapproved, or issue findings and awards.

(c) Agreements that provide for the payment of less than the full amount of compensation due or to become due and undertake to release the employer from all future liability will be approved only where it appears that a reasonable doubt exists as to the rights of the parties or that approval is in the best interest of the parties.

Note: Authority cited: Sections 133 and 5307, Labor Code. Reference: Sections 4646, 5001, 5100.6, 5002 and 5702, Labor Code.

History: 1. Repealer of article 10 heading, new article 12 heading and new section filed 12-17-2019; operative 1-1-2020. Submitted to OAL for printing only pursuant to Government Code section 11351 (Register 2019, No. 51).

§10702. Service of Settlements on Lien Claimants.

Where a lien claim is on file with the Workers' Compensation Appeals Board, and a Compromise and Release agreement or Stipulations with Request for Award is filed, a copy of the Compromise and Release agreement or Stipulations with Request for Award shall be served by the filing party on the lien claimant.

No lien claim shall be disallowed or reduced unless the lien claimant has been given notice and an opportunity to be heard.

Note: Authority cited: Sections 133 and 5307, Labor Code. Reference: Sections 4903, 4903.05, 4903.1, 4903.4, 4904, 4904.1, 4905 and 4906, Labor Code.

History: 1. Renumbering of former section 10886 to section 10702, including amendment of section heading, section and Note, filed 12-17-2019; operative 1-1-2020. Submitted to OAL for printing only pursuant to Government Code section 11351 (Register 2019, No. 51).

§10705. Procedures — Labor Code Section 3761.

Where the insurer has attached a declaration to the Compromise and Release agreement or Stipulations with Request for Award that it has complied with the provisions of Labor Code sections 3761(a) and 3761(b), the Workers' Compensation Appeals Board may approve the Compromise and Release or Stipulations with Request for Award without hearing or further proceedings.

Where a workers' compensation judge or the Appeals Board has approved a Compromise and Release or Stipulations with Request for Award and the insurer has failed to show proof of service pursuant to Labor Code section 3761(b), the workers' compensation judge or the Appeals Board, after giving notice and an opportunity to be heard to the insurer, shall award expenses as provided in Labor Code section 5813 upon request by the employer.

Any request for relief under Labor Code section 3761(b) or Labor Code section 3761(d) shall be made by the filing of a petition pursuant to rule 10510, together with a Declaration of Readiness to Proceed.

Note: Authority cited: Sections 133 and 5307, Labor Code. Reference: Section 3761, Labor Code.

History: 1. Renumbering and amendment of former section 10875 to section 10705 filed 12-17-2019; operative 1-1-2020. Submitted to OAL for printing only pursuant to Government Code section 11351 (Register 2019, No. 51).

§10740. Transcripts. [Renumbered]

Note: Authority cited: Sections 133, 5307, 5309 and 5708, Labor Code. Reference: Sections 5300, 5301, 5309, 5700, 5701 and 5708, Labor Code; and Section 703.5, Evidence Code.

History: 1. Amendment of first paragraph filed 12-19-2002; operative 1-1-2003. Submitted to OAL for printing only pursuant to Government Code section 11351 (Register 2002, No. 51).

2. Repealer of second paragraph and amendment of Note filed 10-15-2014; operative 1-1-2015. Submitted to OAL for printing only pursuant to Government Code section 11351 (Register 2014, No. 42).

3. Editorial correction of History 2 (Register 2017, No. 8).

4. Repealer of article 11 heading and renumbering of former section 10740 to section 10800 filed 12-17-2019; operative 1-1-2020. Submitted to OAL for printing only pursuant to Government Code section 11351 (Register 2019, No. 51).

ARTICLE 13
Hearings

§10742. Declaration of Readiness to Proceed.

(a) Except when a hearing is set on the Workers' Compensation Appeals Board's own motion, no matter shall be placed on calendar unless one of the parties has filed and served a Declaration of Readiness to Proceed in the form prescribed by the Appeals Board. The Declaration of Readiness to Proceed shall be served on all parties in accordance with rule 10610.

(b) A lien claimant shall not file a Declaration of Readiness to Proceed unless:

(1) The underlying case of the injured employee or the dependent(s) of a deceased employee has been resolved or

(2) The injured employee or the dependent(s) of a deceased employee choose(s) not to proceed with their case.

(c) All declarations of readiness to proceed shall state under penalty of perjury that the moving party has made a genuine, good faith effort to resolve the dispute before filing the Declaration of Readiness to Proceed, and shall state with specificity on the Declaration of Readiness to Proceed the efforts made to resolve those issues. Unless a status or priority conference is requested, the declarant shall also state under penalty of perjury that the moving party has completed discovery and is ready to proceed on the issues specified in the Declaration of Readiness to Proceed.

(d) If a party is represented by an attorney or non-attorney representative any Declaration of Readiness to Proceed filed on behalf of the party shall be executed by the attorney or non-attorney representative.

(e) If a Declaration of Readiness to Proceed is filed without complying with the provisions of this section, the Workers' Compensation Appeals Board may order the hearing off calendar and may impose sanctions and award attorney's fees and costs in accordance with Labor Code section 5813 and rule 10421.

Note: Authority cited: Sections 133, 5307, 5309 and 5708, Labor Code. Reference: Sections 4903.05, 4903.06, 5500.3, 5502 and 5813, Labor Code.

History: 1. New article 13 heading and renumbering and amendment of former section 10414 to section 10742 filed 12-17-2019; operative 1-1-2020. Submit-

ted to OAL for printing only pursuant to Government Code section 11351 (Register 2019, No. 51).

§10744. Objection to Declaration of Readiness to Proceed.

(a) Any objection to a Declaration of Readiness to Proceed shall be filed and served within 10 calendar days after service of the declaration. The objection shall set forth, under penalty of perjury, the specific reason why the case should not be set or why the requested proceedings are inappropriate.

(b) A false declaration or certification filed under this rule by any party, petitioner, attorney or non-attorney representative may give rise to proceedings under Labor Code section 134 for contempt or Labor Code section 5813 for sanctions.

(c) If a party is represented by an attorney or non-attorney representative, any objection to the Declaration of Readiness to Proceed shall be executed by the attorney or non-attorney representative.

(d) If a party has received a copy of the Declaration of Readiness to Proceed and has not filed an objection under this rule, that party shall be deemed to have waived any and all objections to proceeding on the issues specified in the declaration, absent extraordinary circumstances.

Note: Authority cited: Sections 133, 5307, 5309 and 5708, Labor Code. Reference: Sections 134, 5500.3, 5502 and 5813, Labor Code.

History: 1. Renumbering of former section 10416 to section 10744, including amendment of section and Note, filed 12-17-2019; operative 1-1-2020. Submitted to OAL for printing only pursuant to Government Code section 11351 (Register 2019, No. 51).

§10745. Setting the Case.

The Workers' Compensation Appeals Board, upon the receipt of a Declaration of Readiness to Proceed, may, in its discretion, set the case for a type of proceeding other than that requested. The Workers' Compensation Appeals Board may, on its own motion, set any case for conference or trial.

Note: Authority cited: Sections 133 and 5307, Labor Code. Reference: Section 5310, Labor Code.

History: 1. Renumbering and amendment of former section 10420 to section 10745 filed 12-17-2019; operative 1-1-2020. Submitted to OAL for printing only pursuant to Government Code section 11351 (Register 2019, No. 51).

§10748. Continuances.

Requests for continuances are inconsistent with the requirement that workers' compensation proceedings be expeditious and are not favored. Continuances will be granted only upon a clear showing of good cause. Where possible, reassignment pursuant to rule 10346 shall be used to avoid continuances.

Note: Authority cited: Sections 133 and 5307, Labor Code. Reference: Article XIV, Section 4, California Constitution; and Sections 5502 and 5502.5, Labor Code.

History: 1. Renumbering and amendment of former section 10548 to section 10748 filed 12-17-2019; operative 1-1-2020. Submitted to OAL for printing only pursuant to Government Code section 11351 (Register 2019, No. 51).

§10750. Notice of Hearing.

The Workers' Compensation Appeals Board shall either serve or, under rule 10629, cause to be served notice on all parties and their attorneys or non-attorney representatives of record of the time and place of each hearing scheduled, whether or not the hearing affects all parties, as provided in rule 10610.

Notice of hearing shall be given at least 10 days before the date of hearing, except where:

(a) Notice is waived; or

(b) A different time is expressly agreed to by all parties and concurred in by the Workers' Compensation Appeals Board.

Note: Authority cited: Sections 133 and 5307, Labor Code. Reference: Section 5504, Labor Code.

History: 1. Amendment of section and Note filed 12-19-2002; operative 1-1-2003. Submitted to OAL for printing only pursuant to Government Code section 11351 (Register 2002, No. 51).
2. Amendment of section and Note filed 11-17-2008; operative 11-17-2008. Submitted to OAL for printing only (Register 2008, No. 47).
3. Amendment of subsection (a) filed 10-15-2014; operative 1-1-2015. Submitted to OAL for printing only pursuant to Government Code section 11351 (Register 2014, No. 42).
4. Editorial correction of History 3 (Register 2017, No. 8).
5. Repealer of article 12 heading, repealer of former section 10750 and renumbering and amendment of former section 10544 to section 10750 filed 12-17-2019; operative 1-1-2020. Submitted to OAL for printing only pursuant to Government Code section 11351 (Register 2019, No. 51).

§10751. Appearances by Non-Attorney Representatives Not Identified on Notice of Representation.

(a) A non-attorney representative may appear on a party's behalf if identified on a notice of representation.

(b) A non-attorney representative who has not been identified on a notice of representation shall file a notice of appearance that includes the full legal name of the represented party and the name, address and telephone number of the attorney or non-attorney representative and associated entity, if any.

Note: Authority cited: Sections 133 and 5307, Labor Code. Reference: Sections 4903, 4903.6 and 4906, Labor Code

History: 1. New section filed 12-19-2002; operative 1-1-2003. Submitted to OAL for printing only pursuant to Government Code section 11351 (Register 2002, No. 51).
2. Amendment of section heading, section and Note filed 11-17-2008; operative 11-17-2008. Submitted to OAL for printing only (Register 2008, No. 47).
3. Amendment filed 10-15-2014; operative 1-1-2015. Submitted to OAL for printing only pursuant to Government Code section 11351 (Register 2014, No. 42).
4. Editorial correction of History 3 (Register 2017, No. 8).
5. Repealer of former section 10751 and new section filed 12-17-2019; operative 1-1-2020. Submitted to OAL for printing only pursuant to Government Code section 11351 (Register 2019, No. 51).

§10752. Appearances Required.

(a) Each applicant and defendant shall appear or have an attorney or non-attorney representative appear at all hearings pertaining to the case in chief. Neither a lien conference nor a lien trial is a hearing pertaining to the case in chief.

(b) Each required party shall have a person available with settlement authority at all hearings. This person need not be present if the party's attorney or non-attorney representative is present and can obtain immediate authority.

(c) A represented injured employee or dependent shall personally appear at any mandatory settlement conference. Failure to personally appear shall not be a basis for dismissal of the application.

(d) A lien claimant need not appear at any mandatory settlement conference or trial in the case in chief, but shall be immediately available by telephone with full settlement authority and shall notify defendant(s) of the telephone number at which the defendant(s) may reach the lien claimant. Failure to comply may give rise to monetary sanctions, attorney's fees and costs under Labor Code section 5813 and rule 10421.

(e) Any appearance required by this rule may be excused by the Workers' Compensation Appeals Board. Any appearance not required by this rule may be ordered by the Workers' Compensation Appeals Board.

Note: Authority cited: Sections 133, 5307, 5309 and 5708, Labor Code. Reference: Sections 5502 and 5700, Labor Code.

History: 1. New section filed 12-17-2019; operative 1-1-2020. Submitted to OAL for printing only pursuant to Government Code section 11351 (Register 2019, No. 51).

§10753. Inspection of Files. [Repealed]

Note: Authority cited: Sections 133, 5307, 5309 and 5708, Labor Code. Reference: Section 126, Labor Code.

History: 1. Amendment of section and Note filed 12-19-2002; operative 1-1-2003. Submitted to OAL for printing only pursuant to Government Code section 11351 (Register 2002, No. 51).
2. Amendment of section and Note filed 11-17-2008; operative 11-17-2008. Submitted to OAL for printing only (Register 2008, No. 47).
3. Amendment filed 10-15-2014; operative 1-1-2015. Submitted to OAL for printing only pursuant to Government Code section 11351 (Register 2014, No. 42).
4. Editorial correction of History 3 (Register 2017, No. 8).
5. Repealer filed 12-17-2019; operative 1-1-2020. Submitted to OAL for printing only pursuant to Government Code section 11351 (Register 2019, No. 51).

§10754. Sealing Documents. [Renumbered]

Note: Authority cited: Sections 133, 5307, 5309 and 5708, Labor Code. Reference: Section 5708, Labor Code; Rule 2.551, California Rules of Court.

History: 1. Amendment filed 12-19-2002; operative 1-1-2003. Submitted to OAL for printing only pursuant to Government Code section 11351 (Register 2002, No. 51).
2. Amendment of section and Note filed 11-17-2008; operative 11-17-2008. Submitted to OAL for printing only (Register 2008, No. 47).
3. Amendment of section heading, repealer and new section and amendment of Note filed 10-15-2014; operative 1-1-2015. Submitted to OAL for printing

only pursuant to Government Code section 11351 (Register 2014, No. 42).
4. Editorial correction of History 3 (Register 2017, No. 8).
5. Renumbering of former section 10754 to section 10813 filed 12-17-2019; operative 1-1-2020. Submitted to OAL for printing only pursuant to Government Code section 11351 (Register 2019, No. 51).

§10755. Failure to Appear at Mandatory Settlement Conference in Case in Chief.

(a) Where an applicant served with notice of a mandatory settlement conference fails to appear either in person or by attorney or non-attorney representative at the mandatory settlement conference, the workers' compensation judge may:

(1) Dismiss the application after issuing a 10-day notice of intention to dismiss, or

(2) Close discovery and set the case in chief for trial.

(b) Where a defendant served with notice of a mandatory settlement conference fails to appear either in person or by attorney or non-attorney representative at the mandatory settlement conference, the workers' compensation judge may:

(1) Close discovery and set the case for trial on all issues, or

(2) Set the case in chief for trial.

(c) Where a required party, after notice, fails to appear at a mandatory settlement conference in the case in chief and good cause is shown for failure to appear, the workers' compensation judge may take the case off calendar or may continue the case to a date certain.

(d) This rule shall not apply to lien conferences, which are governed by rule 10875.

Note: Authority cited: Sections 133 and 5307, Labor Code. Reference: Article XIV, Section 4, California Constitution; and Sections 5502(e) and 5708, Labor Code.

History: 1. Amendment of section and Note filed 11-17-2008; operative 11-17-2008. Submitted to OAL for printing only (Register 2008, No. 47).
2. Amendment filed 10-15-2014; operative 1-1-2015. Submitted to OAL for printing only pursuant to Government Code section 11351 (Register 2014, No. 42).
3. Editorial correction of History 2 (Register 2017, No. 8).
4. Renumbering of former section 10755 to section 10811 and new section 10755 filed 12-17-2019; op-

erative 1-1-2020. Submitted to OAL for printing only pursuant to Government Code section 11351 (Register 2019, No. 51).

§10756. Failure to Appear at Trial in Case in Chief.

(a) Where an applicant served with notice of trial in the case in chief fails to appear either in person or by attorney or non-attorney representative at the trial, the workers' compensation judge may:

(1) Dismiss the application after issuing a 10-day notice of intention to dismiss, or

(2) Hear the evidence and, after service of the minutes of hearing and summary of evidence that shall include a 10-day notice of intention to submit, make such decision as is just and proper.

(b) Where a defendant served with notice of trial in the case in chief fails to appear either in person or by attorney or non-attorney representative at the trial, the workers' compensation judge may hear the evidence and, after service of the minutes of hearing and summary of evidence that shall include a 10-day notice of intention to submit, make such decision as is just and proper.

(c) Where a required party, after notice, fails to appear at a trial in the case in chief and good cause is shown for failure to appear, the workers' compensation judge may take the case off calendar or may continue the case to a date certain.

(d) This rule shall not apply to lien trials, which are governed by rule 10876.

Note: Authority cited: Sections 133 and 5307, Labor Code. Reference: Article XIV, Section 4, California Constitution; and Sections 5502(e) and 5708, Labor Code.

History: 1. New section filed 12-17-2019; operative 1-1-2020. Submitted to OAL for printing only pursuant to Government Code section 11351 (Register 2019, No. 51).

§10757. Appearances in Settled Cases.

When the parties represent to the workers' compensation judge assigned to the case that a case has been settled, the case may be taken off calendar.

Note: Authority cited: Sections 133 and 5307, Labor Code. Reference: Article XIV, Section 4, California Constitution; and Sections 5502 and 5502.5, Labor Code.

History: 1. Renumbering and amendment of former section 10549 to section 10757 filed 12-17-2019;

operative 1-1-2020. Submitted to OAL for printing only pursuant to Government Code section 11351 (Register 2019, No. 51).

§10758. Status Conferences.

At the discretion of the workers' compensation judge, any hearing except a trial may be re-designated as a status conference.

Note: Authority cited: Sections 133 and 5307, Labor Code. Reference: Article XIV, Section 4, California Constitution; and Sections 5502 and 5502.5, Labor Code.

History: 1. New section filed 12-17-2019; operative 1-1-2020. Submitted to OAL for printing only pursuant to Government Code section 11351 (Register 2019, No. 51). For prior history, see Register 2008, No. 47.

§10759. Mandatory Settlement Conferences.

(a) In accordance with Labor Code section 5502, the workers' compensation judge shall have authority to inquire into the adequacy and completeness, including provision for lien claims, of Compromise and Release agreements or Stipulations with Request for Award or orders, and to issue orders approving Compromise and Release agreements or awards or orders based upon approved stipulations. The workers' compensation judge may temporarily adjourn a conference to a time certain to facilitate a specific resolution of the dispute(s) subject to Labor Code section 5502(d)(1).

Subject to the provisions of Labor Code section 5502.5 and rule 10744, upon a showing of good cause, the workers' compensation judge may continue a mandatory settlement conference to a date certain, may continue it to a status conference on a date certain, or may take the case off calendar. In such a case, the workers' compensation judge shall note the reasons for the continuance or order taking off calendar in the minutes. The minutes shall be served on all parties and their representatives.

(b) Absent resolution of the dispute(s), the parties shall file a joint Pre-Trial Conference Statement setting forth the issues and stipulations for trial, witnesses, and a list of exhibits. A defendant that has paid benefits shall have a current computer printout of benefits paid available for inspection at every mandatory settlement conference.

(1) Each exhibit listed must be clearly identified by author/provider, date, and title or type

(e.g., "the July 1, 2008 medical report of John Doe, M.D. (3 pages)"). Each medical report, medical-legal report, medical record, or other paper or record having a different author/provider and/or a different date is a separate "document" and must be listed as a separate exhibit, with the exception that the following documents may be listed as a single exhibit, unless otherwise ordered by the Workers' Compensation Appeals Board:

(A)   Excerpted portions of physician, hospital or dispensary records, provided that the party offering the exhibit designates each excerpted portion by the title of the record or document, by the date or dates of treatment or other service(s) covered by the record or document, by the author or authors of the record or document, and by any available page number(s) (e.g., Bates-numbered pages of records or documents photocopied and numbered by a legal copy service). Only the relevant excerpts of physician, hospital or dispensary records shall be admitted in evidence;

(B)   Excerpted portions of personnel records, wage records and statements, job descriptions, and other business records provided that the party offering the exhibit designates each excerpted portion by the title of the record or document, by the date or dates covered by the record or document, by the author or authors of the record or document, and by any available page number(s) (e.g., Bates-numbered pages of records or documents photocopied and numbered by a legal copy service). Only the relevant excerpts of personnel records, wage records and statements, job descriptions, and other business records shall be admitted in evidence; and

(C)   Explanation of Benefits (EOB) letters.

(c)   The workers' compensation judge may make orders and rulings regarding admission of evidence and discovery matters, including admission of offers of proof and stipulations of testimony where appropriate and necessary for resolution of the dispute(s) by the workers' compensation judge, and may submit and decide the dispute(s) on the record pursuant to the agreement of the parties.

(d)   The joint Pre-Trial Conference Statement, the disposition, and any orders shall be filed by the workers' compensation judge in the record of the proceedings on a form prescribed and approved by the Appeals Board and shall be served on the parties.

Note: Authority cited: Sections 133, 5307 and 5502, Labor Code. Reference: Sections 5502 and 5502.5, Labor Code.

History: 1. New section filed 12-17-2019; operative 1-1-2020. Submitted to OAL for printing only pursuant to Government Code section 11351 (Register 2019, No. 51).

§10760.   Recording of Trial Level Proceedings. [Renumbered]

Note: Authority cited: Sections 133, 5307, 5309 and 5708, Labor Code. Reference: Rule 1.150, California Rules of Court.

History: 1. New section filed 10-15-2014; operative 1-1-2015. Submitted to OAL for printing only pursuant to Government Code section 11351 (Register 2014, No. 42).

2. Editorial correction of History 1 (Register 2017, No. 8).

3. Renumbering former section 10760 to section 10818 filed 12-17-2019; operative 1-1-2020. Submitted to OAL for printing only pursuant to Government Code section 11351 (Register 2019, No. 51).

§10761.   Submission at Conference.

(a)   A workers' compensation judge may receive evidence and submit an issue or issues for decision at a conference hearing if the parties agree.

(b)   If documentary evidence is required to determine the issue or issues being submitted, the parties shall comply with the provisions of rule 10759 regarding the listing and filing of exhibits.

(c)   After submission at a conference, the workers' compensation judge shall prepare minutes of hearing and a summary of evidence as set forth in rule 10787.

Note: Authority cited: Sections 133, 5307, 5309 and 5708, Labor Code. Reference: Sections 5708 and 5709, Labor Code.

History: 1. Renumbering and amendment of former section 10541 to section 10761 filed 12-17-2019; operative 1-1-2020. Submitted to OAL for printing only pursuant to Government Code section 11351 (Register 2019, No. 51).

§10770.   Filing and Service of Lien Claims. [Repealed]

Note: Authority cited: Sections 133, 5307, 5309 and 5708, Labor Code. Reference: Sections 4903, 4903.05, 4903.06, 4903.8, 4903.1, 4903.4, 4903.5, 4903.6, 4904, 4603.2, 4603.3, 4603.6, 4610.5, 4610.6, 4616.3, 4616.4, 4622 and 5813, Labor Code; and

Sections 9792.5, 9794, 9795.4, 10561 and 10770.5, title 8, California Code of Regulations.

History: 1. Amendment exempt from OAL review pursuant to Government Code section 11351 filed 12-19-90; operative 1-1-91 (Register 91, No. 7).

2. Amendment filed 12-23-93; operative 1-1-94. Submitted to OAL for printing only pursuant to Government Code section 11351 (Register 93, No. 52).

3. Amendment filed 12-19-2002; operative 1-1-2003. Submitted to OAL for printing only pursuant to Government Code section 11351 (Register 2002, No. 51).

4. Amendment of section and Note filed 11-17-2008; operative 11-17-2008. Submitted to OAL for printing only (Register 2008, No. 47).

5. Amendment of section heading, section and Note filed 5-21-2012; operative 5-21-2012 pursuant to Government Code section 11343.4. Submitted to OAL for printing only pursuant to Government Code 11351 (Register 2012, No. 21).

6. Amendment of section and Note filed 9-23-2013; operative 10-23-2013. Submitted as a file and print by the Workers' Compensation Appeals Board pursuant to Government Code section 11351 (Register 2013, No. 39).

7. Amendment of subsections (c)(2)-(3) filed 10-15-2014; operative 1-1-2015. Submitted to OAL for printing only pursuant to Government Code section 11351 (Register 2014, No. 42).

8. Editorial correction of History 8 (Register 2017, No. 8).

9. Amendment of subsections (a)(3)(A)-(B), repealer of subsection (c)(3), subsection renumbering, amendment of newly designated subsections (c)(5) and (c)(7) and subsections (d)(1), (d)(1)(C) and (*l*) and amendment of Note filed 2-24-2017; operative 3-26-2017 pursuant to Government Code section 11343.4(b)(3). Submitted as a file and print to OAL pursuant to Government Code section 11351 (Register 2017, No. 8).

10. Repealer of article 13 heading and renumbering of former section 10770.5 to section 10863 filed 12-17-2019; operative 1-1-2020. Submitted to OAL for printing only pursuant to Government Code section 11351 (Register 2019, No. 51).

§10770.1. Lien Conferences and Lien Trials. [Repealed]

Note: Authority cited: Sections 133, 5307, 5309 and 5708, Labor Code. Reference: Sections 4903, 4903.05, 4903.06, 4903.1, 4903.4, 4903.5, 4903.6, 4904, 5502 and 5502.5, Labor Code; Sections 351, 352, 451 and 452, Evidence Code; and Sections 10250, 10205.16, 10301(u), 10301(z), 10364(a), 10561, 10629 and 10770-10772, title 8, California Code of Regulations.

History: 1. New section filed 5-21-2012; operative 5-21-2012 pursuant to Government Code section

11343.4. Submitted to OAL for printing only pursuant to Government Code 11351 (Register 2012, No. 21).

2. Amendment of section and Note filed 9-23-2013; operative 10-23-2013. Submitted as a file and print by the Workers' Compensation Appeals Board pursuant to Government Code section 11351 (Register 2013, No. 39).

3. Amendment of subsections (a)(1), (c)(1)(A), (e) and (i) filed 10-15-2014; operative 1-1-2015. Submitted to OAL for printing only pursuant to Government Code section 11351 (Register 2014, No. 42).

4. Editorial correction of History 3 (Register 2017, No. 8).

5. Repealer filed 12-17-2019; operative 1-1-2020. Submitted to OAL for printing only pursuant to Government Code section 11351 (Register 2019, No. 51).

§10770.5. Verification to Filing of Lien Claim or Application by Lien Claimant. [Renumbered]

Note: Authority cited: Sections 133, 5307, 5309 and 5708, Labor Code. Reference: Sections 4903 and 4903.6, Labor Code.

History: 1. New section filed 11-17-2008; operative 11-17-2008. Submitted to OAL for printing only (Register 2008, No. 47).

2. Amendment filed 9-23-2013; operative 10-23-2013. Submitted as a file and print by the Workers' Compensation Appeals Board pursuant to Government Code section 11351 (Register 2013, No. 39).

3. Renumbering of former section 10770.5 to section 10863 filed 12-17-2019; operative 1-1-2020. Submitted to OAL for printing only pursuant to Government Code section 11351 (Register 2019, No. 51).

§10770.6. Verification to Filing of Declaration of Readiness By or on Behalf of Lien Claimant. [Renumbered]

Note: Authority cited: Sections 133, 5307, 5309 and 5708, Labor Code. Reference: Sections 4903 and 4903.6, Labor Code.

History: 1. New section filed 11-17-2008; operative 11-17-2008. Submitted to OAL for printing only (Register 2008, No. 47).

2. Amendment filed 9-23-2013; operative 10-23-2013. Submitted as a file and print by the Workers' Compensation Appeals Board pursuant to Government Code section 11351 (Register 2013, No. 39).

3. Renumbering of former section 10770.6 to section 10874 filed 12-17-2019; operative 1-1-2020. Submitted to OAL for printing only pursuant to Government Code section 11351 (Register 2019, No. 51).

§10770.7. Requirement for Liens Filed Before January 1, 2017. [Repealed]

Note: Authority cited: Sections 133, 5307 and 5708, Labor Code. Reference: Sections 4903 and 4903.05, and Labor Code; and Sections 9792.5, 9794, 9795.4, 10390 et seq., 10561, 10770 and 10770.5, title 8, California Code of Regulations.

History: 1. New section filed 2-24-2017; operative 3-26-2017 pursuant to Government Code section 11343.4(b)(3). Submitted as a file and print to OAL pursuant to Government Code section 11351 (Register 2017, No. 8).

2. Repealer filed 12-17-2019; operative 1-1-2020. Submitted to OAL for printing only pursuant to Government Code section 11351 (Register 2019, No. 51).

§10772. Unemployment Compensation Disability Liens. [Repealed]

Note: Authority cited: Sections 133 and 5307, Labor Code. Reference: Sections 4903 and 4904, Labor Code.

History: 1. Amendment of last paragraph filed 12-19-2002; operative 1-1-2003. Submitted to OAL for printing only pursuant to Government Code section 11351 (Register 2002, No. 51).

2. Repealer filed 12-17-2019; operative 1-1-2020. Submitted to OAL for printing only pursuant to Government Code section 11351 (Register 2019, No. 51).

§10773. Law Firm Employees. [Repealed]

Note: Authority cited: Sections 133 and 5307, Labor Code. Reference: Section 4907, Labor Code.

History: 1. New section filed 12-19-2002; operative 1-1-2003. Submitted to OAL for printing only pursuant to Government Code section 11351 (Register 2002, No. 51). For prior history, see Register 96, No. 43.

2. Repealer filed 12-17-2019; operative 1-1-2020. Submitted to OAL for printing only pursuant to Government Code section 11351 (Register 2019, No. 51).

§10774. Substitution or Dismissal of Attorneys. [Renumbered]

Note: Authority cited: Sections 133, 5307, Labor Code. Reference: Sections 4903, 4906, Labor Code.

History: 1. Repealer of article 14 heading and renumbering of former section 10774 to section 10402 filed 12-17-2019; operative 1-1-2020. Submitted to OAL for printing only pursuant to Government Code section 11351 (Register 2019, No. 51).

§10774.5. Notices of Representation, Change of Representation, and Non-Representation for Lien Claimants. [Repealed]

Note: Authority: Sections 133, 5307, 5309 and 5708, Labor Code. Reference: Sections 4903(a), 4903.6(b), 4906, 4907, 5501, and 5700; Sections 284, 285 and 286, Code of Civil Procedure; and Sections 10774 and 10779, title 8, California Code of Regulations.

History: 1. New section filed 9-23-2013; operative 10-23-2013. Submitted as a file and print by the Workers' Compensation Appeals Board pursuant to Government Code section 11351 (Register 2013, No. 39).

2. Repealer filed 12-17-2019; operative 1-1-2020. Submitted to OAL for printing only pursuant to Government Code section 11351 (Register 2019, No. 51).

§10775. Reasonable Attorney's Fee. [Renumbered]

Note: Authority cited: Sections 133 and 5307, Labor Code. Reference: Sections 4903 and 4906, Labor Code.

History: 1. Amendment exempt from OAL review pursuant to Government Code section 11351 filed 12-19-90; operative 1-1-91 (Register 91, No. 7).

2. Amendment of first and penultimate paragraphs filed 12-19-2002; operative 1-1-2003. Submitted to OAL for printing only pursuant to Government Code section 11351 (Register 2002, No. 51).

3. Renumbering of former section 10775 to section 10844 filed 12-17-2019; operative 1-1-2020. Submitted to OAL for printing only pursuant to Government Code section 11351 (Register 2019, No. 51).

§10776. Approval of Attorney's Fee. [Renumbered]

Note: Authority cited: Sections 133 and 5307, Labor Code. Reference: Sections 4903 and 4906, Labor Code.

History: 1. Amendment of subsections (a)-(b) filed 12-19-2002; operative 1-1-2003. Submitted to OAL for printing only pursuant to Government Code section 11351 (Register 2002, No. 51).

2. Renumbering of former section 10776 to section 10840 filed 12-17-2019; operative 1-1-2020. Submitted to OAL for printing only pursuant to Government Code section 11351 (Register 2019, No. 51).

§10778. Request for Increase of Attorney's Fee. [Renumbered]

Note: Authority cited: Sections 133, 5307, Labor Code. Reference: Sections 4903, 4906, Labor Code.

History: 1. Renumbering of former section 10778 to section 10842 filed 12-17-2019; operative 1-1-2020. Submitted to OAL for printing only pursuant to Government Code section 11351 (Register 2019, No. 51).

§10779. Disbarred and Suspended Attorneys. [Renumbered]

Note: Authority cited: Sections 133, 5307, 5309 and 5708, Labor Code. Reference: Section 4907, Labor Code; and Section 6126, Business and Professions Code.

History: 1. Amendment of first paragraph filed 12-19-2002; operative 1-1-2003. Submitted to OAL for printing only pursuant to Government Code section 11351 (Register 2002, No. 51).

2. Amendment of section and Note filed 11-17-2008; operative 11-17-2008. Submitted to OAL for printing only (Register 2008, No. 47).

3. Renumbering of former section 10779 to section 10445 filed 12-17-2019; operative 1-1-2020. Submitted to OAL for printing only pursuant to Government Code section 11351 (Register 2019, No. 51).

§10780. Dismissal Orders. [Renumbered]

Note: Authority cited: Sections 133 and 5307, Labor Code.

History: 1. Repealer and new section filed 12-23-93; operative 1-1-94. Submitted to OAL for printing only pursuant to Government Code section 11351 (Register 93, No. 52).

2. Amendment of section and Note filed 12-19-2002; operative 1-1-2003. Submitted to OAL for printing only pursuant to Government Code section 11351 (Register 2002, No. 51).

3. Repealer of article 15 heading and renumbering of former section 10780 to section 10850 filed 12-17-2019; operative 1-1-2020. Submitted to OAL for printing only pursuant to Government Code section 11351 (Register 2019, No. 51).

§10782. Expedited Hearings.

(a) Where injury to any part or parts of the body is accepted as compensable by the employer, a party is entitled to an expedited hearing and decision upon the filing of an Application for Adjudication of Claim and a Declaration of Readiness to Proceed pursuant to rule 10625 establishing a bona fide, good faith dispute pursuant to Labor Code section 5502(b).

(b) An expedited hearing may be set upon request where injury to any part or parts of the body is accepted as compensable by the employer and the issues include medical treatment

or temporary disability for a disputed body part or parts.

(c) A workers' compensation judge assigned to a case may re-designate the expedited hearing as a mandatory settlement conference, receive a Pre-Trial Conference Statement pursuant to Labor Code section 5502, close discovery and schedule the case for trial on the issues presented, if the workers' compensation judge determines that the case is not appropriate for expedited determination.

(d) Grounds for the re-designation of an expedited hearing include, but are not limited to, cases where the direct and cross-examination of the applicant will be prolonged, or where there are multiple witnesses who will offer extensive testimony.

(e) The parties are expected to submit for decision all matters properly in issue at a single trial and to produce all necessary evidence, including witnesses, documents, medical reports, payroll statements and all other matters considered essential in the proof of a party's claim or defense.

Note: Authority cited: Sections 133, 5307 and 5502, Labor Code. Reference: Section 5502, Labor Code.

History: 1. New section filed 11-17-2008; operative 11-17-2008. Submitted to OAL for printing only (Register 2008, No. 47).

2. Renumbering of former section 10782 to section 10430 and renumbering of former section 10552 to section 10782, including amendment of section heading and section, filed 12-17-2019; operative 1-1-2020. Submitted to OAL for printing only pursuant to Government Code section 11351 (Register 2019, No. 51).

§10785. Priority Conferences.

(a) A priority conference shall be set upon the filing of a Declaration of Readiness to Proceed requesting a priority conference that shows that:

(1) The applicant is represented by an attorney and the issues in dispute include employment and/or injury arising out of and in the course of employment; or

(2) The applicant claims to have been employed by an illegally uninsured employer and the issues in dispute include employment and/or injury arising out of and in the course of employment.

(b) To the extent possible, all priority and status conferences in a case shall be conducted by the same workers' compensation judge. When discovery is complete, or when the workers' compensation judge determines that the parties have had sufficient time to complete reasonable discovery, the case shall be set for trial as expeditiously as possible.

Note: Authority cited: Sections 133, 5307 and 5502, Labor Code. Reference: Section 5502, Labor Code.

History: 1. New section filed 11-17-2008; operative 11-17-2008. Submitted to OAL for printing only (Register 2008, No. 47).

2. Repealer of former section 10785 and renumbering former section 10555 to section 10785, including amendment of section heading and section, filed 12-17-2019; operative 1-1-2020. Submitted to OAL for printing only pursuant to Government Code section 11351 (Register 2019, No. 51).

§10786. Determination of Medical-Legal Expense Dispute.

(a)   Within 60 days of service of a medical-legal provider objection to a denial of all or a portion of the medical-legal provider's billing pursuant to Labor Code section 4622(c), the defendant shall file and serve a petition for determination of medical-legal expenses and a Declaration of Readiness to Proceed. Upon filing of a Declaration of Readiness to Proceed, the medical-legal provider shall be added to the official address record.

(b)   If a defendant has failed to file and serve a petition for determination of medical-legal expenses and a Declaration of Readiness in compliance with subdivision (a), a medical-legal provider may file and serve a petition for reimbursement of medical-legal expenses and a Declaration of Readiness to Proceed. Upon filing of a petition for reimbursement of medical-legal expenses and a Declaration of Readiness to Proceed, the medical-legal provider shall be added to the official address record.

(c)   Upon receipt of a Declaration of Readiness in accordance with the provisions of subdivisions (a) and (b) of this rule, the matter shall be set for either a status conference or a mandatory settlement conference, in the discretion of the workers' compensation judge.

(d)   Notwithstanding any other provision of this rule, if there is a threshold issue relating to the case in chief that would entirely defeat the medical-legal expense claim that must be determined prior to adjudicating the medical-legal expense claim dispute, the Workers' Compensa-tion Appeals Board may defer hearing and determining the medical-legal expense claim dispute until the underlying claim of the employee or dependent has been resolved or abandoned.

(e)   A defendant shall be deemed to have waived all objections to a medical-legal provider's billing, other than compliance with Labor Code sections 4620 and 4621, if:

(1)   The provider submitted a properly documented billing to the defendant and, within 60 days thereafter, the defendant failed to serve an explanation of review (EOR) that complies with Labor Code section 4603.3 and any applicable regulations adopted by the Administrative Director; or

(2)   The defendant failed to make payment consistent with an explanation of review (EOR) that complies with Labor Code section 4603.3 and any applicable regulations adopted by the Administrative Director; or

(3)   The provider submitted a timely and proper request for a second review to the defendant and, within 14 days thereafter, the defendant failed to serve a final written determination that complies with any applicable regulations adopted by the Administrative Director; or

(4)   The defendant failed to make payment consistent with a final written determination that complies with any applicable regulations adopted by the Administrative Director.

(f)   A defendant shall be deemed to have waived any objections to a medical-legal provider's billing, other than the amount payable pursuant to the fee schedule(s) in effect on the date the services were rendered and compliance with Labor Code sections 4620 and 4621, if the provider submitted a timely objection to the defendant's EOR regarding a dispute other than the amount payable and the defendant failed to file and serve a petition for determination of medical-legal expenses and a Declaration of Readiness as required by Labor Code section 4622 and subdivision (a) of this rule.

(g)   A medical-legal provider's bill will be deemed satisfied, and neither the employee nor the employer shall be liable for any further payment, if the defendant issued a timely and proper EOR and made payment consistent with that EOR within 60 days after receipt of the provider's written billing and report and the provider failed to make a timely and proper request for second review in the form prescribed by the Rules of the Administrative Director within 90 days after service of the EOR.

(h) A medical-legal provider will be deemed to have waived any objection based on the amount payable under the fee schedule(s) in effect on the date the services were rendered if, within 14 days after receipt of the provider's request for second review, the defendant issued a timely and proper final written determination and made payment consistent with that determination and the provider failed to request IBR within 30 days after service of this second review determination.

(i) Bad Faith Actions or Tactics:

(1) If the Workers' Compensation Appeals Board determines that, as a result of bad faith actions or tactics, a defendant failed to comply with the requirements, timelines and procedures set forth in Labor Code sections 4622, 4603.3 and 4603.6 and the related Rules of the Administrative Director, the defendant shall be liable for the medical-legal provider's reasonable attorney's fees and costs and for sanctions under Labor Code section 5813 and rule 10421. The amount of the attorney's fees, costs and sanctions payable shall be determined by the Workers' Compensation Appeals Board; however, for bad faith actions or tactics occurring on or after October 23, 2013, the monetary sanctions shall not be less than $500.00. These attorney's fees, costs and monetary sanctions shall be in addition to any penalties and interest that may be payable under Labor Code section 4622 or other applicable provisions of law, and in addition to any lien filing fee, lien activation fee or IBR fee that, by statute, the defendant might be obligated to reimburse to the medical-legal provider.

(2) If the Workers' Compensation Appeals Board determines that, as a result of bad faith actions or tactics, a medical-legal provider has improperly asserted that a defendant failed to comply with the requirements, timelines and procedures set forth in Labor Code sections 4622 and 4603.6 and the related Rules of the Administrative Director, the medical-legal provider shall be liable for the defendant's reasonable attorney's fees and costs and for sanctions under Labor Code section 5813 and rule 10421. The amount of the attorney's fees, costs and sanctions payable shall be determined by the Workers' Compensation Appeals Board; however, for bad faith actions or tactics occurring on or after October 23, 2013, the monetary sanctions shall not be less than $500.00.

Note: Authority cited: Sections 133, 4622, 4627 and 5307, Labor Code. Reference: Sections 4603.3, 4603.6, 4622 and 5813, Labor Code.

History: 1. New section filed 12-17-2019; operative 1-1-2020. Submitted to OAL for printing only pursuant to Government Code section 11351 (Register 2019, No. 51).

§10787. Trials.

(a) The parties shall submit for decision all matters properly in issue at a single trial and produce at the trial all necessary evidence, including witnesses, documents, medical reports, payroll statements and all other matters considered essential in the proof of a party's claim or defense. However, a workers' compensation judge may order that the issues in a case be bifurcated and tried separately upon a showing of good cause.

(b) Unless already filed in EAMS, the parties shall have all proposed exhibits available at trial for review by and filing with the trial workers' compensation judge.

(c) Minutes of hearing and summary of evidence shall be prepared at the conclusion of each trial and filed in the record of proceedings. They shall include:

(1) The names of the commissioners, deputy commissioner or workers' compensation judge, reporter, the parties present, attorneys or other agents appearing therefor and witnesses sworn;

(2) The place and date of said trial;

(3) The admissions and stipulations, the issues and matters in controversy, a descriptive listing of all exhibits received for identification or in evidence (with the identity of the party offering the same);

(4) The disposition, and if the disposition is an order taking off calendar or a continuance, the reasons for the order which shall include the time and action, if any, required for submission;

(5) A summary of the evidence required by Labor Code section 5313 that shall include a fair and unbiased summary of the testimony given by each witness;

(6) If motion pictures are shown, a brief summary of their contents or a stipulation that parties waive a summary; and

(7) A fair statement of any offers of proof.

(d) Notwithstanding subdivision (c), the summary of evidence need not be filed upon issuance of a stipulated order, decision or award.

Note: Authority cited: Sections 133 and 5307, Labor Code. Reference: Sections 5708 and 5313, Labor Code.

History: 1. New section filed 12-17-2019; operative 1-1-2020. Submitted to OAL for printing only pursuant to Government Code section 11351 (Register 2019, No. 51).

§10788. Petition for Automatic Reassignment of Trial or Expedited Hearing to Another Workers' Compensation Judge.

A party shall be entitled to automatic reassignment of a trial or expedited hearing to another workers' compensation judge in accordance with the provisions of this rule. Consolidated cases are to be considered as one case within the meaning of this rule.

(a)   An injured worker shall be entitled to one reassignment of a workers' compensation judge for trial or expedited hearing. The defendants shall be entitled to one reassignment of a workers' compensation judge for a trial or expedited hearing, which may be exercised by any of them. This rule is not applicable to conference hearings. In no event shall any motion or petition for reassignment be entertained after the swearing of the first witness at a trial or expedited hearing.

(b)   If the parties are first notified of the identity of the workers' compensation judge assigned for trial at a mandatory settlement conference, at a status conference, at a lien conference, at a priority conference or upon reassignment at the time of trial, to exercise the right to automatic reassignment a party must make an oral motion immediately upon learning the name of the workers' compensation judge to whom the case has been assigned for trial. The motion shall be acted upon immediately by the presiding workers' compensation judge.

(c)   If the parties are first notified of the identity of the workers' compensation judge assigned for trial or expedited hearing by a notice of trial served by mail, to exercise the right to automatic reassignment a party must file a petition requesting reassignment not more than 5 days after receipt of the notice of trial or expedited hearing. The presiding workers' compensation judge shall rule on any petition for automatic reassignment.

(d)   If a petition for automatic reassignment is granted and results in a new trial date, a new notice of trial or expedited hearing shall be served. Unless required for the convenience of the Workers' Compensation Appeals Board, no continuance shall be granted by reason of a petition or motion under this rule. If a continuance is granted, another trial or expedited hearing shall be scheduled as early as possible.

(e)   If a party files a petition or makes a motion for automatic reassignment and no other workers' compensation judge is available in the office, the assignment shall be made by a deputy commissioner of the Appeals Board.

Note: Authority cited: Section 5307, Labor Code. Reference: Section 5310, Labor Code.

History: 1. Renumbering and amendment of former section 10453 to section 10788 filed 12-17-2019; operative 1-1-2020. Submitted to OAL for printing only pursuant to Government Code section 11351 (Register 2019, No. 51).

§10789. Walk-Through Documents.

(a)   The following documents may be submitted on a walk-through basis without a party filing a Declaration of Readiness to Proceed or the Workers' Compensation Appeals Board serving a notice of hearing:

(1)   Compromise and Releases;

(2)   Stipulations with Request for Award;

(3)   Petitions for attorney's fees for representation of the applicant at a deposition;

(4)   Petitions to compel attendance at a medical examination or deposition; and

(5)   Petitions for Costs pursuant to rule 10545.

(b)   The following procedures shall be followed for filing walk-through documents:

(1)   A walk-through settlement document (i.e., a Compromise and Release or a Stipulations with Request for Award), and all supporting medical reports and other supporting documents not previously filed, shall be filed directly with the workers' compensation judge at the date and time of the walk-through. Permanent and stationary medical or medical-legal reports shall be indicated as such. In addition, each walk-through settlement document (i.e., a Compromise and Release or a Stipulations with Request for Award) shall be accompanied by a proof of service showing that the settlement document was served on all other parties to the settlement, on any defendant not executing the settlement who may be liable for the payment of additional compensation, and on all lien claimants whose liens have not been resolved. A case

opening settlement document being submitted for a walk-through shall be submitted no later than noon (12:00 p.m.) of the court day before any action on the walk-through, and shall be designated as a walk-through document. All documents in support of the settlement document shall be submitted at the walk-through with the assigned workers' compensation judge.

(2) A walk-through petition (i.e., a petition for deposition attorney's fees, a petition for costs or a petition to compel attendance at a medical examination or deposition) and all other documents relating to the walk-through petition, including any supporting documentation shall be filed directly with the workers' compensation judge at the date and time of the walk-through. The party presenting the walk-through petition shall use the appropriate form, document cover sheet, and document separator sheet. In addition, at the date and time of the walk-through, the party filing the walk-through petition shall file a proof of service directly to the workers' compensation judge, as follows:

(A) For a petition for attorney's fees for representation of the applicant at a deposition, a proof of service showing service on the injured worker and the defendant alleged to be liable for paying the fees.

(B) For a petition to compel attendance at a medical examination or deposition, a proof of service showing service on the injured worker, the injured worker's attorney and all defendants.

(c) Each district office shall have a designee of the presiding workers' compensation judge available to assign walk-through cases from 8:00 a.m. to 11:00 a.m. and 1:00 p.m. to 4:00 p.m. on court days.

(d) When appearing for the walk-through proceeding, the party filing the walk-through document shall appear before the district office staff person designated by the presiding workers' compensation judge to assign the walk-through document to a workers' compensation judge. The filing party shall then appear before the assigned workers' compensation judge. If the assigned workers' compensation judge is unavailable for any reason, the filing party shall then proceed to the presiding workers' compensation judge for possible reassignment to another workers' compensation judge.

(e) A workers' compensation judge who is presented with a walk-through settlement document shall approve it, disapprove it, suspend action on it, or accept it for later review and action.

(f) A walk-through document may be acted on only by a workers' compensation judge at the district office that has venue. If an injured worker has existing cases at two or more district offices that have venue, a walk-through document may be filed at any office having venue over an existing case that is a subject of the walk-through document. An existing case is a case that has been filed and assigned a case number prior to the filing of the walk-through document.

(g) A walk-through document may be acted on by any workers' compensation judge except as follows:

(1) If a workers' compensation judge has taken testimony, any walk-through document in that case must be acted on by the judge who took testimony if that workers' compensation judge works at the district office to which the case is assigned, unless the presiding workers' compensation judge allows it to be acted on by another workers' compensation judge.

(2) If a workers' compensation judge has reviewed a document and declined to approve it, a walk-through document in that case must be acted on by the same workers' compensation judge, if that workers' compensation judge works at the district office to which the case is assigned, unless the presiding workers' compensation judge allows it to be acted on by another workers' compensation judge.

(h) A workers' compensation judge who is presented with a walk-through petition for attorney's fees, petition for costs or petition to compel attendance shall issue an order in compliance with rule 10832.

Note: Authority cited: Sections 133 and 5307, Labor Code. Reference: Sections 4053, 4054, 5001, 5002, 5702 and 5710, Labor Code.

History: 1. Renumbering and amendment of former section 10417 to section 10789 filed 12-17-2019; operative 1-1-2020. Submitted to OAL for printing only pursuant to Government Code section 11351 (Register 2019, No. 51).

§10790.   Interpreters.

It shall be the responsibility of any party producing a witness requiring an interpreter to arrange for the presence of a qualified interpreter. Subject to the rules of the Administrative Director, the Workers' Compensation Appeals

Board may in any case appoint an interpreter and fix the interpreter's compensation.

Note: Authority: Sections 130, 133, 5307 and 5708, Labor Code. Reference: Sections 4600, 4621, 5710 and 5811, Labor Code.

History: 1. Renumbering of former section 10564 to section 10790, including amendment of section and Note, filed 12-17-2019; operative 1-1-2020. Submitted to OAL for printing only pursuant to Government Code section 11351 (Register 2019, No. 51).

ARTICLE 14
Record of Proceedings

§10800. Transcripts.

Testimony taken at hearings will not be transcribed except upon the written request of a party accompanied by the fee prescribed in the Rules of the Administrative Director, or unless ordered by a commissioner, a deputy commissioner or presiding workers' compensation judge. Any written request shall be served on all parties.

Note: Authority cited: Sections 133, 5307, 5309 and 5708, Labor Code. Reference: Sections 5300, 5301, 5309, 5700, 5701 and 5708, Labor Code; and Section 703.5, Evidence Code.

History: 1. New article 14 heading and renumbering and amendment of former section 10740 to section 10800 filed 12-17-2019; operative 1-1-2020. Submitted to OAL for printing only pursuant to Government Code section 11351 (Register 2019, No. 51).

§10803. Record of Proceedings Maintained in Adjudication File.

(a) The Workers' Compensation Appeals Board's adjudication file shall consist of:

(1) All documents filed by any party, attorney or other agent of record, and as provided in rule 10205.4; and

(2) The record of proceedings, which consists of: the pleadings, minutes of hearing, summaries of evidence, certified transcripts, proofs of service, admitted evidence, exhibits identified but not admitted as evidence, notices, petitions, briefs, findings, orders, decisions and awards, opinions on decision, reports and recommendations on petitions for reconsideration and/or removal, and the arbitrator's file, if any. Each of these documents is part of the record of proceedings, whether maintained in paper or electronic form. Documents that are in the adjudication file but have not been received or

offered as evidence are not part of the record of proceedings.

(b) Upon approval of a Compromise and Release or Stipulations with Request for Award, all medical reports that have been filed as of the date of approval shall be deemed admitted in evidence and part of the record of proceedings.

Note: Authority cited: Sections 133, 5307, 5309 and 5708, Labor Code. Reference: Sections 126 and 5708, Labor Code.

History: 1. New section filed 12-17-2019; operative 1-1-2020. Submitted to OAL for printing only pursuant to Government Code section 11351 (Register 2019, No. 51).

§10807. Inspection of Workers' Compensation Appeals Board Records.

(a) The records and files of the Workers' Compensation Appeals Board shall not be taken from its offices on informal request, in response to a subpoena duces tecum, or in response to any order issued by any other court or tribunal.

(b) Except as precluded by Civil Code section 1798.24 or Government Code section 6254, certified copies of portions of the records desired by litigants shall be delivered upon payment of fees as provided in the Rules of the Administrative Director.

(c) Except as provided by rules 10208.6 and 10813, or as ordered by the presiding workers' compensation judge or the Appeals Board, the adjudication case files of the Workers' Compensation Appeals Board may be inspected in accordance with the provisions of rules 10208.5 and 10208.6.

Note: Authority cited: Sections 133, 5307, 5309 and 5708, Labor Code. Reference: Sections 126, 127, 5811 and 5955, Labor Code; Section 1798.24, Civil Code; and Section 6254, Government Code.

History: 1. New section filed 12-17-2019; operative 1-1-2020. Submitted to OAL for printing only pursuant to Government Code section 11351 (Register 2019, No. 51).

§10811. Destruction of Records.

Except as otherwise provided by these rules, or as ordered by a workers' compensation judge or the Appeals Board, the adjudication case files of the Workers' Compensation Appeals Board shall be retained, returned, and destroyed in accordance with the provisions of rule 10208.7.

Note: Authority cited: Sections 133, 5307, 5309 and 5708, Labor Code. Reference: Section 135, Labor Code.

History: 1. Renumbering and amendment of former section 10755 to section 10811 filed 12-17-2019; operative 1-1-2020. Submitted to OAL for printing only pursuant to Government Code section 11351 (Register 2019, No. 51).

§10813. Sealed Documents.

(a) The presiding workers' compensation judge or the Appeals Board may order sealed medical reports, medical records or other documents filed in a case containing references to or discussions of mental or emotional health of any person, sexual habits or practice, use of or addiction to alcohol or other drugs, or other matters of similar character. Sealed documents shall not be made available for public inspection except by order of the presiding workers' compensation judge or the Appeals Board upon a showing of good cause.

(b) A party requesting that documents be sealed shall file a petition to seal documents or portions thereof with either the district office having venue or with the Appeals Board, if the matter is pending there.

(1) Any petition to seal documents shall demonstrate good cause and shall be accompanied by a declaration containing facts sufficient to justify the sealing consistent with subdivision (c) of this rule.

(2) Documents that have not been filed prior to the petition to seal may be lodged with the Workers' Compensation Appeals Board concurrently with the filing of the petition to seal. A document shall be lodged in a sealed envelope with a coversheet that includes the ADJ number, a general description of the documents and a statement that "the documents are lodged pending the outcome of a petition to seal."

(3) If necessary to prevent disclosure, the petition, any opposition and any supporting documents must be filed in a public redacted version and lodged in a complete version conditionally under seal.

(4) If the presiding worker's compensation judge or the Appeals Board denies the petition to seal, the clerk shall return the lodged record to the submitting party and shall not place it in the adjudication file.

(5) Subsequently-filed documents shall not disclose material contained in a document previously sealed, conditionally sealed, or subject to a pending petition to seal.

(c) The presiding workers' compensation judge or the Appeals Board may order that a document be filed under seal or sealed only after expressly finding facts that establish:

(1) There exists an overriding public interest that overcomes the right of public access to the record;

(2) The overriding public interest supports sealing the record;

(3) A substantial probability exists that the overriding public interest will be prejudiced if the record is not sealed;

(4) The proposed sealing is narrowly tailored; and

(5) No less restrictive means exists to achieve the overriding public interest.

(d) Documents may be ordered sealed on the motion of the presiding workers' compensation judge or the Appeals Board if the injured employee is unrepresented or other good cause exists for sealing the documents. All parties shall be given notice and opportunity to be heard. After the issuance of a notice of intention to seal documents, the documents shall be lodged conditionally under seal pending the issuance of an order sealing the documents or an order finding no good cause to seal the documents.

(e)(1) An order sealing a document or documents shall be filed in the record of the proceedings. The order shall set forth the facts that support the findings and direct the sealing of only those documents and pages, or, if practicable, portions of those documents and pages containing the material that requires placement under seal.

(2) If the order directs that an entire document shall be sealed, and if the sealed document is contained in a paper adjudication file, the sealed document shall be placed in a sealed envelope, which shall be removed from the file before the file is made available for public inspection. If the sealed document is in an electronic adjudication file, the document shall be marked as sealed. No entirely sealed document in a paper file or an electronic file shall be available for public inspection.

(3) If the order directs that a portion or portions of a document be sealed, and if the partially sealed document is contained in a paper adjudication file, the partially sealed document shall be placed in a sealed envelope, however, a version of the document with the sealed portion redacted shall be made available for public inspection. If the sealed document is in an

electronic adjudication file, a version of the document with the sealed portion redacted also shall be electronically maintained and shall be made available for public inspection.

(f) Sealed documents shall be made available for inspection by any party to the case or by their representative, subject to any reasonable conditions and limitations as the presiding workers' compensation judge or the Appeals Board may impose.

Note: Authority cited: Sections 133, 5307, 5309 and 5708, Labor Code. Reference: Section 5708, Labor Code; and Rule 2.551, California Rules of Court.

History: 1. Renumbering and amendment of former section 10754 to section 10813 filed 12-17-2019; operative 1-1-2020. Submitted to OAL for printing only pursuant to Government Code section 11351 (Register 2019, No. 51).

§10818. Recording of Proceedings.

(a) For the purposes of this rule, "recording" means any photographing, recording, or broadcasting of trial level proceedings using video, film, audio, any digital media or other equipment.

(b) Except as provided in this rule, proceedings shall not be photographed, recorded, or broadcast. This rule does not prohibit the Division of Workers' Compensation (DWC) from photographing or videotaping sessions for judicial education or publications and is not intended to apply to closed-circuit television broadcasts solely within DWC or among DWC facilities if the broadcasts are controlled by DWC and DWC personnel.

(c) Recording shall be permitted only on written order by the assigned workers' compensation judge. The workers' compensation judge may permit, refuse or limit recording.

(1) Any person who wishes to record a proceeding shall make a written request to the assigned workers' compensation judge and shall serve the written request on all parties at least 10 business days before the proceeding commences unless good cause to shorten time is shown.

(2) The workers' compensation judge may hold a hearing on the request or rule on the request without a hearing.

(3) In ruling on the request, the workers' compensation judge shall consider the following factors:

(A) Importance of maintaining public trust and confidence in the workers' compensation system;

(B) Importance of promoting public access to the workers' compensation system;

(C) Parties' support of or opposition to the request;

(D) Nature of the case;

(E) Privacy rights of all participants in the proceeding, including witnesses;

(F) Effect on any minor who is a party, prospective witness, or other participant in the proceeding;

(G) Effect on any ongoing law enforcement activity in the case;

(H) Effect on any subsequent proceedings in the case;

(I) Effect of coverage on the willingness of witnesses to cooperate, including the risk that coverage will engender threats to the health or safety of any witness;

(J) Effect on excluded witnesses who would have access to the televised testimony of prior witnesses;

(K) Security and dignity of the trial level proceeding;

(L) Undue administrative or financial burden to DWC or participants;

(M) Interference with neighboring hearing rooms;

(N) Maintaining orderly conduct of the proceeding;

(O) Any other factor the workers' compensation judge deems relevant.

(4) The workers' compensation judge's ruling on the request to permit recording is not required to make findings or a statement of decision. The workers' compensation judge may condition the order permitting recording of the proceedings on the requestor's agreement to pay any increased costs incurred by DWC resulting from recording the proceeding (for example, for additional security). The requestor shall be responsible for ensuring that any person who records the trial level proceedings on their behalf know and follow the provisions of the order and this rule.

(5) The order permitting recordation may be modified or terminated on the workers' compensation judge's own motion or upon application to the workers' compensation judge without the necessity of a prior hearing or

written findings. Notice of the application and any modification or termination ordered pursuant to the application shall be given to the parties and each person permitted by the previous order to record the proceeding.

(6) The workers' compensation judge shall not permit recording of the following:

(A) Proceedings held in chambers that are not transcribed by a hearing reporter;

(B) Proceedings closed to the public; and

(C) Conferences between an attorney and a client, witness, or aide, between attorneys, or between counsel and the workers' compensation judge at the bench, unless transcribed by a hearing reporter.

(7) The workers' compensation judge may require a demonstration that people and equipment comply with this rule. The workers' compensation judge may specify the placement of equipment to minimize disruption of the proceedings.

(8) The following rules shall apply to all recording:

(A) One video recording device and one still photographer shall be permitted.

(B) The equipment used shall not produce distracting sound or light. Signal lights or devices to show when equipment is operating shall not be visible.

(C) Microphones and wiring shall be unobtrusively located in places approved by the workers' compensation judge and shall be operated by one person.

(D) Operators shall not move equipment or enter or leave the courtroom while the proceeding is in session, or otherwise cause a distraction.

(E) Equipment or clothing shall not bear the insignia or marking of a media agency.

(9) If two or more people request recordation of a proceeding, they shall file a statement of agreed arrangements. If they are unable to agree, the workers' compensation judge may deny a request to record the proceeding.

(d) Any violation of this rule or an order made under this rule is an unlawful interference with the proceedings and may be the basis for an order terminating recording, a citation for contempt, or an order imposing monetary or other sanctions as provided by law.

(e) Notwithstanding (a) through (d), a workers' compensation judge may permit inconspicuous personal recording devices to be used by parties in a courtroom to make sound recordings as personal notes of the proceedings. A person proposing to use a recording device shall obtain advance permission from the workers' compensation judge before recording the proceeding. The recording shall not be used for any purpose other than as personal notes, and shall not constitute evidence as to any matter recorded. The right of any individual to use a personal recording device shall be suspended if, in the workers' compensation judge's sole discretion, it appears that:

(1) The continued recording of the proceedings will inhibit any party or witness from participation in the proceeding; or

(2) The recording is done in a manner that threatens to disrupt the proceeding.

(f) Only the stenographic recording provided by an Official Hearing Reporter shall be deemed the official recording of a proceeding.

Note: Authority cited: Sections 133, 5307, 5309 and 5708, Labor Code. Reference: Rule 1.150, California Rules of Court.

History: 1. Renumbering former section 10760 to section 10818, including amendment of section heading and section, filed 12-17-2019; operative 1-1-2020. Submitted to OAL for printing only pursuant to Government Code section 11351 (Register 2019, No. 51).

§10820.   When Certified Copies Will Issue.

(a) Certified copies of findings, awards and other final orders for the purpose of having judgment entered and execution issued by the clerk of a superior court shall be issued by the presiding workers' compensation judge only upon written request of the person seeking to have judgment entered and execution issued, or by their attorney or non-attorney representative, and upon payment of the fees prescribed by the Rules of the Administrative Director.

(b) Certified copies of such orders and awards against authorized insurance carriers, authorized self-insured employers, the State of California and all political subdivisions thereof shall be issued only upon receipt of a written request showing good cause therefor.

(c) Every request for a certified copy of any final order must state whether proceedings are pending on reconsideration or judicial review, whether a petition for reconsideration or a writ of review has been filed, and whether the decision, a certified copy of which is requested has become final.

(d)   Nothing in these rules shall limit the power of the Workers' Compensation Appeals Board to issue a certified copy at any time upon its own motion without charge.

Note: Authority cited: Sections 133 and 5307, Labor Code. Reference: Sections 5806, 5807 and 5808, Labor Code.

History: 1. Amendment of section and Note filed 12-19-2002; operative 1-1-2003. Submitted to OAL for printing only pursuant to Government Code section 11351 (Register 2002, No. 51).
2. Repealer of article 16 heading and amendment of section filed 12-17-2019; operative 1-1-2020. Submitted to OAL for printing only pursuant to Government Code section 11351 (Register 2019, No. 51).

§10825.   Withholding Certified Copies.

As an alternative to the issuance of an order staying execution, the Workers' Compensation Appeals Board may direct by order that no certified copy be issued. Such an order shall have the same effect as an order staying execution issued under similar circumstances.

(a)   Before staying execution or issuing an order withholding issuance of a certified copy of an order, decision or award, the Workers' Compensation Appeals Board in its discretion may require the filing of a bond from an approved surety equivalent to twice the probable amount of liability in the case.

(b)   The bond shall be filed in the record of the case.

Note: Authority cited: Sections 133 and 5307, Labor Code. Reference: Sections 130, 134, 5105, 5806, 5807, 5808, 5809, 6000, 6001 and 6002, Labor Code.

History: 1. Amendment of subsection (a) filed 12-17-2019; operative 1-1-2020. Submitted to OAL for printing only pursuant to Government Code section 11351 (Register 2019, No. 51).

§10828.   Necessity for Bond.
[Repealed]

Note: Authority cited: Sections 133 and 5307, Labor Code. Reference: Sections 5808, 5956, 6000, 6001 and 6002, Labor Code.

History: 1. Amendment of section and Note filed 12-19-2002; operative 1-1-2003. Submitted to OAL for printing only pursuant to Government Code section 11351 (Register 2002, No. 51).
2. Repealer filed 12-17-2019; operative 1-1-2020. Submitted to OAL for printing only pursuant to

Government Code section 11351 (Register 2019, No. 51).

ARTICLE 15
Findings, Awards and Orders

§10832.   Notices of Intention and Orders after Notices of Intention.

(a)   The Workers' Compensation Appeals Board may issue a notice of intention for any proper purpose, including but not limited to:

(1)   Allowing or disallowing a lien;

(2)   Allowing or disallowing a petition for costs;

(3)   Sanctioning a party;

(4)   Submitting the matter on the record after a party fails to appear; or

(5)   Dismissing an application.

(b)   A Notice of Intention may be served by designated service in accordance with rule 10629.

(c)   If an objection is filed within the time provided, the Workers' Compensation Appeals Board, in its discretion may:

(1)   Sustain the objection;

(2)   Issue an order consistent with the notice of intention together with an opinion on decision; or

(3)   Set the matter for hearing.

(d)   Any order issued after a notice of intention shall be served by the Workers' Compensation Appeals Board pursuant to rule 10628.

(e)   An order with a clause rendering the order null and void if an objection is received is not a Notice of Intention and must be served by the Workers' Compensation Appeals Board.

Note: Authority cited: Sections 133 and 5307, Labor Code. Reference: Section 5307, Labor Code.

History: 1. New article 15 heading and new section filed 12-17-2019; operative 1-1-2020. Submitted to OAL for printing only pursuant to Government Code section 11351 (Register 2019, No. 51). For prior history, see Register 96, No. 43.

§10833.   Minute Orders.

Interlocutory or interim orders, including but not limited to orders of dismissal of improper or unnecessary parties, may be entered upon the minutes of hearing and will become the order of the Workers' Compensation Appeal Board upon the filing thereof.

Note: Authority cited: Sections 133 and 5307, Labor Code. Reference: Section 5307.5, Labor Code.

History: 1. Renumbering and amendment of former section 10570 to section 10833 filed 12-17-2019; operative 1-1-2020. Submitted to OAL for printing only pursuant to Government Code section 11351 (Register 2019, No. 51).

§10835. Effect of Stipulations.

(a) Findings, awards and orders may be based upon stipulations of parties in open court or upon written stipulation signed by the parties.

(b) No finding shall be made contrary to a stipulation of the parties without giving the parties notice and an opportunity to be heard.

Note: Authority cited: Sections 133 and 5307, Labor Code. Reference: Section 5702, Labor Code.

History: 1. New section filed 12-17-2019; operative 1-1-2020. Submitted to OAL for printing only pursuant to Government Code section 11351 (Register 2019, No. 51).

§10840. Approval of Attorney's Fee by Workers' Compensation Appeals Board Required.

(a) No attorney or agent shall request, demand or accept any money from a worker or dependent of a worker for the purpose of representing the worker or dependent of a worker before the Workers' Compensation Appeals Board or in any appellate procedure related thereto until the fee has been approved or set by the Workers' Compensation Appeals Board or an appellate court.

(b) Any agreement between any attorney or agent and a worker or dependent of a worker for payment of a fee shall be submitted to the Workers' Compensation Appeals Board for approval within 10 days after the agreement is made.

Note: Authority cited: Sections 133 and 5307, Labor Code. Reference: Sections 4903 and 4906, Labor Code.

History: 1. Repealer and new section filed 12-16-92; operative 2-1-93 and exempt from OAL review pursuant to Government Code section 11351 (Register 92, No. 51).

2. Amendment of section heading and text filed 12-23-93; operative 1-1-94. Submitted to OAL for printing only pursuant to Government Code section 11351 (Register 93, No. 52).

3. Amendment of article heading, section heading, section and Note filed 11-17-2008; operative 11-17-2008. Submitted to OAL for printing only (Register 2008, No. 47).

4. Repealer of article 17 heading, repealer of former section 10840 and renumbering former section 10776 to section 10840, including amendment of section heading and section, filed 12-17-2019; operative 1-1-2020. Submitted to OAL for printing only pursuant to Government Code section 11351 (Register 2019, No. 51).

§10842. Request for Increase of Attorney's Fee

All requests for an increase in attorney's fee shall be accompanied by proof of service on the applicant of written notice of the attorney's adverse interest and of the applicant's right to seek independent counsel. Failure to notify the applicant may constitute grounds for dismissal of the request for increase in fee.

Note: Authority cited: Sections 133 and 5307, Labor Code. Reference: Sections 4903 and 4906, Labor Code.

History: 1. New section filed 5-25-82; designated effective 7-1-82 (Register 82, No. 22).

2. Amendment of section heading and text filed 12-23-93; operative 1-1-94. Submitted to OAL for printing only pursuant to Government Code section 11351 (Register 93, No. 52).

3. Amendment of last paragraph filed 12-19-2002; operative 1-1-2003. Submitted to OAL for printing only pursuant to Government Code section 11351 (Register 2002, No. 51).

4. Amendment of section heading, section and Note filed 11-17-2008; operative 11-17-2008. Submitted to OAL for printing only (Register 2008, No. 47).

5. Renumbering of former section 10842 to section 10945 and renumbering and amendment of former section 10778 to section 10842 filed 12-17-2019; operative 1-1-2020. Submitted to OAL for printing only pursuant to Government Code section 11351 (Register 2019, No. 51).

§10843. Petitions for Removal and Answers. [Renumbered]

Note: Authority cited: Sections 133, 5307, 5309 and 5708, Labor Code. Reference: Section 5310, Labor Code.

History: 1. New section filed 12-23-93; operative 1-1-94. Submitted to OAL for printing only pursuant to Government Code section 11351 (Register 93, No. 52).

2. Amendment filed 12-12-2000; operative 1-1-2001. Submitted to OAL for printing only pursuant to Government Code section 11351 (Register 2000, No. 50).

5. Renumbering of former section 10842 to section 10945 and renumbering and amendment of former section 10778 to section 10842 filed 12-17-2019;

operative 1-1-2020. Submitted to OAL for printing only pursuant to Government Code section 11351 (Register 2019, No. 51).

3. Amendment filed 12-19-2002; operative 1-1-2003. Submitted to OAL for printing only pursuant to Government Code section 11351 (Register 2002, No. 51).

4. Amendment of section heading, section and Note filed 11-17-2008; operative 11-17-2008. Submitted to OAL for printing only (Register 2008, No. 47).

5. Renumbering of former section 10843 to section 10955 filed 12-17-2019; operative 1-1-2020. Submitted to OAL for printing only pursuant to Government Code section 11351 (Register 2019, No. 51).

§10844. Reasonable Attorney's Fee.

In establishing a reasonable attorney's fee, the workers' compensation judge or arbitrator shall consider the:

(a) Responsibility assumed by the attorney;

(b) Care exercised in representing the applicant;

(c) Time involved; and

(d) Results obtained.

Note: Authority cited: Sections 133 and 5307, Labor Code. Reference: Sections 4903 and 4906, Labor Code.

History: 1. New section filed 11-17-2008; operative 11-17-2008. Submitted to OAL for printing only (Register 2008, No. 47).

2. Repealer of former section 10844 and renumbering and amendment of former section 10775 to section 10844 filed 12-17-2019; operative 1-1-2020. Submitted to OAL for printing only pursuant to Government Code section 11351 (Register 2019, No. 51).

§10845. General Requirements for Petitions for Reconsideration, Removal, and Disqualification, and for Answers and Other Documents. [Repealed]

Note: Authority cited: Sections 133, 5307, 5309 and 5708, Labor Code. Reference: Sections 5310, 5311, 5900 and 5905, Labor Code.

History: 1. New section filed 11-17-2008; operative 11-17-2008. Submitted to OAL for printing only (Register 2008, No. 47).

2. Amendment of subsection (a) filed 9-23-2013; operative 10-23-2013. Submitted as a file and print by the Workers' Compensation Appeals Board pursuant to Government Code section 11351 (Register 2013, No. 39).

3. Amendment of subsection (a) filed 10-15-2014; operative 1-1-2015. Submitted to OAL for printing only pursuant to Government Code section 11351 (Register 2014, No. 42).

4. Editorial correction of History 3 (Register 2017, No. 8).

5. Repealer filed 12-17-2019; operative 1-1-2020. Submitted to OAL for printing only pursuant to Government Code section 11351 (Register 2019, No. 51).

§10846. Skeletal Petitions. [Renumbered]

Note: Authority cited: Sections 133, 5307, 5309 and 5708, Labor Code. Reference: Sections 5310, 5311, 5902, 5903 and 5904, Labor Code.

History: 1. Amendment of section and Note filed 11-17-2008; operative 11-17-2008. Submitted to OAL for printing only (Register 2008, No. 47).

2. Renumbering of former section 10846 to section 10972 filed 12-17-2019; operative 1-1-2020. Submitted to OAL for printing only pursuant to Government Code section 11351 (Register 2019, No. 51).

§10848. Supplemental Petitions. [Renumbered]

Note: Authority cited: Sections 133, 5307, 5309 and 5708, Labor Code. Reference: Sections 5310, 5311 and 5900, Labor Code.

History: 1. Repealer and new section filed 12-23-93; operative 1-1-94. Submitted to OAL for printing only pursuant to Government Code section 11351 (Register 93, No. 52).

2. Amendment of section and Note filed 11-17-2008; operative 11-17-2008. Submitted to OAL for printing only (Register 2008, No. 47).

3. Renumbering of former section 10848 to section 10964 filed 12-17-2019; operative 1-1-2020. Submitted to OAL for printing only pursuant to Government Code section 11351 (Register 2019, No. 51).

§10850. Order Dismissing Application.

(a) Orders of dismissal of Applications for Adjudication of Claim shall issue forthwith upon request by the employee unless there is good cause to not issue an order.

(b) All other orders of dismissal of Applications for Adjudication of Claim shall issue only after service of a notice of intention allowing at least 10 days for any adverse party to show good cause to the contrary, and not by an order with a clause rendering the order null and void if an objection showing good cause is filed.

Note: Authority cited: Sections 133 and 5307, Labor Code. Reference: Section 5307, Labor Code.

History: 1. Amendment of section and Note filed 12-19-2002; operative 1-1-2003. Submitted to OAL for printing only pursuant to Government Code section 11351 (Register 2002, No. 51).

2. Amendment of section and Note filed 11-17-2008; operative 11-17-2008. Submitted to OAL for printing only (Register 2008, No. 47).

3. Repealer of former section 10850 and renumbering of former section 10780 to section 10850, including amendment of section heading, section and Note, filed 12-17-2019; operative 1-1-2020. Submitted to OAL for printing only pursuant to Government Code section 11351 (Register 2019, No. 51).

§10852.   Insufficiency of Evidence. [Repealed]

Note: Authority cited: Sections 133 and 5307, Labor Code. Reference: Sections 5902 and 5903, Labor Code.

History: 1. Amendment filed 12-19-2002; operative 1-1-2003. Submitted to OAL for printing only pursuant to Government Code section 11351 (Register 2002, No. 51).

2. Repealer filed 12-17-2019; operative 1-1-2020. Submitted to OAL for printing only pursuant to Government Code section 11351 (Register 2019, No. 51).

§10856.   Allegations of Newly Discovered Evidence and Fraud. [Renumbered]

Note: Authority cited: Sections 133 and 5307, Labor Code. Reference: Sections 5902 and 5903, Labor Code.

History: 1. Amendment filed 12-19-2002; operative 1-1-2003. Submitted to OAL for printing only pursuant to Government Code section 11351 (Register 2002, No. 51).

2. Renumbering of former section 10856 to section 10974 filed 12-17-2019; operative 1-1-2020. Submitted to OAL for printing only pursuant to Government Code section 11351 (Register 2019, No. 51).

§10858.   Correction of Errors. [Renumbered]

Note: Authority cited: Sections 133 and 5307, Labor Code. Reference: Section 5309, Labor Code.

History: 1. Renumbering of former section 10858 to section 10966 filed 12-17-2019; operative 1-1-2020. Submitted to OAL for printing only pursuant to Government Code section 11351 (Register 2019, No. 51).

§10859.   Orders After Filing of Petition for Reconsideration. [Reunumbered]

Note: Authority cited: Section 5307, Labor Code. Reference: Sections 5906, 5907 and 5908.5, Labor Code.

History: 1. Repealer and new section filed 12-16-92; operative 2-1-93 and exempt from OAL review pursuant to Government Code section 11351 (Register 92, No. 51).

2. Amendment filed 12-19-2002; operative 1-1-2003. Submitted to OAL for printing only pursuant to Government Code section 11351 (Register 2002, No. 51).

3. Renumbering of former section 10859 to section 10961 filed 12-17-2019; operative 1-1-2020. Submitted to OAL for printing only pursuant to Government Code section 11351 (Register 2019, No. 51).

§10860.   Report of Workers' Compensation Judge. [Renumbered]

Note: Authority cited: Sections 133, 5307, 5309 and 5708, Labor Code. Reference: Sections 5900 and 5906, Labor Code.

History: 1. Amendment filed 12-23-93; operative 1-1-94. Submitted to OAL for printing only pursuant to Government Code section 11351 (Register 93, No. 52).

2. Amendment filed 12-19-2002; operative 1-1-2003. Submitted to OAL for printing only pursuant to Government Code section 11351 (Register 2002, No. 51).

3. Amendment of section and Note filed 11-17-2008; operative 11-17-2008. Submitted to OAL for printing only (Register 2008, No. 47).

4. Renumbering of former section 10860 to section 10962 filed 12-17-2019; operative 1-1-2020. Submitted to OAL for printing only pursuant to Government Code section 11351 (Register 2019, No. 51).

ARTICLE 16
Liens

§10862.   Filing and Service of Lien Claims and Supporting Documents.

(a)   A lien claim may be filed only if permitted by Labor Code section 4900 et seq. An otherwise permissible lien claim shall not be filed if doing so would violate the premature filing restrictions of Labor Code section 4903.6(a).

(b)   A section 4903(b) lien shall only be filed electronically in accordance with section 4903.05 and not by any other method.

(c)   All other lien claims may be filed utilizing an optical character recognition (OCR) lien claim form approved by the Appeals Board.

(d)   The claims of two or more providers of goods or services shall not be merged into a single lien. An individual provider may claim more than one type of lien on a single lien form by marking the "Other Lien(s)" checkbox on the form and by specifying the nature and statutory basis for each lien in that checkbox's associated text box.

(e) The following documents shall be concurrently filed with each lien claim:

(1) A proof of service;

(2) The verification under penalty of perjury outlined in rule 10863, if required; and

(4) Any other declaration or form required by law to be concurrently filed with a lien claim, including but not limited to documents required by Labor Code sections 4903.05, 4903.06 and 4903.8.

(f) Nothing in this rule shall preclude a medical treatment lien claimant from filing a lien claim if there are other outstanding disputes, including but not limited to injury, employment, jurisdiction, or the statute of limitations.

(g) All original and amended lien claims, and all related documents, including a full statement or itemized voucher for any section 4903(b) lien and any document listed in rule 10862(e) shall be served on:

(1) The injured worker or, if deceased, the worker's dependent(s), unless:

(A) The worker or dependent(s) is represented by an attorney or other agent of record, in which event service may be made solely upon the attorney or agent of record; or

(B) The underlying case of the worker or dependent(s) has been resolved; or

(C) The worker or the dependent(s) chooses not to proceed with the case.

(2) Any employer(s) or insurance carrier(s) that are parties to the case and, if represented, their attorney(s) or other agent(s) of record.

(h) The service of a lien claim on a defendant, or the service of notice of any claim that would be allowable as a lien, shall not constitute the filing of a lien within the meaning of these rules unless allowed by statute.

(i) Where a lien has been served on a party, that party shall have no obligation to file that lien with the Workers' Compensation Appeals Board.

(j) When serving an amended lien claim, the lien claimant shall indicate in the box set forth on the lien form that it is an "amended" lien claim and shall provide the name, mailing address and telephone number of a person with authority to resolve the lien claim on behalf of the lien claimant.

(k) Any lien claim filed in violation of the provisions of this rule may be deemed not filed for any purpose, including tolling or extending the time for filing the lien claim, and may not be acknowledged or returned to the filer and may be destroyed at any time without notice.

Note: Authority cited: Sections 133, 5307 and 5708, Labor Code. Reference: Sections 4900 et seq., 4903, 4903.05, 4903.06, 4903.8, 4903.1, 4903.4, 4903.5, 4903.6, 4904, 4603.2, 4603.3, 4603.6, 4610.5, 4610.6, 4616.3, 4616.4, 4622 and 5813, Labor Code.

History: 1. Amendment of section and Note filed 12-19-2002; operative 1-1-2003. Submitted to OAL for printing only pursuant to Government Code section 11351 (Register 2002, No. 51).

2. New article 16 heading, renumbering of former section 10862 to section 10984 and new section 10862 filed 12-17-2019; operative 1-1-2020. Submitted to OAL for printing only pursuant to Government Code section 11351 (Register 2019, No. 51).

§10863. Verification of Compliance with Labor Code Section 4903.6 on Filing of Lien Claim or Application by Lien Claimant.

(a) Any section 4903(b) lien, any lien for medical-legal costs and any application related to any such lien shall have attached to it a verification under penalty of perjury which shall contain a statement specifying in detail the facts establishing that both of the following have occurred:

(1) Sixty days have elapsed since after the date of acceptance or rejection of liability for the claim, or the time provided for investigation of liability pursuant to Labor Code section 5402(b) has elapsed, whichever is earlier; and

(2) Either of the following:

(A) The time provided for payment of medical treatment bills pursuant to Labor Code section 4603.2 has expired and, if the employer objected to the amount of the bill, the reasonable fee has been determined pursuant to Labor Code section 4603.6, and, if authorization for the medical treatment has been disputed pursuant to Labor Code section 4610, the medical necessity of the medical treatment has been determined pursuant to Labor Code sections 4610.5 and 4610.6; or

(B) The time provided for payment of medical-legal expenses pursuant to Labor Code section 4622 has expired and, if the employer objected to the amount of the bill, the reasonable fee has been determined pursuant to Labor Code section 4603.6.

(b) The verification under penalty of perjury shall also contain a statement declaring that the lien is not being filed solely because of a dispute subject to the independent medical review and/or the independent bill review process.

(c) In addition, if an Application for Adjudication of Claim is also being filed, the verification under penalty of perjury shall contain:

(1) A statement specifying in detail the facts establishing that venue in the district office being designated is proper pursuant to Labor Code section 5501.5(a)(1) or Labor Code section 5501.5(a)(2); and

(2) A statement specifying in detail the facts establishing that the filing lien claimant has made a diligent search and has determined that no adjudication case number exists for the same injured worker and same date of injury at any district office. A diligent search shall include contacting the injured worker, contacting the employer or carrier, or inquiring at the district office with appropriate venue pursuant to Labor Code section 5501.5(a)(1) or Labor Code section 5501.5(a)(2).

(d) The verification shall be in the following form:

I declare under penalty of perjury under the laws of the State of California:

(1) That the time periods set forth in rule 10863(a) have elapsed;

(2) That the section 4903(b) lien, the lien for medical-legal costs, or the application is not being filed solely because of a dispute subject to the independent medical review and/or independent bill review process; and

(3) That, if an Application for Adjudication of Claim is being filed, that venue is proper as set forth in rule 10863(b) and that I have made a diligent search and have determined that no adjudication case number exists for the same injured worker and the same date of injury. In determining that no adjudication case number exists for the same injured worker and the same date of injury, I have made a diligent search consisting of the following efforts (specify):

—————————————————————

—————————————————————

———————————————————— s/s

———————————————————— on

Failure to attach the verification or an incorrect verification may be a basis for sanctions.

(e) If the Appeals Board approves an e-form or optical character recognition (OCR)

form for this declaration, lien claimants shall file the declaration using the adopted form.

Note: Authority cited: Sections 133, 5307, 5309 and 5708, Labor Code. Reference: Sections 4603.2, 4603.6, 4610.5, 4610.6, 4622, 4903, 4903.6, 5402 and 5501.5, Labor Code.

History: 1. Renumbering of former section 10770.5 to section 10863, including amendment of section heading, section and Note, filed 12-17-2019; operative 1-1-2020. Submitted to OAL for printing only pursuant to Government Code section 11351 (Register 2019, No. 51).

§10864. Authority of Workers' Compensation Judge After Decision After Reconsideration. [Renumbered]

Note: Authority cited: Sections 133 and 5307, Labor Code. Reference: Sections 5900, 5910 and 5911, Labor Code.

History: 1. Amendment filed 5-25-82; designated effective 7-1-82 (Register 82, No. 22).

2. Amendment filed 12-19-2002; operative 1-1-2003. Submitted to OAL for printing only pursuant to Government Code section 11351 (Register 2002, No. 51).

3. Renumbering of former section 10864 to section 10986 and new section 10862 filed 12-17-2019; operative 1-1-2020. Submitted to OAL for printing only pursuant to Government Code section 11351 (Register 2019, No. 51).

§10865. Reconsideration of Arbitration Decisions Made Pursuant To Labor Code Sections 3201.5 and 3201.7. [Renumbered]

Note: Authority cited: Sections 133, 5307, 5309 and 5708, Labor Code. Reference: Sections 3201.5 and 3201.7, Labor Code.

History: 1. New section filed 12-23-93; operative 1-1-94. Submitted to OAL for printing only pursuant to Government Code section 11351 (Register 93, No. 52).

2. Amendment of section heading, section and Note filed 12-19-2002; operative 1-1-2003. Submitted to OAL for printing only pursuant to Government Code section 11351 (Register 2002, No. 51).

3. Amendment of section heading, section and Note filed 11-17-2008; operative 11-17-2008. Submitted to OAL for printing only (Register 2008, No. 47).

4. Renumbering of former section 10865 to section 10990 filed 12-17-2019; operative 1-1-2020. Submitted to OAL for printing only pursuant to Government Code section 11351 (Register 2019, No. 51).

§10866. Reconsideration of Arbitrator's Decisions or Awards Made Pursuant to the Mandatory or Voluntary Arbitration Provisions of Labor Code Sections 5270 through 5275. [Renumbered]

Note: Authority cited: Sections 133, 5307, 5309 and 5708, Labor Code. Reference: Sections 5273, 5275, 5277(c) and 5900-5911, Labor Code.

History: 1. New section filed 12-23-93; operative 1-1-94. Submitted to OAL for printing only pursuant to Government Code section 11351 (Register 93, No. 52).
2. Amendment of section and Note filed 12-19-2002; operative 1-1-2003. Submitted to OAL for printing only pursuant to Government Code section 11351 (Register 2002, No. 51).
3. Amendment of section heading, section and Note filed 11-17-2008; operative 11-17-2008. Submitted to OAL for printing only (Register 2008, No. 47).
4. Renumbering of former section 10866 to section 10995 filed 12-17-2019; operative 1-1-2020. Submitted to OAL for printing only pursuant to Government Code section 11351 (Register 2019, No. 51).

§10868. Notices of Representation for Lien Claimants.

(a) Whenever any lien claimant obtains representation after a lien has been filed, or changes such representation, the lien claimant shall, within 5 days, file and serve a notice of representation in accordance with rules 10390, 10400, 10401 and 10402. If a copy of the notice of representation is not in the record at the time of the hearing, the lien claimant's representative shall lodge a copy at the hearing and shall personally serve a copy on all parties appearing. Unless a representative signs an initial lien document on behalf of a lien claimant, a notice of representation is required.

(b) In addition to the requirements of rules 10390, 10400 and 10401, the notice shall:

(1) Include the caption, the case title (i.e., the name of the injured employee and the name of the defendant or primary defendant(s)) and the adjudication case number(s) to which the notice relates; and

(2) Set forth the full legal name, mailing address and telephone number of the lien claimant.

(c) The notice shall be verified by a declaration signed by the lien claimant and the lien claimant's representative under penalty of perjury stating:

(1) "I declare that the named initial or new representative has consented to represent the interests of the named lien claimant and that the named lien claimant has consented to this representation.";

(2) "This representation began on _____, _____, 20_____.

(A) "I am not aware of any other attorney or non-attorney who was previously representing the lien claimant."; or

(B) "I am aware that _____ [specify person or entity] was previously representing the lien claimant. This Notice of Representation supersedes any previous Notice of Representation. I hereby certify that I have notified the previous attorney or non-attorney representative in writing.";

(3) "By signing below, the representative affirms that they are not disqualified from appearing under Labor Code section 4907, WCAB rule 10445 (Cal. Code Regs., tit. 8, § 10445) or by any other rule, order or decision of the Workers' Compensation Appeals Board, the State Bar of California, or any court."

(d) Any violation of this rule may give rise to monetary sanctions, attorney's fees and costs under Labor Code section 5813 and rule 10421.

Note: Authority cited: Sections 133, 5307, 5309 and 5708, Labor Code. Reference: Sections 130, 4907 and 5710, Labor Code; Sections 284, 285 and 286, Code of Civil Procedure; and Sections 10390 and 10445, title 8, California Code of Regulations.

History: 1. New section filed 12-17-2019; operative 1-1-2020. Submitted to OAL for printing only pursuant to Government Code section 11351 (Register 2019, No. 51). For prior history, see Register 2002, No. 51.

§10870. Approval of Compromise and Release. [Repealed]

Note: Authority cited: Sections 133 and 5307, Labor Code. Reference: Sections 4646, 5001, 5002 and 5100.6, Labor Code.

History: 1. Amendment of article 18 heading and amendment of section and Note filed 12-19-2002; operative 1-1-2003. Submitted to OAL for printing only pursuant to Government Code section 11351 (Register 2002, No. 51).
2. Repealer of article 18 heading and section filed 12-17-2019; operative 1-1-2020. Submitted to OAL for printing only pursuant to Government Code section 11351 (Register 2019, No. 51).

§10872. Notification of Resolution or Withdrawal of Lien Claims.

(a) Within seven days after a lien has been

resolved or withdrawn, the lien claimant shall file and serve a notification of resolution or a withdrawal of the lien claim. For purposes of this rule, a lien is not resolved unless payment in accordance with an order or an informal agreement has been made and received.

(b) The lien claimant shall appear at any hearing that was noticed prior to the resolution or withdrawal of the lien unless excused by the Workers' Compensation Appeals Board. The lien claimant shall be excused from appearing at any subsequently noticed hearing.

(c) Any violation of this rule may give rise to monetary sanctions, attorney's fees and costs under Labor Code section 5813 and rule 10421.

Note: Authority cited: Sections 133, 5307, 5309 and 5708, Labor Code. Reference: Sections 4903, 4903.05, 4903.06, 4903.8, 4903.1, 4903.4, 4903.5, 4903.6, 4904, 4603.2, 4603.3, 4603.6, 4610.5, 4610.6, 4616.3, 4616.4, 4622 and 5813, Labor Code.

History: 1. New section filed 12-17-2019; operative 1-1-2020. Submitted to OAL for printing only pursuant to Government Code section 11351 (Register 2019, No. 51).

§10873. Lien Claimant Declarations of Readiness to Proceed.

(a) A lien conference shall be set when any party files a Declaration of Readiness to Proceed in accordance with rule 10742 on any issue(s) relating to lien claim other than in the case in chief, or by the Workers' Compensation Appeals Board on its own motion at any time.

(1) Based upon resources available and such other considerations as the Workers' Compensation Appeals Board in its discretion may deem appropriate, a lien conference may be set at any district office without the necessity of an order changing venue.

(2) Unless otherwise expressly stated in the notice of hearing, all unresolved lien claims and lien issues shall be heard at the lien conference, whether or not listed in any Declaration of Readiness to Proceed. An agreement to "pay, adjust or litigate" a lien claim, or its equivalent, or an award leaving a lien claim to be adjusted, is not a resolution of the lien claim or lien issue.

(3) Once a Declaration of Readiness to Proceed for a lien conference has been filed, it cannot be withdrawn. If the lien of a lien claimant that has filed a Declaration of Readiness to Proceed has been resolved, that lien claimant shall request that its lien be withdrawn in accordance with rule 10872.

(4) To the extent feasible, the date of the lien conference shall be no sooner than 60 days after the date the notice of hearing for it is served.

(b) When a party files and serves a Declaration of Readiness to Proceed on an issue relating to a lien claim other than in the case in chief, the party shall designate on the Declaration of Readiness to Proceed form that it is requesting a lien conference and shall not designate any other kind of conference. If a status conference or any other type of conference is requested or is set on the calendar, that status conference or other type of conference shall be deemed a lien conference and shall be governed by any and all rules applying to a lien conference.

(c) Nothing in this rule shall preclude the Workers' Compensation Appeals Board, in its discretion, from setting a type of hearing other than that requested in the Declaration of Readiness to Proceed.

(d) After a lien conference or lien trial has been ordered off calendar, no party or lien claimant shall file a new Declaration of Readiness to Proceed for at least 90 days. The Declaration of Readiness to Proceed shall designate that a lien conference is requested and shall state under penalty of perjury that there has been no hearing on the lien claim(s) or lien issue(s) within the preceding 90 days. Nothing in this subdivision shall preclude the Workers' Compensation Appeals Board from:

(1) Restoring the lien claim(s) or lien issue(s) to the lien conference or lien trial calendar on its own motion; or

(2) Restoring the lien claim(s) or lien issue(s) to the lien conference or lien trial calendar less than 90 days after the most recent hearing.

Note: Authority cited: Sections 133, 5307, 5309 and 5708, Labor Code. Reference: Sections 4903, 4903.05, 4903.06, 4903.1, 4903.4, 4903.5, 4903.6, 4904, 5502 and 5502.5, Labor Code.

History: 1. New section filed 12-17-2019; operative 1-1-2020. Submitted to OAL for printing only pursuant to Government Code section 11351 (Register 2019, No. 51).

§10874. Verification to Filing of Declaration of Readiness to Proceed by or on Behalf of Lien Claimant.

No Declaration of Readiness to Proceed shall be filed for a section 4903(b) lien, or for a lien claim for medical-legal costs, without an attached verification executed under penalty of perjury:

(a) Stating either that:

(1) The Declaration of Readiness to Proceed is not being filed because of a dispute solely subject to the independent medical review and/or independent bill review process; or

(2) A timely petition appealing the Administrative Director's determination regarding independent medical review and/or independent bill review has been filed; and

(b) Stating either that:

(1) The underlying case has been resolved; or

(2) At least six months have elapsed from the date of injury and the injured worker has chosen not to proceed with their case.

The declarant shall make a diligent search to determine that the injured worker has chosen not to proceed with their case and the verification shall specify the efforts made in conducting the diligent search. A diligent search shall include contacting the injured worker, contacting the employer or carrier, or inquiring at the district office with appropriate venue pursuant to Labor Code section 5501.5(a)(1) or Labor Code section 5501.5(a)(2).

The verification shall be in the following form:

I declare under penalty of perjury under the laws of the State of California that:

☐ The Declaration of Readiness to Proceed is not being filed because of a dispute subject to the independent medical review and/or independent bill review process; or

☐ A timely petition appealing the Administrative Director's determination regarding independent medical review and/or independent bill review has been filed (Check one box); and

☐ The underlying case has been resolved; or

☐ At least six months have elapsed from the date of injury and the injured worker has chosen not to proceed with their case (Check one box). In determining that the injured worker has chosen not to proceed with their case, I have made a diligent search consisting of the following efforts (specify):

_____

_____

_____ s/s

_____ on

_____

Failure to attach the verification or an incorrect verification may be a basis for sanctions.

(c) If the Appeals Board approves an e-form or optical character recognition (OCR) form for this declaration, lien claimants shall file the declaration using the adopted form.

Note: Authority cited: Sections 133, 5307, 5309 and 5708, Labor Code. Reference: Sections 4903, 4903.6 and 5501.5, Labor Code.

History: 1. Repealer of former section 10874 and renumbering of former section 10770.6 to section 10874, including amendment of section heading, section and Note, filed 12-17-2019; operative 1-1-2020. Submitted to OAL for printing only pursuant to Government Code section 11351 (Register 2019, No. 51).

§10875. Lien Conferences.

(a) All defendants and lien claimants shall appear at all lien conferences, either in person or by attorney or non-attorney representative. Each defendant, lien claimant, attorney and non-attorney representative appearing at any lien conference:

(1) Shall have sufficient knowledge of the lien dispute(s) to inform the workers' compensation judge as to all relevant factual and/or legal issues in dispute;

(2) Shall have authority to enter into binding factual stipulations; and

(3) Shall either have full settlement authority or have full settlement authority immediately available by telephone.

(b) If a lien claimant fails to appear at a lien conference, the worker's compensation judge may issue a notice of intention to dismiss consistent with rule 10888, or defer the lien.

(c) If a defendant does not appear, or for any other reason any lien claim(s) or lien issue(s) cannot be fully resolved at the lien conference, the workers' compensation judge shall take one of the following actions:

(1) Set a lien trial and close discovery;

(2) Upon a showing of good cause, allow a continuance of the lien conference to another lien conference; or

(3) Upon a showing of good cause, order the lien conference off calendar.

Good cause shall not include the delayed or late appointment of an attorney or non-attorney representative by a defendant or lien claimant or the delayed receipt of the defendant's or lien claimant's file by that attorney or non-attorney representative.

The action taken shall apply to all unresolved lien claim(s) or lien issue(s).

(d) For any lien claim(s) or lien issue(s) not fully resolved at the lien conference by an order signed by a workers' compensation judge and set for trial, the defendant(s) and lien claimant(s) shall prepare, sign, and file with the workers' compensation judge a Pre-Trial Conference Statement, which shall include:

(1) All stipulations;

(2) The specific issues in dispute;

(3) All documentary evidence that might be offered at the lien trial; and

(4) All witnesses who might testify at the lien trial.

The right to present any issue, documentary evidence, or witness not listed in the Pre-Trial Conference Statement shall be deemed waived, absent a showing of good cause. Evidence not disclosed on the Pre-Trial Conference Statement or obtained thereafter shall not be admissible unless the proponent of the evidence can demonstrate that it was not available or could not have been discovered by the exercise of due diligence prior to the lien conference.

(e) Any violation of the provisions of this rule may give rise to monetary sanctions, attorney's fees and costs under Labor Code section 5813 and rule 10421.

Note: Authority cited: Sections 133, 5307, 5309 and 5708, Labor Code. Reference: Sections 4903, 4903.05, 4903.06, 4903.1, 4903.4, 4903.5, 4903.6, 4904, 5502 and 5502.5, Labor Code.

History: 1. New section filed 12-23-93; operative 1-1-94. Submitted to OAL for printing only pursuant to Government Code section 11351 (Register 93, No. 52).

2. Amendment of penultimate paragraph filed 12-19-2002; operative 1-1-2003. Submitted to OAL for printing only pursuant to Government Code section 11351 (Register 2002, No. 51).

3. Renumbering of former section 10875 to section 10705 and new section 10875 filed 12-17-2019; operative 1-1-2020. Submitted to OAL for printing only pursuant to Government Code section 11351 (Register 2019, No. 51).

§10876. Fees Required at Lien Conference.

(a) No lien claimant that is required to pay a lien filing or lien activation fee shall file a Declaration of Readiness to Proceed or partici-

pate in any lien conference, including obtaining an order allowing its lien in whole or in part, without submitting written proof of prior timely payment of the fee.

(b) At the lien conference, there shall be a rebuttable presumption that a lien claimant is required to pay a lien filing fee or activation fee.

(1) If a lien claimant asserts it is an entity listed in Labor Code sections 4903.05(c)(7) or 4903.06(b), it shall be prepared to file proof or submit a stipulation to that effect at the lien conference upon request by the workers' compensation judge. The workers' compensation judge, however, may formally or informally take judicial notice that the lien claimant is such an entity. This may include, but is not necessarily limited to, taking judicial notice of prior decisions of the Workers' Compensation Appeals Board and taking judicial notice based on the "common knowledge" or the "not reasonably subject to dispute" provisions of Evidence Code section 452(g) and (h).

(2) If a lien claimant asserts under Labor Code section 4903.06(a) that it already paid a filing fee as required by former Labor Code section 4903.05 as added by Chapter 639 of the Statutes of 2003, it shall submit written proof of such payment at the lien conference.

(c) The following requirements must be met to satisfy the lien claimant's burden of demonstrating prior timely payment:

(1) Proof of prior timely payment shall be in the form provided by the Rules of the Administrative Director or by a printout from the Public Information Search Tool of EAMS. An offer of proof or a stipulation that payment was made shall not be adequate.

(2) Proof of prior timely payment of a filing fee must establish that the fee was paid contemporaneously with the filing of the lien.

(3) Proof of prior timely payment of an activation fee must establish that the fee was paid before the scheduled starting time of the lien conference set forth in the notice of hearing, except that, if the lien claimant filed the Declaration of Readiness to Proceed, the proof shall establish that the activation fee was paid contemporaneously with the filing of the Declaration of Readiness to Proceed.

(d) If a lien claimant fails to submit proper written proof of prior timely payment, the Workers' Compensation Appeals Board may elect to conduct a search within the Electronic Adjudication Management System to confirm prior timely payment, but is not obligated to do so, and a failure to conduct such a search shall not be a proper basis for a petition for reconsideration, removal, or disqualification.

(e) If a lien claimant that is required to pay a lien filing or activation fee fails to provide proper written proof of prior timely payment, then:

(1) If the proof of prior timely payment of the activation fee is not submitted, the lien claim shall be dismissed with prejudice. This provision shall apply even if, but for the lien conference, the activation fee would not have been due until December 31, 2013.

(2) If the proof of prior timely payment of the filing fee is not submitted, the lien claim shall be deemed dismissed by operation of law as of the time of its filing, except that if the lien claimant filed a Declaration of Readiness to Proceed its lien shall be dismissed with prejudice; however, in neither case shall the dismissed lien toll, preserve, or extend any applicable statute of limitations.

(f) A lien claimant shall not avoid dismissal by attempting to pay the fee at or after the hearing.

Note: Authority cited: Sections 133, 5307, 5309 and 5708, Labor Code. Reference: Sections 4903, 4903.05, 4903.06, 4903.1, 4903.4, 4903.5, 4903.6, 4904, 5502 and 5502.5, Labor Code; and Sections 351, 352, 451 and 452, Evidence Code.

History: 1. New section filed 12-17-2019; operative 1-1-2020. Submitted to OAL for printing only pursuant to Government Code section 11351 (Register 2019, No. 51).

§10878. Submission at Lien Conferences.

(a) The workers' compensation judge may order that any unresolved lien claim(s) or lien issue(s) be submitted for decision solely on the exhibits listed in the Pre-Trial Conference Statement if no witnesses are listed in the Pre-Trial Conference Statement.

(b) If the disputed lien claim(s) or lien issue(s) are submitted for decision at the lien conference, the workers' compensation judge shall prepare minutes of hearing and a summary of evidence as set forth in rule 10787.

Note: Authority cited: Sections 133, 5307, 5309 and 5708, Labor Code. Reference: Sections 4903, 4903.05, 4903.06, 4903.1, 4903.4, 4903.5, 4903.6,

4904, 5502 and 5502.5, Labor Code; and Sections 351, 352, 451 and 452, Evidence Code.

History: 1. Amendment of section heading, section and Note filed 12-19-2002; operative 1-1-2003. Submitted to OAL for printing only pursuant to Government Code section 11351 (Register 2002, No. 51).

2. Repealer and new section filed 12-17-2019; operative 1-1-2020. Submitted to OAL for printing only pursuant to Government Code section 11351 (Register 2019, No. 51).

§10880. Lien Trials.

(a) All defendants and lien claimants shall appear at all lien trials, either in person or by attorney or non-attorney representative. Each defendant, lien claimant, attorney and non-attorney representative appearing at any lien trial:

(1) Shall have sufficient knowledge of the lien dispute(s) to inform the workers' compensation judge as to all relevant factual and/or legal issues in dispute;

(2) Shall have authority to enter into binding factual stipulations; and

(3) Shall either have full settlement authority or have full settlement authority immediately available by telephone.

(b) Where a lien claimant or defendant served with notice of a lien trial fails to appear either in person or by attorney or non-attorney representative, the workers' compensation judge may:

(1) Dismiss the lien claim after issuing a 10-day notice of intention to dismiss with or without prejudice, or

(2) Hear the evidence and, after service of the minutes of hearing and summary of evidence that shall include a 10-day notice of intention to submit, make such decision as is just and proper, or

(3) Defer the issue of the lien and submit the case on the remaining issues.

(c) If the workers' compensation judge defers a lien issue, upon the issuance of a decision on the remaining issues, the workers' compensation judge shall:

(1) Issue a 10-day notice of intention to order payment of the lien in full or in part, or

(2) Issue a 10-day notice of intention to disallow the lien, or

(3) Continue the lien issue to a lien conference.

(d) At the conclusion of a lien trial, the workers' compensation judge shall prepare minutes of hearing and a summary of evidence as set forth in rule 10787.

(e) Any violation of the provisions of this rule may give rise to monetary sanctions, attorney's fees and costs under Labor Code section 5813 and rule 10421.

Note: Authority cited: Sections 133 and 5307, Labor Code. Reference: Article XIV, Section 4, California Constitution; and Sections 5502(e) and 5708, Labor Code.

History: 1. New section filed 12-17-2019; operative 1-1-2020. Submitted to OAL for printing only pursuant to Government Code section 11351 (Register 2019, No. 51).

§10882.   Action on Settlement Agreement. [Repealed]

Note: Authority cited: Sections 133 and 5307, Labor Code. Reference: Sections 5001, 5002 and 5702, Labor Code.

History: 1. Amendment of section heading, section and Note filed 12-19-2002; operative 1-1-2003. Submitted to OAL for printing only pursuant to Government Code section 11351 (Register 2002, No. 51).
2. Repealer filed 12-17-2019; operative 1-1-2020. Submitted to OAL for printing only pursuant to Government Code section 11351 (Register 2019, No. 51).

§10886.   Service on Lien Claimants. [Renumbered]

Note: Authority cited: Sections 133 and 5307, Labor Code. Reference: Sections 4903, 4903.05, 4903.1, 4903.4, 4904, 4904.1, 4905 and 4906, Labor Code.

History: 1. Amendment exempt from OAL review pursuant to Government Code section 11351 filed 12-19-90; operative 1-1-91 (Register 91, No. 7).
2. Amendment filed 12-19-2002; operative 1-1-2003. Submitted to OAL for printing only pursuant to Government Code section 11351 (Register 2002, No. 51).
3. Amendment of section and Note filed 9-23-2013; operative 10-23-2013. Submitted as a file and print by the Workers' Compensation Appeals Board pursuant to Government Code section 11351 (Register 2013, No. 39).
4. Renumbering of former section 10886 to section 10702 filed 12-17-2019; operative 1-1-2020. Submitted to OAL for printing only pursuant to Government Code section 11351 (Register 2019, No. 51).

§10888.   Dismissal of Lien Claims.

(a) The Appeals Board or a workers' compensation judge may order a lien dismissed for lack of prosecution, non-appearance by the lien claimant or failure to comply with the provisions of the Labor Code or these rules.

(b) A lien claim may be dismissed for lack of prosecution on a petition filed by a party or on the Appeals Board's or the workers' compensation judge's own motion if the lien claimant fails to file a Declaration of Readiness to Proceed within:

(1) 180 days after the underlying case of the injured employee or the dependent(s) of a deceased employee has been resolved or the injured employee or the dependent(s) of a deceased employee choose(s) not to proceed with the case; or

(2) 180 days after a lien conference or lien trial is ordered off calendar if the lien claim was at issue.

(c) A dismissal for failure to appear at a hearing shall only issue if the lien claimant was provided with notice of the lien conference or lien trial.

(d) A dismissal for failure to comply with the Labor Code or these rules shall only be issued if the lien claimant has failed to comply with a statute or rule that provides that a lien may be dismissed for non-compliance.

(e) Before issuing an Order dismissing a lien, the Workers' Compensation Appeals Board shall issue a Notice of Intention to Dismiss the lien claim consistent with rule 10832 that provides at least 10 days for the lien claimant to file and serve a response showing good cause why an Order dismissing the lien should not issue.

Note: Authority cited: Sections 133, 5307, 5309 and 5708, Labor Code. Reference: Sections 4903, 4903.05, 4903.06, 4903.1, 4903.4, 4903.5, 4903.6, 4904, 5502, 5502.5 and 5404.5, Labor Code.

History: 1. New section filed 12-19-2002; operative 1-1-2003. Submitted to OAL for printing only pursuant to Government Code section 11351 (Register 2002, No. 51).
2. Repealer and new section filed 12-17-2019; operative 1-1-2020. Submitted to OAL for printing only pursuant to Government Code section 11351 (Register 2019, No. 51).

§10899.   Unemployment Compensation Disability Liens.

When an unemployment compensation disability lien is filed by the Employment Development Department, there shall be a rebuttable presumption that the amounts stated therein have been paid to the injured worker by the Employment Development Department.

In any case involving a lien claim for unemployment compensation disability benefits or unemployment compensation benefits and extended duration benefits where it appears that further benefits may have been paid subsequent to the filing of the claim of lien, the workers' compensation judge shall notify the lien claimant when the case is ready for decision or for Order Approving Compromise and Release, and the lien claimant shall have five 5 days thereafter in which to file and serve an amended lien reflecting all payments made to and including the date of filing of the amended lien.

In cases where a Compromise and Release is filed and continuing unemployment compensation disability benefits or unemployment compensation benefits and extended duration benefits are being paid, the workers' compensation judge will ascertain the full amount of the lien claim as of the time of the approval of the Compromise and Release so that the allocation made under the authority of Labor Code section 4904 may be changed to reflect unemployment compensation disability or unemployment compensation and extended duration payments to the date of decision.

Note: Authority cited: Sections 133 and 5307, Labor Code. Reference: Sections 4903 and 4904, Labor Code.

History: 1. Renumbering and amendment of former section 10772 to section 10899 filed 12-17-2019; operative 1-1-2020. Submitted to OAL for printing only pursuant to Government Code section 11351 (Register 2019, No. 51).

ARTICLE 17
Arbitration

§10900.   Mandatory Arbitration.

Unless the applicant is not represented by an attorney, any party may file an arbitration submittal form after a defendant denies liability for benefits because it disputes insurance coverage.

Any party may file an arbitration submittal form after a petition for contribution pursuant to Labor Code section 5500.5 has been filed.

Any party may file a petition objecting to arbitration submittal if the party asserts the issues in dispute are not subject to mandatory arbitration pursuant to Labor Code section 5275(a). Upon receipt of an arbitration submittal

form or an objection to an arbitration submittal form, the presiding workers' compensation judge may set the matter for a status conference to determine if the issues in dispute are subject to mandatory arbitration.

Note: Authority cited: Sections 133, 5307, 5309 and 5708, Labor Code. Reference: Sections 5270, 5272, 5275, 5276, 5277 and 5500.5, Labor Code

History: 1. New article 17 heading and new section filed 12-17-2019; operative 1-1-2020. Submitted to OAL for printing only pursuant to Government Code section 11351 (Register 2019, No. 51).

§10905.   Voluntary Arbitration.

The parties agreeing to submit an issue or issues to voluntary arbitration shall jointly submit an arbitration submittal form outlining the issues they propose to submit to arbitration.

Unless there is an existing ADJ number, an Application for Adjudication of Claim shall be concurrently filed with an arbitration submittal form.

Upon receipt of an arbitration submittal form, the presiding workers' compensation judge may set the matter for a status conference to clarify the issues submitted to the arbitrator or to ensure compliance with Labor Code section 5270.

Note: Authority cited: Sections 133, 5307, 5309 and 5708, Labor Code. Reference: Sections 5270, 5271, 5272, 5273, 5275, 5276 and 5277, Labor Code.

History: 1. New section filed 12-17-2019; operative 1-1-2020. Submitted to OAL for printing only pursuant to Government Code section 11351 (Register 2019, No. 51).

§10910.   Selection of Arbitrator.

(a)   If the parties agree on an arbitrator, the parties shall file a proposed order appointing arbitrator concurrently with the arbitration submittal form. The presiding workers' compensation judge shall, within 10 days of receipt of the arbitration submittal form and proposed order, issue an Order Appointing Arbitrator or set the matter for a status conference.

(b)   If the arbitration submittal form requests a panel pursuant to Labor Code section 5271, the presiding workers' compensation judge shall, within 10 days of receipt of the arbitration submittal form, serve on each of the parties an identical list of arbitrators selected at random pursuant to Labor Code 5271(b).

(1)   Within 10 days of service of the list of arbitrators, any party may file a petition to disqualify an arbitrator for reasons set forth in

section 170.1 of the Code of Civil Procedure. A timely petition for disqualification suspends the arbitrator selection process until the presiding workers' compensation judge acts on the petition. Together with any order issued regarding the petition for disqualification, the presiding workers' compensation judge shall set forth time limits for striking names.

(2)　Within 15 days of service of the list of arbitrators, each party may strike two names from the list and serve notice of the names struck on all parties to the arbitration. Failure to serve notice waives a party's right to participate in the arbitrator selection process.

(3)　The presiding workers' compensation judge shall, within 30 days of receipt of the arbitration submittal form, issue an Order Appointing Arbitrator or set the matter for a status conference.

(c)　Only the arbitrator named in the Order Appointing Arbitrator shall conduct the arbitration.

(d)　An arbitrator shall not communicate with any party regarding the merits of the issues to be arbitrated until appointed as the named arbitrator in the Order Appointing Arbitrator.

Note: Authority cited: Sections 133, 5307, 5309 and 5708, Labor Code. Reference: Sections 5271, 5272, 5273, 5275, 5276 and 5277, Labor Code; and Section 170.1, Code of Civil Procedure.

History: 1. New section filed 12-17-2019; operative 1-1-2020. Submitted to OAL for printing only pursuant to Government Code section 11351 (Register 2019, No. 51).

§10912.　Disqualification of Arbitrator.

After service of a list of panel members pursuant to rule 10910, any party may, within 10 days, petition the presiding workers' compensation judge to remove any member from the panel pursuant to section 170.1 of the Code of Civil Procedure. If the presiding workers' compensation judge finds cause under section 170.1 of the Code of Civil Procedure, the presiding workers' compensation judge shall remove the member or members of the panel challenged and add to the original list the appropriate number of arbitrators at random to make a full panel and, within 10 days, serve the list on the parties.

If the presiding workers' compensation judge selects an arbitrator pursuant to rule 10910, the parties will have 10 days after service of the name of the arbitrator to petition to disqualify that arbitrator pursuant to section 170.1 of the

Code of Civil Procedure. If the presiding workers' compensation judge finds cause, the presiding workers' compensation judge shall assign another arbitrator pursuant to Labor Code section 5271(d) and order the issue or issues in dispute submitted to that arbitrator.

Note: Authority cited: Sections 133, 5307, 5309 and 5708, Labor Code. Reference: Sections 5271, 5272, 5273, 5275, 5276 and 5277, Labor Code; and Section 170.1, Code of Civil Procedure.

History: 1. Renumbering of former section 10998 to section 10912, including amendment of section and Note, filed 12-17-2019; operative 1-1-2020. Submitted to OAL for printing only pursuant to Government Code section 11351 (Register 2019, No. 51).

§10914.　Record of Arbitration Proceeding.

(a)　The arbitrator shall make and maintain the record of the arbitration proceeding and shall file the record with the Appeals Board when required by this rule or rule 10940.

(b)　The parties shall provide the arbitrator with a copy of the Arbitration Submittal Form and the Order Appointing Arbitrator.

(c)　The record of arbitration proceedings shall include the following:

(1)　Order Appointing Arbitrator;

(2)　Notices of appearance of the parties involved in the arbitration;

(3)　Minutes of the arbitration proceedings, identifying those present, the date of the proceeding, the disposition and those served with the minutes or the identification of the party designated to serve the minutes;

(4)　Pleadings, petitions, objections, briefs and responses filed by the parties with the arbitrator;

(5)　Exhibits filed by the parties;

(6)　Stipulations and issues entered into by the parties;

(7)　Arbitrator's Summary of Evidence containing evidentiary rulings, a description of exhibits admitted into evidence, the identification of witnesses who testified and summary of witness testimony;

(8)　Verbatim transcripts of witness testimony if witness testimony was taken under oath.

(9)　Findings, orders, awards, decisions and opinions on decision made by the arbitrator; and

(10)　Arbitrator's report on petition for reconsideration, removal or disqualification.

(d) The arbitrator shall file any finding, order or award together with the opinion on decision with the Appeals Board when it is served on the parties.

Note: Authority cited: Sections 133, 5307, 5309 and 5708, Labor Code. Reference: Sections 5271, 5272, 5273, 5275, 5276 and 5277, Labor Code.

History: 1. New section filed 12-17-2019; operative 1-1-2020. Submitted to OAL for printing only pursuant to Government Code section 11351 (Register 2019, No. 51).

§10920. Arbitrator Fee and Cost Disputes.

Any dispute involving an arbitrator's fee or cost shall be resolved by the presiding workers' compensation judge of the district office having venue.

Any request to resolve a dispute about arbitrator fees or costs must be accompanied by any written agreement pertaining to arbitrator fees or costs and a statement that shall include the nature of the dispute and an itemization of the hours spent in actual arbitration hearing, in preparation for arbitration, and in preparation of the decision. The statement shall also include an itemization of the verifiable costs including use of facility, reporters and transcript preparation.

An arbitrator's fee shall not exceed a reasonable amount. In establishing a reasonable fee, the presiding workers' compensation judge shall consider:

(a) Responsibility assumed by the arbitrator;

(b) Experience of the arbitrator;

(c) Number and complexity of the issues being arbitrated;

(d) Time involved; and

(e) Expeditiousness and completeness of issue resolution.

The presiding workers' compensation judge of each district office shall maintain statistics on all arbitration fees awarded pursuant to Labor Code section 5273(c) including the amount and rationale for the award pursuant to (a) through (e) above.

Arbitration costs will be allowed in a reasonable amount pursuant to Labor Code section 5273(a).

Note: Authority: Sections 133, 5307, 5309 and 5708, Labor Code. Reference: Sections 5271, 5273, 5275, 5276 and 5277, Labor Code.

History: 1. Renumbering of former section 10999 to section 10920, including amendment of section and

Note, filed 12-17-2019; operative 1-1-2020. Submitted to OAL for printing only pursuant to Government Code section 11351 (Register 2019, No. 51).

ARTICLE 18
Reconsideration, Removal and Disqualification

§10940. Filing and Service of Petitions for Reconsideration, Removal, Disqualification and Answers.

(a) Petitions for reconsideration, removal, or disqualification and answers shall be filed in EAMS or with the district office having venue in accordance with Labor Code section 5501.5 unless otherwise provided. Petitions for reconsideration of decisions after reconsideration of the Appeals Board shall be filed with the office of the Appeals Board. Petitions filed in EAMS pursuant to this rule must comply with rules 10205.10-10205.14.

(b) No duplicate copies shall be filed with any district office or with the Appeals Board. No documents sent directly to the Appeals Board by fax or e-mail will be accepted for filing, unless otherwise ordered by the Appeals Board.

(c) Every petition and answer shall be verified upon oath in the manner required for verified pleadings in courts of record. A verification and a proof of service shall be attached to each petition and answer. Failure to file a proof of service shall constitute valid ground for dismissing the petition.

(d) A petition shall not exceed 25 pages and an answer shall not exceed 10 pages unless allowed by the Appeals Board. Any verification, proof of service, exhibit, document cover sheet or document separator sheet filed with the petition or answer shall not be counted in determining the page limitation. Upon its own motion or upon a showing of good cause, the Appeals Board may allow the filing of a petition or answer that exceeds the page limitations. A request to exceed the page limitations shall be made by a separate petition, made under penalty of perjury, that specifically sets forth reasons why the request should be granted.

(e) If the petition seeks removal or reconsideration of an arbitrator's decision or disqualification of an arbitrator, the petition and any answer shall be served on the arbitrator and all affected parties in accordance with rule 10610.

Note: Authority cited: Sections 133, 5307, 5309 and 5708, Labor Code. Reference: Sections 5501.5, 5900, 5902 and 5905, Labor Code.

History: 1. Amendment filed 6-28-83; designated effective 7-1-83 pursuant to Government Code Section 11346.2(d) (Register 83, No. 27).
2. Amendment of last paragraph filed 12-19-2002; operative 1-1-2003. Submitted to OAL for printing only pursuant to Government Code section 11351 (Register 2002, No. 51).
3. Repealer of article 19 heading, new article 18 heading and repealer and new section filed 12-17-2019; operative 1-1-2020. Submitted to OAL for printing only pursuant to Government Code section 11351 (Register 2019, No. 51).

§10942. Service. [Repealed]

Note: Authority cited: Sections 133 and 5307, Labor Code. Reference: Sections 4750, 4751, 4753, 4753.5 and 4754.5, Labor Code.

History: 1. Amendment filed 6-28-83; designated effective 7-1-83 pursuant to Government Code Section 11346.2(d) (Register 83, No. 27).
2. Amendment filed 12-19-2002; operative 1-1-2003. Submitted to OAL for printing only pursuant to Government Code section 11351 (Register 2002, No. 51).
3. Repealer filed 12-17-2019; operative 1-1-2020. Submitted to OAL for printing only pursuant to Government Code section 11351 (Register 2019, No. 51).

§10945. Required Content of Petitions for Reconsideration, Removal, Disqualification and Answers.

(a) Every petition for reconsideration, removal or disqualification shall fairly state all of the material evidence relative to the point or points at issue. Each contention shall be separately stated and clearly set forth. A failure to fairly state all of the material evidence may be a basis for denying the petition.

(b) Every petition and answer shall support its evidentiary statements by specific references to the record.

(1) References to any stipulations, issues or testimony contained in any Minutes of Hearing, Summary of Evidence or hearing transcript shall specify:

(A) The date and time of the hearing; and

(B) If available, the page(s) and line number(s) of the Minutes, Summary, or transcript to which the evidentiary statement relates (e.g., "Summary of Evidence, 5/1/08 trial, 1:30pm session, at 6:11-6:15").

(2) References to any documentary evidence shall specify:

(A) The exhibit number or letter of the document;

(B) Where applicable, the author(s) of the document;

(C) Where applicable, the date(s) of the document; and

(D) The relevant page number(s) (e.g., "Exhibit M, Report of John A. Jones, M.D., 6/16/08 at p. 7.").

(3) References to any deposition transcript shall specify:

(A) The exhibit number or letter of the document;

(B) The name of the person deposed;

(C) The date of the deposition; and

(D) The relevant page number(s) and line(s) (e.g., "Exh. 3, 6/20/08 depo of William A. Smith, M.D., at 21:20-22:5]").

(c)(1) Copies of documents that have already been received in evidence or that have already been made part of the adjudication file shall not be attached or filed as exhibits to petitions for reconsideration, removal, or disqualification or answers. Documents attached in violation of this rule may be detached from the petition or answer and discarded.

(2) A document that is not part of the adjudication file shall not be attached to or filed with a petition for reconsideration or answer unless a ground for the petition for reconsideration is newly discovered evidence.

(3) A document shall not be attached to or filed with a petition for removal or disqualification or answer unless the document is not part of the adjudication file and is relevant to a petition for removal or disqualification.

Note: Authority cited: Sections 133, 5307, 5309 and 5708, Labor Code. Reference: Sections 126, 5310, 5311, 5900, 5902 and 5904, Labor Code.

History: 1. Renumbering of former section 10842 to section 10945, including amendment of section heading and section, filed 12-17-2019; operative 1-1-2020. Submitted to OAL for printing only pursuant to Government Code section 11351 (Register 2019, No. 51).

§10946. Medical Reports in Subsequent Injuries Benefits Trust Fund Cases. [Repealed]

Note: Authority cited: Sections 133, 5307, 5309 and 5708, Labor Code.

History: 1. Amendment filed 6-28-83; designated effective 7-1-83 pursuant to Government Code Section 11346.2(d) (Register 83, No. 27).

2. Amendment of section and Note filed 12-19-2002; operative 1-1-2003. Submitted to OAL for printing only pursuant to Government Code section 11351 (Register 2002, No. 51).

3. Amendment of section heading, section and Note filed 11-17-2008; operative 11-17-2008. Submitted to OAL for printing only (Register 2008, No. 47).

4. Repealer filed 12-17-2019; operative 1-1-2020. Submitted to OAL for printing only pursuant to Government Code section 11351 (Register 2019, No. 51).

§10950. Petitions Appealing Orders Issued by the Administrative Director. [Repealed]

Note: Authority cited: Sections 133, 5307, 5309 and 5708, Labor Code. Reference: Sections 129, 4603, 4604, 5300, 5301 and 5302, Labor Code.

History: 1. Amendment of section and Note filed 12-19-2002; operative 1-1-2003. Submitted to OAL for printing only pursuant to Government Code section 11351 (Register 2002, No. 51).

2. Amendment of section heading, section and Note filed 11-17-2008; operative 11-17-2008. Submitted to OAL for printing only (Register 2008, No. 47).

3. Repealer of article 20 heading and section filed 12-17-2019; operative 1-1-2020. Submitted to OAL for printing only pursuant to Government Code section 11351 (Register 2019, No. 51).

§10953. Petition Appealing Audit Penalty Assessment — Labor Code Section 129.5(g). [Renumbered]

Note: Authority cited: Sections 133, 5307, 5309 and 5708, Labor Code. Reference: Section 129.5(g), Labor Code.

History: 1. New section filed 12-19-2002; operative 1-1-2003. Submitted to OAL for printing only pursuant to Government Code section 11351 (Register 2002, No. 51).

2. Amendment of section and Note filed 11-17-2008; operative 11-17-2008. Submitted to OAL for printing only (Register 2008, No. 47).

3. Renumbering of former section 10953 to section 10590 filed 12-17-2019; operative 1-1-2020. Submitted to OAL for printing only pursuant to Government Code section 11351 (Register 2019, No. 51).

§10955. Petitions for Removal and Answers.

(a) At any time within 20 days after the service of the order or decision, or of the occurrence of the action in issue, any party may petition for removal based upon one or more of the following grounds:

(1) The order, decision or action will result in significant prejudice.

(2) The order, decision or action will result in irreparable harm.

The petitioner must also demonstrate that reconsideration will not be an adequate remedy after the issuance of a final order, decision or award. Failure to file the petition to remove timely shall constitute valid ground for dismissing the petition for removal.

(b) The petition for removal and any answer shall be verified upon oath in the manner required for verified pleadings in courts of record.

(c) A copy of the petition for removal shall be served forthwith upon all parties by the petitioner. Any adverse party may file an answer within 10 days after service. No supplemental petitions, pleadings or responses shall be considered unless requested or approved by the Appeals Board.

(d) A workers' compensation judge may, within 15 days of the filing of the petition for removal, rescind the order or decision in issue, or take action to resolve the issue raised in the petition. If the workers' compensation judge so acts, or if the petitioner withdraws the petition at any time, the petition for removal will be deemed automatically dismissed, requiring no further action by the Appeals Board. The issuance of a new order or decision, or the occurrence of a new action, will recommence the time period for filing a petition for removal as described above.

(e) The filing of a petition for removal does not terminate the workers' compensation judge's authority to proceed in a case or require the workers' compensation judge to continue or cancel a previously scheduled hearing absent direction from the Appeals Board. After a petition for removal has been filed, the workers' compensation judge shall consult with the presiding workers' compensation judge prior to proceeding in the case or continuing or canceling a scheduled hearing.

Note: Authority cited: Sections 133, 5307, 5309 and 5708, Labor Code. Reference: Section 5310, Labor Code.

History: 1. Renumbering and amendment of former section 10843 to section 10955 filed 12-17-2019; operative 1-1-2020. Submitted to OAL for printing only pursuant to Government Code section 11351 (Register 2019, No. 51). For prior history, see Register 2008, No. 47.

§10957. Petition Appealing Independent Bill Review Determination of the Administrative Director. [Renumbered]

Note: Authority: Sections 133, 5307, 5309 and 5708, Labor Code. Reference: Sections 4603.6, 5500, 5501, 5502, 5700 et seq., 5800 et seq. and 5900 et seq., Labor Code; and Sections 10250, 10409, 10507, 10508, 10842, 10845, 10846, 10852, 10856, 10859 and 10860, California Code of Regulations, title 8.

History: 1. New section filed 9-23-2013; operative 10-23-2013. Submitted as a file and print by the Workers' Compensation Appeals Board pursuant to Government Code section 11351 (Register 2013, No. 39). For prior history, see Register 2008, No. 47.
2. Renumbering of former section 10957 to section 10567 filed 12-17-2019; operative 1-1-2020. Submitted to OAL for printing only pursuant to Government Code section 11351 (Register 2019, No. 51).

§10957.1. Petition Appealing Independent Medical Review Determination of the Administrative Director. [Renumbered]

Note: Authority: Sections 133, 5307, 5309 and 5708, Labor Code. Reference: Sections 4610.6, 5500, 5501, 5502, 5700 et seq., 5800 et seq. and 5900 et seq., Labor Code; and Sections 10250, 10409, 10507, 10508, 10842, 10845, 10846, 10852, 10856, 10859 and 10860, California Code of Regulations, title 8.

History: 1. New section filed 9-23-2013; operative 10-23-2013. Submitted as a file and print by the Workers' Compensation Appeals Board pursuant to Government Code section 11351 (Register 2013, No. 39).
2. Amendment of subsections (c) and (i) filed 10-15-2014; operative 1-1-2015. Submitted to OAL for printing only pursuant to Government Code section 11351 (Register 2014, No. 42).
3. Editorial correction of History 2 (Register 2017, No. 8).
4. Renumbering of former section 10957.1 to section 10575 filed 12-17-2019; operative 1-1-2020. Submitted to OAL for printing only pursuant to Government Code section 11351 (Register 2019, No. 51).

§10959. Petition Appealing Medical Provider Network Determination of the Administrative Director. [Renumbered]

Note: Authority: Sections 133, 5307, 5309 and 5708, Labor Code. Reference: Sections 4616 et seq., 5300(f) and 5900 et seq., Labor Code.

History: 1. New section filed 9-23-2013; operative 10-23-2013. Submitted as a file and print by the Workers' Compensation Appeals Board pursuant to Government Code section 11351 (Register 2013, No. 39).
2. Renumbering of former section 10959 to section 10580 filed 12-17-2019; operative 1-1-2020. Submitted to OAL for printing only pursuant to Government Code section 11351 (Register 2019, No. 51).

§10960. Petition for Disqualification of Workers' Compensation Judge.

Proceedings to disqualify a workers' compensation judge under Labor Code section 5311 shall be initiated by the filing of a petition for disqualification supported by an affidavit or declaration under penalty of perjury stating in detail facts establishing one or more of the grounds for disqualification specified in section 641 of the Code of Civil Procedure. The petition to disqualify a workers' compensation judge and any answer shall be verified upon oath in the manner required for verified pleadings in courts of record.

If the workers' compensation judge assigned to hear the matter and the grounds for disqualification are known, the petition for disqualification shall be filed not more than 10 days after service of notice of hearing or after grounds for disqualification are known.

A petition for disqualification shall be referred to and determined by a panel of three commissioners of the Appeals Board in the same manner as a petition for reconsideration.

Note: Authority cited: Section 5307, Labor Code. Reference: Section 641, Code of Civil Procedure; and Sections 5310 and 5311, Labor Code.

History: 1. Repealer of article 21 heading, renumbering of former section 10452 to section 10960, including amendment of section heading, section and Note, filed 12-17-2019; operative 1-1-2020. Submitted to OAL for printing only pursuant to Government Code section 11351 (Register 2019, No. 51).

§10961. Actions by Workers' Compensation Judge After Petition for Reconsideration is Filed.

Within 15 days of the timely filing of a petition for reconsideration, a workers' compensation judge shall perform one of the following actions:

(a) Prepare a Report and Recommendation on Petition for Reconsideration in accordance with rule 10962;

(b)   Rescind the entire order, decision or award and initiate further proceedings within 30 days; or

(c)   Rescind the order, decision or award and issue an amended order, decision or award. The time for filing a petition for reconsideration pursuant to Labor Code section 5903 will run from the filing date of the amended order, decision or award.

After 15 days have elapsed from the filing of a petition for reconsideration, a workers' compensation judge shall not issue any order in the case until the Appeals Board has denied or dismissed the petition for reconsideration or issued a decision after reconsideration.

Note: Authority cited: Section 5307, Labor Code. Reference: Sections 5903, 5906, 5907 and 5908.5, Labor Code.

History: 1. Renumbering of former section 10859 to section 10961, including amendment of section heading, section and Note, filed 12-17-2019; operative 1-1-2020. Submitted to OAL for printing only pursuant to Government Code section 11351 (Register 2019, No. 51).

§10962.   Report of Workers' Compensation Judge.

Petitions for reconsideration, petitions for removal and petitions for disqualification shall be referred to the workers' compensation judge from whose decisions or actions relief is sought. If the workers' compensation judge prepares a report, it shall contain:

(a)   A statement of the contentions raised by the petition;

(b)   A discussion of the support in the record for the findings of fact and the conclusions of law that serve as a basis for the decision or order as to each contention raised by the petition, or, in the case of a petition for disqualification, a specific response to the allegations and, if appropriate, a discussion of any failure by the petitioner to comply with the procedures set forth in rule 10960; and

(c)   The action recommended on the petition.

The workers' compensation judge shall submit the report to the Appeals Board within 15 days after the petition is filed unless the Appeals Board grants an extension of time. The workers' compensation judge shall serve a copy of the report on the parties and any lien claimant, the validity of whose lien is specifically questioned by the petition, at the time the report is submitted to the Appeals Board.

If the workers' compensation judge assigned to the case is unavailable, the presiding workers' compensation judge shall prepare and serve the report.

Note: Authority cited: Sections 133, 5307, 5309 and 5708, Labor Code. Reference: Sections 5900 and 5906, Labor Code.

History: 1. Renumbering and amendment of former section 10860 to section 10962 filed 12-17-2019; operative 1-1-2020. Submitted to OAL for printing only pursuant to Government Code section 11351 (Register 2019, No. 51).

§10964.   Supplemental Petitions.

(a)   When a petition for reconsideration, removal or disqualification has been timely filed, supplemental petitions or pleadings or responses other than the answer shall be considered only when specifically requested or approved by the Appeals Board.

(b)   A party seeking to file a supplemental pleading shall file a petition setting forth good cause for the Appeals Board to approve the filing of a supplemental pleading and shall attach the proposed pleading.

(c)   Supplemental petitions or pleadings or responses other than the answer shall neither be accepted nor deemed filed for any purpose except as provided by this rule.

Note: Authority cited: Sections 133, 5307, 5309 and 5708, Labor Code. Reference: Sections 5310, 5311 and 5900, Labor Code.

History: 1. Renumbering and amendment of former section 10848 to section 10964 filed 12-17-2019; operative 1-1-2020. Submitted to OAL for printing only pursuant to Government Code section 11351 (Register 2019, No. 51).

§10966.   Correction of Errors.

Before a petition for reconsideration is filed, a workers' compensation judge may correct the decision for clerical, mathematical or procedural error or amend the decision for good cause under the authority and subject to the limitations set out in sections 5803 and 5804 of the Labor Code.

Note: Authority cited: Sections 133 and 5307, Labor Code. Reference: Sections 5309, 5803 and 5804, Labor Code.

History: 1. Renumbering of former section 10858 to section 10966, including amendment of Note, filed 12-17-2019; operative 1-1-2020. Submitted to OAL for printing only pursuant to Government Code section 11351 (Register 2019, No. 51).

§10972.　Skeletal Petitions.

A petition for reconsideration, removal or disqualification may be denied or dismissed if it is unsupported by specific references to the record and to the principles of law involved.

Note: Authority cited: Sections 133, 5307, 5309 and 5708, Labor Code. Reference: Sections 126, 5310, 5311, 5900, 5902, 5903 and 5904, Labor Code.

History: 1. Renumbering of former section 10846 to section 10972, including amendment of Note, filed 12-17-2019; operative 1-1-2020. Submitted to OAL for printing only pursuant to Government Code section 11351 (Register 2019, No. 51).

§10974.　Allegations of Newly Discovered Evidence and Fraud.

Where reconsideration is sought on the ground of newly discovered evidence that could not with reasonable diligence have been produced before submission of the case or on the ground that the decision had been procured by fraud, the petition must contain an offer of proof, specific and detailed, providing:

(a)　The names of witnesses to be produced;

(b)　A summary of the testimony to be elicited from the witnesses;

(c)　A description of any documentary evidence to be offered;

(d)　The effect that the evidence will have on the record and on the prior decision; and

(e)　As to newly discovered evidence, a full and accurate statement of the reasons why the testimony or exhibits could not reasonably have been discovered or produced before submission of the case.

A petition for reconsideration sought upon these grounds may be denied if it fails to meet the requirements of this rule, or if it is based upon cumulative evidence.

Note: Authority cited: Sections 133 and 5307, Labor Code. Reference: Sections 5902 and 5903, Labor Code.

History: 1. Renumbering and amendment of former section 10856 to section 10974 filed 12-17-2019; operative 1-1-2020. Submitted to OAL for printing only pursuant to Government Code section 11351 (Register 2019, No. 51).

§10984.　Hearing After Reconsideration Granted.

Where reconsideration has been granted and the case referred to a workers' compensation judge for proceedings on reconsideration, the workers' compensation judge shall, upon the conclusion thereof, prepare and serve upon the parties a summary of evidence received in the proceedings after reconsideration granted.

Unless otherwise instructed by the panel before which a case is pending, the workers' compensation judge to whom the case has been assigned for further proceedings may rule on requests for postponement and continuance of further hearing, join additional parties, dismiss unnecessary parties where such dismissal is not opposed by any other party to the case, make all interlocutory or procedural orders that are agreed to by all parties, issue subpoenas, rule on motions for discovery, rule on all evidentiary motions and objections and make all other rulings necessary to expedite and facilitate the trial and disposition of the case. The workers' compensation judge shall not order a medical examination, obtain a recommended disability evaluation, make an order taking the case off calendar nor make an order approving or disapproving Compromise and Release.

Note: Authority cited: Sections 133 and 5307, Labor Code. Reference: Sections 5309 and 5313, Labor Code.

History: 1. Renumbering and amendment of former section 10862 to section 10984 filed 12-17-2019; operative 1-1-2020. Submitted to OAL for printing only pursuant to Government Code section 11351 (Register 2019, No. 51).

§10986.　Authority of Workers' Compensation Judge After Decision After Reconsideration.

After a decision after reconsideration has become final, subsequent orders and decisions in a case shall be made by any trial level workers' compensation judge.

An order correcting a decision after reconsideration for clerical, mathematical or procedural error shall be made by the panel that made the decision or, if the composition of the Appeals Board has changed, by the successor panel.

Note: Authority cited: Sections 133 and 5307, Labor Code. Reference: Sections 5900, 5910 and 5911, Labor Code.

History: 1. Renumbering and amendment of former section 10864 to section 10986 filed 12-17-2019; operative 1-1-2020. Submitted to OAL for printing only pursuant to Government Code section 11351 (Register 2019, No. 51).

§10990. Reconsideration of Arbitration Decisions Made Pursuant to Labor Code Sections 3201.5 and 3201.7.

(a)   A petition for reconsideration from an arbitration decision made pursuant to Labor Code section 3201.5(a)(1) or section 3201.7(a)(1) (known as "carve-out" cases) shall be filed directly with the office of the Appeals Board within 20 days of the service of the final order, decision or award made and filed by the arbitrator or board of arbitrators. A copy of the petition for reconsideration shall be served on the arbitrator or arbitration board.

(b)   Notwithstanding any other provision of these rules, a petition for reconsideration in a carve-out case shall be filed directly with the office of the Appeals Board, and not with any district office, including the San Francisco district office. Any petition for reconsideration in a carve-out case that is received by any district office shall neither be accepted for filing nor deemed filed for any purpose. If a carve-out petition for reconsideration is submitted to a district office in violation of this rule, the petition shall be returned to the petitioner with a letter referencing this rule, noting that the petition was improperly submitted to a district office and has been rejected, and indicating that the petition should be filed directly with the Appeals Board consistent with this rule.

(c)   The petition for reconsideration in a carve-out case, which shall be submitted with a document cover sheet, shall also comply with each of the following requirements:

(1)   It shall be captioned so as to identify it as a "Petition for Reconsideration from Arbitrator's Decision Under Labor Code section 3201.5 or 3201.7" and it shall include:

(A)   The injured employee's first and last names;

(B)   The name(s) of the defendant(s);

(C)   The alternative dispute resolution (ADR) case number (i.e., the carve-out arbitration case number); and

(D)   The Workers' Compensation Appeals Board adjudication case number, if previously assigned;

(2)   It shall set forth the date on which the arbitrator or board of arbitrators served the arbitration decision. Proof of service of the arbitration decision on the parties shall be either by a verified statement of the arbitrator or the board of arbitrators indicating the date of service and listing the names and addresses of the persons served or by written acknowledgment of receipt by the parties at the time of the arbitration proceedings;

(3)   It shall append, under a document separator sheet a copy of that portion of the collective bargaining agreement relating to the workers' compensation arbitration and reconsideration processes;

(4)   It shall append, under a document separator sheet, a completed Application for Adjudication of Claim (but without any venue designation), which is required solely for the purpose of obtaining the information set forth therein (e.g., the injured employee's date(s) of injury and date of birth; the names and mailing addresses of the parties); therefore, it shall not be deemed an application for purposes of Labor Code section 4064(c); and

(5)   It shall contain a proof of service of the petition, including service on the arbitrator or board of arbitrators.

(d)   After the filing of the carve-out petition for reconsideration, an adjudication file will be created and an adjudication case number will be assigned, if there is no existing adjudication case number. Any new adjudication case number will be served by the Appeals Board on the parties and attorneys, and on the arbitrator or board of arbitrators, at the addresses listed in the proof of service to the petition.

(e)   Following the Appeals Board's service of the adjudication case number (or, if there is an existing case, following the filing of the carve-out petition for reconsideration), and until the Appeals Board issues a decision disposing of all issues raised in the petition, all further documents shall be filed directly with the office of the Appeals Board, and not with any district office.

(f)   Within 15 days after receiving the petition for reconsideration, the arbitrator or board of arbitrators shall perform one of the following actions:

(1) Rescind the entire order, decision or award and initiate further proceedings within 30 days; or

(2) Rescind the order, decision or award and issue an amended order, decision or award. The time for filing a petition for reconsideration pursuant to Labor Code section 5903 will run from the filing date of the amended order, decision or award; or

(3) Submit to the Appeals Board an electronic copy of the complete record of proceedings, including:

(A) The transcript of proceedings, if any;

(B) A summary of testimony if the proceedings were not transcribed;

(C) The documentary evidence submitted by each of the parties;

(D) An opinion that sets forth the rationale for the decision; and

(E) A report on the petition for reconsideration, consistent with the provisions of rule 10962. The original arbitration record shall not be filed.

(g) Upon receipt of the electronic copy of the complete record of proceedings, the Appeals Board may enter the petition for reconsideration, any answer and the record of the arbitration proceedings into the adjudication file within EAMS.

(h) The petition for reconsideration, any answer, and the arbitration record shall be deemed part of the Workers' Compensation Appeals Board's record of proceedings under rule 10803.

(i) After an arbitration decision has been made, the arbitrator or board of arbitrators shall maintain possession of the original record of the arbitration proceedings until the time for filing a petition for reconsideration has passed. Thereafter, one of the parties may be designated custodian of the arbitration record as provided for in the collective bargaining agreement.

Note: Authority cited: Sections 133, 5307, 5309 and 5708, Labor Code. Reference: Sections 3201.5, 3201.7 and 4064, Labor Code.

History: 1. Renumbering of former section 10865 to section 10990, including amendment of section and Note, filed 12-17-2019; operative 1-1-2020. Submitted to OAL for printing only pursuant to Government Code section 11351 (Register 2019, No. 51).

§10995. Reconsideration of Arbitrator's Decisions or Awards Made Pursuant to the Mandatory or Voluntary Arbitration Provisions of Labor Code Sections 5270 through 5275.

(a) Any final order, decision or award filed by an arbitrator under the mandatory or voluntary arbitration provisions of Labor Code sections 5270 through 5275 shall be subject to the reconsideration process.

(b) A petition for reconsideration from any final order, decision or award filed by an arbitrator under the mandatory or voluntary arbitration provisions of Labor Code sections 5270 through 5275, and any answer, shall be filed in EAMS or with the district office having venue in accordance with Labor Code section 5501.5. No duplicate copies of petitions shall be filed with any other district office or with the Appeals Board.

(c) Within 15 days after receiving the petition for reconsideration, the arbitrator shall perform one of the following actions:

(1) Rescind the entire order, decision or award and initiate further proceedings within 30 days; or

(2) Rescind the order, decision or award and issue an amended order, decision or award. The time for filing a petition for reconsideration pursuant to Labor Code section 5903 will run from the filing date of the amended order, decision or award; or

(3) Prepare and serve a report on reconsideration as provided in rule 10962. Upon completion of the report on reconsideration, the arbitrator shall concurrently forward an electronic copy of the arbitrator's report and an electronic copy of the complete arbitration file directly to the presiding workers' compensation judge of the district office having venue over the matter. Upon receipt of the arbitrator's report and the record of arbitration proceedings, the district office shall enter the report and the file into the EAMS adjudication file.

(d) The petition for reconsideration, any answer, and the arbitration record shall be deemed part of the Workers' Compensation Appeals Board's record of proceedings under rule 10803.

Note: Authority cited: Sections 133, 5307, 5309 and 5708, Labor Code. Reference: Sections 5270-5275, 5501.5 and 5900-5911, Labor Code.

History: 1. New section filed 10-15-2014; operative 1-1-2015. Submitted to OAL for printing only pursuant to Government Code section 11351 (Register 2014, No. 42). For prior history, see Register 2008, No. 47.

2. Editorial correction of History 1 (Register 2017, No. 8).

3. Repealer of article 22 heading, repealer of former section 10995 and renumbering of former section 10866 to section 10995, including amendment of section and Note, filed 12-17-2019; operative 1-1-2020. Submitted to OAL for printing only pursuant to Government Code section 11351 (Register 2019, No. 51).

§10996. Voluntary Arbitration. [Repealed]

Note: Authority cited: Sections 133, 5307, 5309 and 5708, Labor Code. Reference: Sections 5270-5278, Labor Code.

History: 1. New section filed 10-15-2014; operative 1-1-2015. Submitted to OAL for printing only pursuant to Government Code section 11351 (Register 2014, No. 42). For prior history, see Register 2008, No. 47.

2. Editorial correction of History 1 (Register 2017, No. 8).

3. Repealer filed 12-17-2019; operative 1-1-2020. Submitted to OAL for printing only pursuant to Government Code section 11351 (Register 2019, No. 51).

§10997. Request for Arbitration. [Repealed]

Note: Authority cited: Sections 133 and 5307, Labor Code. Reference: Sections 5270 through 5277, Labor Code.

History: 1. New section filed 1-12-90; operative 1-12-90 (Register 90, No. 5). This section is exempt from review by OAL pursuant to Government Code section 11351.

2. Change without regulatory effect filed 1-26-90 (Register 90, No. 5).

3. Amendment exempt from OAL review pursuant to Government Code section 11351 filed 12-19-90; operative 1-1-91 (Register 91, No. 7).

4. Amendment filed 12-19-2002; operative 1-1-2003. Submitted to OAL for printing only pursuant to Government Code section 11351 (Register 2002, No. 51).

5. Repealer filed 12-17-2019; operative 1-1-2020. Submitted to OAL for printing only pursuant to Government Code section 11351 (Register 2019, No. 51).

§10998. Disqualification of Arbitrator. [Renumbered]

Note: Authority cited: Sections 133 and 5307, Labor Code. Reference: Section 5271(d), Labor Code.

History: 1. New section filed 1-12-90; operative 1-12-90 (Register 90, No. 5). This section is exempt from review by OAL pursuant to Government Code section 11351.

2. Change without regulatory effect filed 1-26-90 (Register 90, No. 5).

3. Amendment exempt from OAL review pursuant to Government Code section 11351 filed 12-19-90; operative 1-1-91 (Register 91, No. 7).

4. Amendment of first paragraph and Note filed 12-19-2002; operative 1-1-2003. Submitted to OAL for printing only pursuant to Government Code section 11351 (Register 2002, No. 51).

5. Renumbering of former section 10998 to section 10912 filed 12-17-2019; operative 1-1-2020. Submitted to OAL for printing only pursuant to Government Code section 11351 (Register 2019, No. 51).

§10999. Arbitrator Fee and Cost Disputes. [Renumbered]

Note: Authority cited: Sections 133 and 5307, Labor Code. Reference: Section 5273(c), Labor Code.

History: 1. New section filed 1-12-90; operative 1-12-90 (Register 90, No. 5). This section is exempt from review by OAL pursuant to Government Code section 11351.

2. Change without regulatory effect filed 1-26-90 (Register 90, No. 5).

3. Amendment exempt from OAL review pursuant to Government Code section 11351 filed 12-19-90; operative 1-1-91 (Register 91, No. 7).

4. Amendment of section and Note filed 12-19-2002; operative 1-1-2003. Submitted to OAL for printing only pursuant to Government Code section 11351 (Register 2002, No. 51).

5. Renumbering of former section 10999 to section 10920 filed 12-17-2019; operative 1-1-2020. Submitted to OAL for printing only pursuant to Government Code section 11351 (Register 2019, No. 51).

CHAPTER 7
DEPARTMENT OF INDUSTRIAL RELATIONS

SUBCHAPTER 1
OCCUPATIONAL INJURY OR ILLNESS REPORTS AND RECORDS

ARTICLE 2
Employer Records of Occupational Injury or Illness

§14300.35. Employee Involvement.

(a) Basic requirement. Your employees and

their representatives must be involved in the recordkeeping system in several ways.

(1)   You must inform each employee of how he or she is to report a work-related injury or illness to you.

(2)   You must provide access to your injury and illness records for your employees and their representatives as described in paragraph (b)(2) of this section.

(b)   Implementation.

(1)   What must I do to make sure that employees report work-related injuries and illnesses to me?

(A)   You must set up a way for employees to report work-related injuries and illnesses promptly and

(B)   You must tell each employee how to report work-related injuries and illnesses to you.

(2)   Do I have to give my employees and their representatives access to the injury and illness records required by this article?

Yes. Your employees, former employees, their personal representatives, and their authorized employee representatives have the right to access the injury and illness records required by this article, with some limitations, as discussed below.

(A)   Who is an authorized employee representative?

An authorized employee representative is an authorized collective bargaining agent of employees.

(B)   Who is a "personal representative" of an employee or former employee?

A personal representative is:

1.   Any person that the employee or former employee designates as such, in writing; or

2.   The legal representative of a deceased or legally incapacitated employee or former employee.

(C)   If an employee or his or her representative asks for access to the Cal/OSHA Form 300 and annual summary when do I have to provide it?

When an employee, former employee, personal representative, or authorized employee representative asks for copies of your current or stored Cal/OSHA 300 forms or a current or stored annual summary for an establishment the employee or former employee has worked in, you must give the requester a copy of the relevant Cal/OSHA 300 forms and annual summaries by the end of the next business day.

Exception: If your establishment is in NAICS Code 5121, you must give the requester the information within seven (7) calendar days.

(D)   May I remove the names of the employees or any other information from the Cal/OSHA Form 300 before I give copies to an employee, former employee, or employee representative?

No. You must leave the names on the Cal/OSHA Form 300. However, to protect the privacy of injured and ill employees, you may not record the employee's name on the Cal/OSHA Form 300 for certain "privacy concern cases," as specified in Sections 14300.29(b)(6) through 14300.29(b)(9).

(E)   If an employee or representative asks for access to the Cal/OSHA 301 Incident Report, when do I have to provide it?

1.   When an employee, former employee, or personal representative asks for a copy of the Cal/OSHA Form 301 Incident Report describing an injury or illness to that employee or former employee, you must give the requester a copy of the Cal/OSHA 301 Incident Report containing that information by the end of the next business day.

Exception: If your establishment is in NAICS Code 5121, you must give the requester the information within seven (7) calendar days.

2.   When an authorized employee representative asks for copies of the Cal/OSHA 301 Incident Reports or equivalent forms for an establishment where the agent represents employees under a collective bargaining agreement, you must give copies of those forms to the authorized employee representative within seven (7) calendar days but with the following personally identifying information deleted:

1.   Name;

2.   Address;

3.   Date of birth;

4.   Date of hire;

5.   Gender;

6.   Name of physician;

7.   Location where treatment was provided;

8.   Whether the employee was treated in an emergency room; and

9.   Whether the employee was hospitalized overnight as an in-patient.

(F)   May I charge for the copies?

No. You may not charge for these copies the first time they are provided. However, if one of the designated persons asks for additional copies, you may assess a reasonable charge for retrieving and copying the records.

(c)   With the exception of provisions to protect the privacy of employees in subsections (b)(2)(D) and (b)(2)(E) of this section and in subsections (b)(6) through (b)(10) in Section 14300.29, nothing in this section shall be deemed to preclude employees and employee representatives from collectively bargaining to obtain access to information relating to occupational injuries and illnesses in addition to the information made available under this section.

Note: Authority cited: Sections 150(b) and 6410, Labor Code. Reference: Section 6410, Labor Code.

History: 1. New section filed 1-15-2002; operative 1-15-2002 pursuant to Government Code section 11343.4 (Register 2002, No. 3).

2. Amendment of subsections (a)(1)-(2), (b)(1)(A), (b)(2)(C) and (b)(2)(E)1. filed 11-1-2018 as an emergency; operative 11-1-2018 (Register 2018, No. 44). A Certificate of Compliance must be transmitted to OAL by 4-30-2019 or emergency language will be repealed by operation of law on the following day.

3. Amendment of subsections (a)(1)-(2), (b)(1)(A), (b)(2)(C) and (b)(2)(E)1. refiled 4-25-2019 as an emergency; operative 5-1-2019 pursuant to Government Code section 11346.1(d) (Register 2019, No. 17). A Certificate of Compliance must be transmitted to OAL by 7-30-2019 or emergency language will be repealed by operation of law on the following day.

4. Amendment of subsections (a)(1)-(2), (b)(1)(A), (b)(2)(C) and (b)(2)(E)1. refiled 7-29-2019 as an emergency; operative 7-31-2019 pursuant to Government Code section 11346.1(d) (Register 2019, No. 31). A Certificate of Compliance must be transmitted to OAL by 10-29-2019 or emergency language will be repealed by operation of law on the following day.

5. Certificate of Compliance as to 7-29-2019 order, including amendment of Note, transmitted to OAL 10-29-2019 and filed 12-11-2019 (Register 2019, No. 50).

§14300.41.   Electronic Submission of Injury and Illness Records to OSHA.

(a)   Basic requirement.

(1)   Annual electronic submission of Cal/OSHA injury and illness records by establishments with 250 or more employees. If your establishment had 250 or more employees at any time during the previous calendar year, and this article requires your establishment to keep re-

cords, then you must electronically submit information from the Cal/OSHA Form 300A Summary of Work-Related Injuries and Illnesses that you keep under this part to OSHA or OSHA's designee. You must submit the information once a year, no later than the date listed in paragraph (c) of this section of the year after the calendar year covered by the forms.

(2)   Annual electronic submission of Cal/OSHA Form 300A Summary of Work-Related Injuries and Illnesses by establishments with 20 or more employees but fewer than 250 employees in designated industries. If your establishment had 20 or more employees but fewer than 250 employees at any time during the previous calendar year, and your establishment is classified in an industry listed in Appendix H for Title 8 Sections 14300–14300.48, then you must electronically submit information from Cal/OSHA Form 300A Summary of Work-Related Injuries and Illnesses to OSHA or OSHA's designee. You must submit the information once a year, no later than the date listed in paragraph (c) of this section of the year after the calendar year covered by the form.

(3)   Electronic submission of records upon notification. Upon notification, you must electronically submit the requested information from your Cal/OSHA injury and illness records to OSHA or OSHA's designee.

(4)   Electronic submission of the Employer Identification Number (EIN). For each establishment that is subject to these reporting requirements, you must provide the EIN used by the establishment.

(b)   Implementation.

(1)   Does every employer have to routinely submit information from the Cal/OSHA injury and illness records to OSHA or its designee?

No, only two categories of employers must routinely submit information from their Cal/OSHA injury and illness records. First, if your establishment had 250 or more employees at any time during the previous calendar year, and this article requires your establishment to keep records, then you must submit the required Cal/OSHA Form 300A information to OSHA once a year. Second, if your establishment had 20 or more employees but fewer than 250 employees at any time during the previous calendar year, and your establishment is classified in an industry listed in Appendix H for Title 8 Sections 14300–14300.48, then you must submit the required Cal/OSHA Form 300A information to OSHA once a year. Employers in these two categories must submit the required information by the date listed in paragraph (c) of this section of the year after the calendar year covered by the form or forms (for example, 2018 for the 2017 forms). If you are not in either of these two categories, then you must submit information from the injury and illness records to OSHA only if OSHA notifies you to do so for an individual data collection.

(2)   If I have to submit information under paragraph (a)(1) of this section, do I have to submit all of the information from the record-keeping form?

Yes, you are required to submit all of the information from the Form 300A.

(3)   Do part-time, seasonal, or temporary workers count as employees in the criteria for number of employees in paragraph (a) of this section?

Yes, each individual employed in the establishment at any time during the calendar year counts as one employee, including full-time, part-time, seasonal, and temporary workers.

(4)   How will OSHA notify me that I must submit information from the injury and illness records as part of an individual data collection under paragraph (a)(3) of this section?

OSHA will notify you by mail if you will have to submit information as part of an individual data collection under paragraph (a)(3). OSHA will also announce individual data collections through publication in the Federal Register and the OSHA newsletter, and announcements on the OSHA Web site. If you are an employer who must routinely submit the information, then OSHA will not notify you about your routine submittal.

(5)   Does this section affect the Division of Occupational Safety and Health's authority to inspect my workplace?

No. Nothing in this section affects the Division of Occupational Safety and Health's statutory authority to investigate conditions related to occupational safety and health.

(6)   How often do I have to submit the information from the injury and illness records?

If you are required to submit information under paragraph (a)(1) or (2) of this section,

then you must submit the information once a year, by the date listed in paragraph (c) of this section of the year after the calendar year covered by the form or forms. If you are submitting information because OSHA notified you to submit information as part of an individual data collection under paragraph (a)(3) of this section, then you must submit the information as often as specified in the notification.

(7)   How do I submit the information?

You must submit the information electronically. OSHA will provide a secure Web site for the electronic submission of information. For individual data collections under paragraph (a)(3) of this section, OSHA will include the Web site's location in the notification for the data collection.

(8)   Do I have to submit information if my establishment is partially exempt from keeping Cal/OSHA injury and illness records?

If you are partially exempt from keeping injury and illness records under §§ 14300.1 and/or 14300.2, then you do not have to routinely submit Article 2 information under paragraphs (a)(1) and (2) of this section. You will have to submit information under paragraph (a)(3) of this section if OSHA informs you in writing that it will collect injury and illness information from you. If you receive such a notification, then you must keep the Cal/OSHA injury and illness records required by Article 2 and submit information as directed.

(9)   Do I have to submit information if I am located in a State Plan State?

Yes, the requirements apply to employers located in State Plan States.

(10)   May an enterprise or corporate office electronically submit Cal/OSHA injury and illness records for its establishment(s)?

Yes, if your enterprise or corporate office had ownership of or control over one or more establishments required to submit information under paragraph (a)(1) or (2) of this section, then the enterprise or corporate office may collect and electronically submit the information for the establishment(s).

(c)   Reporting dates.

(1)   In 2018, establishments required to submit under paragraph (a)(1) or (2) of this section must submit the required information for 2017 according to the table in this paragraph (c)(1):

Submission year	Establishments submitting under paragraph (a)(1) of this section must submit the required information from this form/these forms:	Establishments submitting under paragraph (a)(2) of this section must submit the required information from this form:	Submission deadline
2018	300A	300A	December 31, 2018

(2)   Beginning in 2019, establishments that are required to submit under paragraph (a)(1) or (2) of this section will have to submit all of the required information by March 2 of the year after the calendar year covered by the form or forms (for example, by March 2, 2019, for the forms covering 2018).

Note: Authority cited: Sections 150(b) and 6410, Labor Code. Reference: Section 6410, Labor Code.

History: 1. New section filed 1-15-2002; operative 1-15-2002 pursuant to Government Code section 11343.4 (Register 2002, No. 3).

2. Amendment of section heading and section filed 11-1-2018 as an emergency; operative 11-1-2018 (Register 2018, No. 44). A Certificate of Compliance must be transmitted to OAL by 4-30-2019 or emergency language will be repealed by operation of law on the following day.

3. Amendment of section heading and section refiled 4-25-2019 as an emergency; operative 5-1-2019 pursuant to Government Code section 11346.1(d) (Register 2019, No. 17). A Certificate of Compliance must be transmitted to OAL by 7-30-2019 or emergency language will be repealed by operation of law on the following day.

4. Amendment of section heading and section refiled 7-29-2019 as an emergency; operative 7-31-2019 pursuant to Government Code section 11346.1(d) (Register 2019, No. 31). A Certificate of Compliance must be transmitted to OAL by 10-29-2019 or emergency language will be repealed by operation of law on the following day.

5. Certificate of Compliance as to 7-29-2019 order, including new subsection (a)(4) and amendment of Note, transmitted to OAL 10-29-2019 and filed 12-11-2019 (Register 2019, No. 50).

§14300.48.   Effective Date.

The provisions of this article take effect on January 1, 2002 or on the effective date of the regulation, whichever is later.

Note: Authority cited: Section 6410, Labor Code. Reference: Section 6410, Labor Code.

History: 1. New section and Appendices A-G filed 1-15-2002; operative 1-15-2002 pursuant to Government Code section 11343.4 (Register 2002, No. 3).

2. Amendment of appendices A, B, D and E and amendment of Notes for appendices D and E filed 4-23-2004; operative 4-23-2004 pursuant to Government Code section 11343.4 (Register 2004, No. 17).

3. Change without regulatory effect amending appendices A, B, D and E filed 8-22-2007 pursuant to section 100, title 1, California Code of Regulations (Register 2007, No. 34).

4. New Appendix H filed 11-1-2018 as an emergency; operative 11-1-2018 (Register 2018, No. 44). A Certificate of Compliance must be transmitted to OAL by 4-30-2019 or emergency language will be repealed by operation of law on the following day.

5. New Appendix H refiled 4-25-2019 as an emergency; operative 5-1-2019 pursuant to Government Code section 11346.1(d) (Register 2019, No. 17). A Certificate of Compliance must be transmitted to OAL by 7-30-2019 or emergency language will be repealed by operation of law on the following day.

6. Amendment of Appendix H refiled 7-29-2019 as an emergency; operative 7-31-2019 pursuant to Government Code section 11346.1(d) (Register 2019, No. 31). A Certificate of Compliance must be transmitted to OAL by 10-29-2019 or emergency language will be repealed by operation of law on the following day.

7. Certificate of Compliance as to 7-29-2019 order, including amendment of appendices B and E, transmitted to OAL 10-29-2019 and filed 12-11-2019 (Register 2019, No. 50).

Appendix B. Cal/OSHA Form 300A (Rev. 4/2019) Annual Summary of Work-Related Injuries and Illnesses

Editor's Note: For the text of Appendix B, please see Barclays *Official California Code of Regulations.*

Appendix E. Required Elements for the Cal/OSHA Form 300A, Annual Summary of Work-Related Injuries and Illnesses Equivalent Form.

A. Employers who are required to complete the Cal/OSHA Form 300A may use an equivalent form that provides all of the following information:

1. The number of cases:

(G) The total number of deaths

(H) The total number of cases with days away from work

(I) The total number of cases with job transfers or restriction

(J) The total number of other recordable cases

2. The number of days:

(K) The total number of days of job transfer or restriction

(L) The total number of days away from work

(M) Injury and Illness Types, the total numbers of:

1. Injuries

2. Skin disorders

3. Respiratory conditions

4. Poisonings

5. Hearing Loss

6. All other illnesses

3. Posting requirement statement: "Post this Annual Summary from February 1 to April 30 of the year following the year covered by the form."

4. Establishment information:

● The establishment name

● Street address

● City, State, Zip

● Industry description

● The North American Industrial Classification System, if known.

5. Employment information

● The annual average number of employees.

● The total hours worked by all employees last year.

(For assistance in calculating the annual average number of employees, and total hours worked, refer to Appendix G.)

6. Sign Here:

● Admonition: "Knowingly falsifying this statement may result in a fine."

● Certification statement: "I certify that I have examined this document and that to the best of my knowledge the entries are true, accurate, and complete."

● Space for the signature of the company executive, and title.

● Phone number of signatory.

● Date of the certification.

Note: Authority cited: Sections 150(b) and 6410, Labor Code. Reference: Section 6410, Labor Code.

THIS BOOK
DOES NOT
CIRCULATE